US Passenger Liners since 1945

US Passenger Liners
since 1945

Milton H. Watson

PSL

Patrick Stephens

First published in 1988

British Library Cataloguing in Publication Data

Watson, Milton H.
  U.S. passenger liners since 1945.
  1. Passenger transport. Shipping. American
  liners 1945-1987
  I. Title
  387.2'432

  ISBN 1-85260-917-2

Title page President Cleveland *departing from San Francisco* (Al Palmer collection, courtesy of American President Lines Archives).

Photograph opposite contents page *The almost completed* United States *minus the portholes in the superstructure* (Courtesy Peter M. Warner).

Patrick Stephens Limited is part of the
Thorsons Publishing Group, Wellingborough, Northamptonshire,
NN8 2RQ England.

Printed and bound in Great Britain by
Butler & Tanner Ltd, Frome and London
Typeset by MJL Limited, Hitchin, Hertfordshire

10 9 8 7 6 5 4 3 2 1

To

Theodore W. Scull

Thanks for encouraging me to write

Contents

Acknowledgements

No work such as this is undertaken without the assistance and encouragement of many people.

I would like to thank Mr Frank O. Braynard, maritime historian, curator of the American Merchant Marine Museum and official historian for the Port of New York. He allowed me to explore and select from the contents of his vast collection and offered many anecdotes. Ms Kathy McLoughlin, a fine colleague, shared her crew experiences with Grace Line and Moore McCormack with me. Mr William H. Miller Jr, noted maritime historian and lecturer, provided photos and interesting titbits. Mr Theodore W. Scull guided me along the right path when I strayed, and finally I would like to thank Mr Peter M. Warner for being at the right place at the right time and sharing his files with me.

Others who have contributed to this project are: Mr Ernest Arroyo; Ms Laura Brown, librarian at the Steamship Historical Society of America at the University of Baltimore (referred to in picture credits as 'SSHSA Collection'); Mr Ray Christianson; Mr Francis J. Duffy of Moran Towing & Transportation Company; Mr James Shaw; Mr Antonio Scrimali; Mr C. Spanton Ashdown of Alcoa; Mr Lloyd Stadum of Puget Sound Maritime Historical Society; and M/M Willie Tinnemeyer.

Many of the individual companies dealt with in this volume have long since ceased passenger operations or have withdrawn from the maritime field. The survivors, under a new name or parent company, in addition to the new firms that assisted with information, are: Alaska Marine Highway System; Mr Luther Blount, American Canadian Line; Mr Andrew C. Peterson, American Cruise Lines; American President Companies; Al Wolfe Associates for Carnival Cruise Lines and Coastwise Cruise Line; Bethlehem Steel Corporation; CP Rail; Clipper Cruise Line; Exploration Cruise Lines; Farrell Lines; W. R. Grace & Company; Great Pacific Cruise Lines, Ingalls Shipbuilding; Lockheed Shipbuilding Company; Matson Navigation Company; Peterson Builders Inc; Premier Cruise Lines; Princess Cruises; Prudential Lines Inc; Society Expeditions; United States Cruises; US Department of Transportation; and the United States Navy.

I would like to extend a warm thanks to a friend and colleague, Ms Maura Gouck, for taking time from correcting tons of English papers to proofread my manuscript. Finally to Patrick Stephens, a round of applause for publishing this work.

Introduction and explanatory notes

Of the voluminous literature that has emerged on passenger ships within the last couple of years, very little has been written about American ships and their respective owners. To shed some light on this unexplored area, I have compiled brief histories and fleet lists of all the post-war American-owned and/or American-flagged passenger steamship companies.

Many of the companies surveyed in this book were well established before 1945, and include the few surviving coastal companies that were in their death throes following the war. Each company, including coastal ones, is listed alphabetically with a brief history of the founding of the company followed by events since 1945. At the end of each company's entry is a complete fleet list, arranged chronologically, of all the ships each owned or operated since 1945.

Included in this work are American-flagged cruise companies that today ply the intracoastal (along the same coast) and inter-coastal (between east and west coasts) waterways of America's eastern and western seaboards, and American-owned but foreign-flagged vessels that carry holidaying passengers to the Caribbean and South Pacific. Why are these companies succeeding while their forebears died? Part of the answer is the lack of unionization.

Information has been obtained from many sources. Most valuable was the companies' own literature in the form of brochures. For the ships' statistics, I relied heavily on *Lloyd's Register of Shipping*, and, where available, statistics were cross-checked with literature issued by the shipping lines. Where wide discrepancies existed, particularly with regard to tonnage and passenger capacity, I have chosen the more reliable of the two sources or listed both.

At the moment there seems no end to the announcements of new companies seeking to capture that other 97% of Americans who have never cruised before. To be as up-to-date as possible, I have included a section entitled 'New companies'. Some have been established since 1978 with nothing more than an idea or pencil sketch, while others are currently under negotiation for the building or purchasing of a vessel. Therefore, this book will include all announcements made up to July 1987.

Gone are the days of sailing in an American ship to Southampton, Genoa, Mombasa, Bombay, Yokohama or Rio de Janeiro. What I hope this book does, therefore, is to rekindle those fond memories you may have had on an American liner; and, thanks to the ingenuity of a few spirited men and women, you can again sail the waterways and seas on an American-owned liner.

Milton H. Watson
The Bronx, NY

Left Brasil's *maiden arrival in New York* (Courtesy Peter M. Warner).

Explanatory notes

Below is a sample entry for one the ships included in the book; the numbers refer to the individual explanatory notes following the example.

Santa Mercedes[1] 1978-1984[2] (c)[3]

Bethlehem Shipbuilding Corporation, Sparrow's Point, Maryland, 1963.[4]

11,188 tons[5]; 547 × 79 ft (167 × 24 m)[6]; steam turbines[7]; single screw[8]; 20 knots[9]; 121 first[10]. Launched 30/7/1963.[11]

1 Name of ship.
2 Date of operation — the year(s) the vessel operated for the company.
3 Indicates that the ship was chartered by the company.
4 Builder and shipyard where the ship was built and year completed.
5 Tonnage — all tonnages listed are gross tons (the amount of permanent enclosed space, ie hull, superstructure and deckhouses, in a ship calculated by 100 cubic feet volume being equal to one gross ton.

Because of differences in measurement, many American ships have been given two official tonnages, one US and one British. American tonnage is calculated on an 1865 law whereby only the cubic content of the hull and the first deck attached directly to the hull are measured. This was acceptable at that time since ship design had not progressed towards permitting any passenger decks above the weather deck. British law, however, advanced with the times and is calculated to take into account the ship's entire superstructure. American companies always listed the British tonnage in their literature since it was larger, but officially used American tonnage to save on docking and other port charges. This is why the *United States* went from 53,329 to 38,216 gross tons, and why *Independence* of American Hawaii is listed at 30,090 tons in company brochures and 20,220 tons in *Lloyd's*. Therefore, to satisfy both purist and novice, the official tonnage as cited in *Lloyd's Register of Shipping* will appear in the fleet list and, where

necessary, 'A' will indicate American and 'B' British tonnage. Where Lloyd's and company literature coincide, only one figure will appear.

A recent international tonnage agreement has meant a substantial increase in gross tonnage for new vessels.

6 Dimensions — the length and breadth of the ship in both feet and (metres). Length is cited in overall feet (metres) (ie from the extreme forward point of the vessel to a similar point aft) while breadth is the widest part of the ship.
7 Type of engines.
8 Propulsion — a single screw indicates one propeller, twin screw is two propellers, triple screw is three propellers and quadruple screw is four propellers.
9 Service speed in knots. One knot equals one nautical mile (6,080 ft) per hour.
10 Passenger/vehicle capacity — this figure can vary greatly in a ship's career. The figures listed are taken from company literature when the ship was new or what the chartering company stated in its promotional material.
11 Launch date (where available) — day/month/year.

There then follows a résumé of each ship's activities. All dates are given as day/month/year.

MV = Maiden Voyage — the first sailing the ship undertakes.
FV = First Voyage — the first sailing on a particular route (or cruise) or for that particular company.
LV = Last Voyage — the last sailing of the ship on a particular route.
RV = Round Voyage — the number of round trips the ship made on a particular route, usually on Atlantic and Pacific sailings.

Some liners appear in two or more fleet lists, in which case all specifications will be given for each entry, with emphasis given to the ship's activity for each particular operator. Such multiple entries are cross-referenced.

Alaska Marine Highway

(1963 to date)

Alaska has more coastline than the rest of the United States combined, and more than half of its largest cities are not accessible by conventional roads. These are the reasons why Alaskans in 1960 voted the necessary bonding to establish the state's waterborne highway system. Operating as a division of the Department of Transportation and Public Facilities, the Marine Highway System started with the snub-nosed *Chilkat*, and by the end of its first operational year a fleet of four ships, including the *Malaspina*, *Taku* and *Matanuska*, served the company.

Chilkat, the smallest vessel, today serves between Ketchikan and Hollis and carries only day passengers. *Malaspina*, *Taku* and *Matanuska* are sister ships produced by the same Puget Sound shipyard; the two 'M's carry 120 standard vehicles and *Taku* 105. Cabins

are provided for over 500 passengers, together with a dining room, cocktail lounge and solarium. The ships ply the route along Alaska's coast from Seattle and Skagway with many intermediate stops.

Tustamena was introduced in August 1964 and placed on the Seldovia, Homer, Port Lions and Kodiak service. She carried 220 passengers, in two-berth and four-berth cabins, and 50 vehicles. In May 1968 she was renovated and lengthened by the insertion of a 56-ft mid-section at San Francisco.

In 1968, *Stena Britannica* was chartered from the Swedish firm of Stena Line, renamed *Wickersham* (registered in Panama) and placed on the Seattle-

Alaska Marine's smallest vessel Chilkat (Alaska Marine Highway).

Skagway run. She was returned to her Scandinavian owners at the end of 1973. In 1969 the newly built cabinless *Le Bartlett* was introduced and placed on the Cordova-Valdez-Whittier route.

In 1974, Alaska Marine took delivery of their new flagship, *Columbia*. She was placed on the Seattle-Skagway run carrying 1,000 passengers (of whom 324 occupied cabins) and 180 vehicles. A lounge, dining room and solarium were provided for the passengers' enjoyment.

The final additions to Alaska Marine Highway's fleet were in 1974 and 1977 with the introduction of *Le Conte* and *Aurora*. Both these small vessels are stationed at Cordova and ferry 250 passengers in lounges and 47 vehicles to Valdez and Whittier.

Alaska Marine Highway is a year-round operation providing an alternative to the cruise ships. Types of accommodation are a plain ticket, entitling the holder to passage only (sleep is taken in a lounge chair), a dormitory berth, an inside four-berth cabin with facilities, and an outside two-berth with private facilities. None of the fares includes meals, which can be purchased on board.

As of the summer of 1987 (summer is the most popular time to travel, when cabins should be booked months in advance), Alaska Marine deployed its vessels as follows: *Columbia* and *Matanuska*

Malaspina which serves on the Prince Rupert-Skagway run (Alaska Marine Highway).

undertook the Seattle-Skagway route, a four-day run; *Malaspina* and *Taku* handled the Prince Rupert-Skagway route in two days; *Le Conte* was dispatched on the two-day Petersburg-Skagway run; *Aurora* sailed on the Ketchikan-Hollis route; and *Tustumena* and *Le Bartlett* carried out services in the south-west system (Cordova-Valdez-Seward-Kodiak-Seldovia area). During the winter, when Alaska is basically snow-covered, services are reduced and some of the ships laid up.

1 *Chilkat* 1957

J.M. Martinac Shipbuilding Corp, Tacoma, Washington, 1957.

256 gross tons; 93 × 33 ft (28 × 10 m); diesel engines; twin screw; 10 knots; 75 passengers, 15 vehicles.

MV 1957 Ketchikan-Metlakatla-Hollis.

2 *Malaspina* 1963

Puget Sound Bridge & Drydock Company, Seattle, Washington, 1963.

2,928 gross tons; 352 × 73 ft (107 × 22 m); motorship; twin screw; 17 knots; 750 passengers, 134 vehicles. Launched 4/6/1962.

MV 1/2/1963 Prince Rupert-Skagway. 1971-72 Rebuilt and lengthened by 56 ft to 408 ft (17 to 124 m). FV 2/6/1972 Seattle-Skagway.

3 *Taku* 1963

Puget Sound Bridge & Drydock Company, Seattle, Washington, 1963.

2,458 gross tons; 352 × 73 ft (107 × 22 m); motorship; twin screw; 16 knots; 500 passengers, 109 vehicles. Launched 2/7/1963.

MV 4/1963 Seattle-Skagway.

4 *Matanuska* 1963

Puget Sound Bridge & Drydock Company, Seattle, Washington, 1963.

2,458 gross tons; 352 × 73 ft (107 × 22 m); motorship; twin screw; 16 knots; 750 passengers, 109 vehicles. Launched 12/5/1962.

MV 10/6/1963 Prince Rupert-Skagway. 1977-78 Rebuilt and lengthened by 56 ft to 408 ft (17 to 124 m). FV 15/8/1978 Seattle-Skagway.

Below *Alaska Marine's* Matanuska (Alaska Marine Highway).

Bottom *Operating the south-west service for Alaska Marine is* Le Bartlett (Alaska Marine Highway).

Left *The flagship of Alaska Marine's fleet is* Columbia *(Alaska Marine Highway).*

Below left Aurora *is employed on the Ketchikan-Hollis route, a five-hour trip (Peterson Builders Inc).*

5 *Tustamena* 1964

Christy Corporation, Sturgeon Bay, Wisconsin, 1964.

2,174 gross tons; 239 × 60 ft (73 × 18 m); steam turbines; twin screw; 14.5 knots; 220 passengers, 54 vehicles. Launched 14/12/1963.

MV 8/1964 Seward-Kodiak-Seldovia-Homer. 5/1968 Lengthened by 56 ft to 295 ft (17 to 90 m), to sleep 58 passengers.

6 *Wickersham* 1968-1973 (c)

A/S Langesunds MV, Mangesund, Norway, 1968.

5,073 gross tons; 364 × 60 ft (111 × 18 m); diesel engines; twin screw; 23 knots; 1,300 passengers. Launched as *Stena Britannica* (Stena Line).

1968 *Wickersham* (Alaska Marine). Route: Seattle-Skagway. 1974 *Viking 6* (Rederi AB Sally). 1981 *Goelo* (Rederi AB Sally). 1983 *Sol Olympia* (Sol Maritime Services). 1985 *Sun Express* (Rederi AB Sally).

7 *Le Bartlett* 1969

Jefferson Shipbuilders, Jeffersonville, Indiana, 1969.

934 gross tons; 193 × 53 ft (59 × 16 m); diesel engines; twin screw; 15 knots; 165 passengers, 54 vehicles.

MV 4/5/1969 Seattle-Cordova. Route: Cordova-Valdez-Whittier.

8 *Columbia* 1974

Lockheed Shipbuilding & Construction Company, Seattle, Washington, 1974.

3,946 gross tons; 418 × 85 ft (127 × 26 m); motorship; twin screw; 21 knots; 1,000 passengers, 184 vehicles. Launched 3/5/1973.

MV 5/7/1974 Seattle-Skagway. 10/13/1974 Ran aground in Peril Strait, Alaska. Laid up for four months. 2/1975 Returned to service.

9 *Le Conte* 1974

Peterson Shipbuilders, Sturgeon Bay, Wisconsin, 1974.

1,328 gross tons; 235 × 57 ft (71 × 17 m); steam turbines; twin screw; 15.5 knots; 250 passengers, 47 vehicles. Launched 26/5/1974.

MV 17/5/1974 Seattle-Juneau.

10 *Aurora* 1977

Peterson Shipbuilders, Sturgeon Bay, Wisconsin, 1977.

1,281 gross tons; 236 × 57 ft (72 × 17 m); steam turbines; twin screw; 15.5 knots; 250 passengers, 47 vehicles. Launched 1/5/1977.

MV 8/1977 Seattle-Ketchikan.

Alaska Steamship Company

(1895-1954)

The goal of Messrs Charles E. Peabody, George Lent, Frank E. Burns, Walter Oakes, Captain Melville Nichols and Captain George Roberts was to form a steamship company that would provide an inexpensive and reliable service from Seattle to Alaska, and at the same time challenge the monopoly of the Pacific Coast Steamship Company. In December 1894, the men incorporated the Alaska Steamship Company in Port Townsend; it was capitalized at $30,000 in 30 shares of $100 each, and its first steamer, *Willapa*, departed Seattle on 3 March 1895 for Juneau. Sustaining the company's growth was the completion of a railroad into the interior, encouraging mining activity for precious metals that brought both fortune-seekers and tourists. By 1905, activity shifted from the Juneau/Skagway area to Valdez/Cordova, then eventually to Nome, where Alaska Steamship was ready to capitalize on the bonanza by switching its ships accordingly.

The prospect of riches attracted even wealthy East Coast folks, and, with the blessings of the J.P. Morgan-Guggenheim syndicate, Alaska Steamship was able to purchase the Northwestern Steamship Company in 1909. After amalgamating the two companies, Charles Peabody designed the company's house flag: a black ball centred on a red flag. After his retirement, the flag was modified to include an 'A' across the black ball and a white rim between and ball and the red field.

At the outbreak of the Second World War, Alaska Steamship had a fleet of 16 vessels operating out of Seattle to Skagway, Seward and Nome. After the attack on Pearl Harbor, the company became an agent for the War Administration, was assigned its own ships and was given sixty others to manage. It returned to peacetime operations under the ownership of Skinner and Eddy Corporation, Seattle, which purchased Alaska Steamship in August 1944 for $4,290,000.

The first passenger sailing out of Seattle was undertaken by *Alaska* in January 1946. She was subsequently followed by *Yukon, Aleutian, Baranof* and *Denali*. Ports of call northbound were Ketchikan (two days), Juneau (three days) and Seward (five days), with occasional calls at Wrangell, Petersburg, Skagway, Sitka, Cordova, Valdez, Kodiak and Seldovia. Southbound, the steamers called at the same ports they stopped at heading north. All steamers had accommodation for over 200 passengers ranging from steerage (men only with no blankets supplied) which in 1949 cost $66 (£16), to a de luxe cabin with private bath for $153.50 (£38). It was during this period that the company decided to concentrate on tourism, and issued an illustrated booklet entitled *How to be a Salt* describing the ship's vocabulary and departments and suggesting how passengers could relax and make themselves at home.

The Inside Passage to Alaska was a hazardous journey and Alaska Steamship was no stranger to its perils. On 4 February 1946 at 4 am during a blinding snowstorm and strong north-easterly winds, Captain Chris Trondsen, in command of *Yukon*, changed course and in the process ran aground near Cape Fairfield. Heavy seas prevented the launching of boats until daylight, by which time rescue vessels arrived to take off the frightened passengers and crew. Some years later another calamity was the collision of *Baranof* with the Greek steamer *Triton* on 26 July 1952 near Namaimo with the loss of two of the crew of the latter.

Many factors contributed to Alaska Steamship's eventual termination of passenger service. Firstly, there were continued labour problems caused by longshoremen, seamen and stewards. Secondly, the arrival of an air service (partly subsidized by the Government) to Alaska took away potential passengers and freight bookings, and thirdly was the end of charter privileges and subsidy payments. Alaska Steamship was facing insurmountable financial difficulties that even a new fleet of steamers could not remedy.

On 6 July 1954, therefore, Mr D.E. Skinner, president of Alaska Steamship Company, announced that his firm was moving out of the passenger business. *Baranof* was immediately laid up, *Alaska* sailed until August, then *Denali* made the company's last sailing in September 1954. In quick succession they were sold off. *Aleutian*, which was on charter to Hawaiian-Pacific in 1953, was sold to Caribbean Atlantic Lines

Below Alaska *was the only vessel built for Alaska Steamship* (Frank O. Braynard collection).

Bottom Yukon *in Alaskan waters* (Everett E. Viez, SSHSA Collection).

and renamed *Tradewind*; *Denali* was purchased by Peninsular & Occidental SS Co, *Alaska* went to Margo-Pacific Lines and *Baranof* was sold to Japanese scrappers in 1955.

Alaska Steamship now concentrated on the carriage of cargo, with the emphasis on increased efficiency. Though this was achieved in the late 'fifties, continued modernization was necessary to remain competitive. Declining revenues, rising operation costs and a devastating fire at Cordova all conspired to force management to cease operations in January 1971.

1 *Alaska* 1923-1954

Todd Drydock & Construction Corporation, Tacoma, Washington, 1923.

4,515 gross tons; 366 × 49 ft (112 × 15 m); turbo-electric; twin screw; 16 knots; 240 first class, 109 steerage passengers. Launched 19/4/1923.
MV 9/6/1923 Seattle-Alaska. 27/10/1940 Struck reef in Arthur Passage. 1942-1945 Chartered to War Shipping Administration. 1/1946 Returned to service. 1955 *Mazatlan* (Margo-Pacific Lines). 1956 Scrapped.

2 *Yukon* 1924-1946
Yukon 1946 (c)

William Cramp & Sons Shipbuilding Company, Philadelphia, Pennsylvania, 1899.
5,747 gross tons; 374 × 50 ft (114 × 15 m); triple expansion engines; twin screw; 15 knots; 266 first class passengers. Launched 4/4/1899 as *Mexico* (NY Cuba Mail).
1905 *Mexico* (Panama Railroad). 1923 *Yukon* (Alaska Steamship). FV 17/5/1924 Seattle-Alaska. 1942 War Administration. 1946 Chartered to Alaska Steamship. 4/2/1946 Ran aground in Johnstone Bay, Prince William Sound.

Below Denali *was the last passenger ship to sail for Alaska Steamship* (Frank O. Braynard collection).

3 *Aleutian* 1930-1953

William Cramp & Sons Shipbuilding Company, Philadelphia, Pennsylvania, 1906.

6,361 gross tons; 416× 50 ft (127 × 15 m); triple expansion engines; twin screw; 17 knots; 334 first class, 162 steerage passengers. Launched 21/3/1906 as *Mexico* (New York & Cuba Mail).

1929 *Aleutian* (Alaska Steamship). FV 3/5/1930 Seattle-Alaska. 1942-1946 Army transport. 11/1946 Returned to service. 1953 Chartered to Hawaiian-Pacific Line (see page 125). 1954 *Tradewind* (Caribbean Atlantic Line) (see page 76). 1956 Scrapped in Belgium 76).

4 *Baranof* 1936-1954

New York Shipbuilding Corporation, Camden, New Jersey, 1919.

4,990 gross tons; 374 × 51 ft (114 × 16 m); quadruple expansion engines; single screw; 110 passengers. Launched 23/9/1918 for Grace Line and taken over by US Navy as transport.

1920 *Santa Elisa* (Grace Line). 1936 *Baranof* (Alaska Steamship). FV 17/6/1936. 1942-1946 Chartered to the War Shipping Administration. 5/1946 Returned to service. 26/7/1952 Collided with Greek steamer *Triton*, 2 killed. 1954 Laid up. 1955 Broken up in Japan.

5 *Denali* 1938-1954

Newport News Shipbuilding & Drydock Company, Newport News, Virginia, 1927.

4,302 gross tons; 336 × 51 ft (102 × 16 m); steam turbines; twin screw; 12 knots; 354 passengers. Launched 30/6/1927 as *Caracas* (Atlantic & Caribbean Steam Navigation).

1938 *Denali* (Alaska Steamship). FV 26/4/1938 Seattle-Alaska. 1941-1946 Chartered by War Shipping Administration. 5/1946 Returned to service. 1954 *Cuba* (Peninsular & Occidental SS Co) (see page 159). 1955 *Southern Cross* (P&O SS Co). 1960 Scrapped at Antwerp.

Alaska Transportation Company

(1948)

Founded in 1935, Alaska Transportation Company operated a fleet of small freighters in the Puget Sound area. After the war, the company counted on the return of tourism to Alaska and in anticipation of the hordes of travellers, the company purchased *George Washington* in 1948 from the US Maritime Commission. After a light refit, *George Washington* was sent northwards from Seattle in May of that year. She sailed for three months, after which she was laid up as a result of industrial action. The company was unable to settle with the strikers and decided to lay up the ship. It may be presumed that the service was not a success, as it was eventually abandoned and the company ceased all operations shortly thereafter.

George Washington 1948

Newport News Shipbuilding & Drydock Company, Newport News, Virginia, 1924.

5,184 gross tons; 390 × 54 ft (119 × 16 m); steam turbines; twin screw; 16 knots; approx 350 passengers. Laid down for Old Dominion Line and launched 20/8/1924 for Eastern Steamship. 1946 Chartered to Alcoa (see page 26). 1947 Laid up. 1948 Sold to Alaska Transportation Company. FV 31/5/1948 Seattle-Alaska. LV 8/1948. Laid up. 1949 *Gascogne* (French Line). 1952 *Gascogne* (Messageries Maritimes). 1955 Scrapped at Hong Kong.

The unsuccessful George Washington *at Ketchikan, Alaska* (SSHSA Collection).

Alcoa Steamship Company

(1940-1960)

In 1886, Charles Martin Hall and a group of other men formed the Pittsburgh Reduction Company to further the commercial development of aluminium. The name of the company was changed in 1907 to the Aluminum Company of America (ALCOA) which started in the shipping business in 1917 by purchasing the small wooden-hulled steamer *Mohegan*. Two additional steamers were built in 1919, but thereafter Alcoa relied on chartered vessels. By the 1930s, the company was operating the following services: Gulf ports to the Caribbean under the Aluminum Line banner; East Coast ports to the Caribbean under the American Caribbean Line house-flag; and the Canada-West Indies route under the trade name of Ocean Dominion Steamship Corporation. On 25 September 1940, Alcoa consolidated its three operations and trade names to form the Alcoa Steamship Company Inc, with the simultaneous announcement that all company ship names would use the prefix 'Alcoa'.

During 1941, Alcoa entered the passenger business by chartering three ships from Eastern Steamship Lines. The purpose was to fill the void on the New York-Bermuda run vacated by United States Lines and run a service between New York and the West Indies. The first ship to sail under the colours of Alcoa was *Acadia* on 11 April 1941, followed on 3 May by *Evangeline*. Both liners remained in service until December 1941.

After the war, Alcoa again turned its attention to acquiring ships fitted with passenger accommodation. Three 'Victory' hulls under construction by the Oregon Shipbuilding Corporation were purchased and redesigned by George G. Sharp for the accommodation of 98 passengers. Each ship was 8,481 tons, 455 feet long and featured such passenger amenities as all outside staterooms with private bath, a swimming pool and modern public rooms. A unique feature in their construction was the use of aluminium in the superstructure, a new trend in shipbuilding.

Waiting for its 'Victory' ships to take shape, Alcoa 'bareboat chartered' the 5,184-ton *George Washington* from the US Maritime Commission (this meant that Alcoa was virtual owner of the vessel responsible for crewing, liability, maintenance and provisioning). Alcoa dispatched the 'GW' on 1 February 1946 on the New York-Bermuda service which lasted until April 1947, a month before the delivery of the first unit of Alcoa's new trio.

Alcoa Cavalier was the first Alcoa-designed passenger ship to sail under their banner. She departed on her maiden voyage from New York on 2 May 1947, and thereafter provided a 17-day voyage every three weeks. The next vessel was *Alcoa Clipper*, which departed New Orleans on 23 May 1947, with *Alcoa Clipper*, which departed New Orleans on 23 May 1947, with *Alcoa Corsair* completing the trio by sailing on 3 June 1947. The New Orleans schedule provided voyages of 24-day duration every two weeks; the voyages were later reduced to seventeen days. During the late 1940s and into the 1950s, additional tonnage was added to the line, but each either carried only twelve passengers or no passengers at all.

As airlines introduced jet aircraft, followed by a resurgence of travel to Europe, Alcoa was one of the first companies to see the 'writing on the wall'. From 1960, Alcoa withdrew from the passenger business. The first ship to go was the *Alcoa Corsair*, which was not able to complete her last voyage as on 22 October 1960 she collided with the Italian motorship *Lorenzo*

Marcello. A 150 ft gash was ripped in *Alcoa Corsair's* starboard side, forcing her to return to port. In 1961 she was sold at public auction. *Alcoa Cavalier* and *Alcoa Clipper* were withdrawn from service and laid up at Mobile, Alabama. In 1963 they were purchased by the Maritime Administration and continued in lay-up until scrapped in 1968 and 1969 respectively.

Today, Alcoa Steamship is a subsidiary of the Aluminum Company of America, operating a fleet of 25 bulk carriers worldwide.

Below George Washington *sailed on Alcoa's New York-Bermuda run* (C. Spanton Ashdown collection).

Bottom *Note the vertical pairs of portholes in the hull of* Alcoa Clipper (Alcoa Steamship Company Inc).

Alcoa Cavalier *docking at New Orleans. The bottom set of portholes was covered up after 1961 when Alcoa's ships started to carry bauxite (Alcoa Steamship Company Inc).*

1 *George Washington* 1946-1947 (c)

Newport News Shipbuilding & Drydock Company, Newport News, Virginia, 1924.

5,184 gross tons; 390 × 54 ft (119 × 16 m); steam turbines; twin screw; 16 knots; 322 first class, 58 third class, 290 steerage passengers. Laid down for Old Dominion. Launched 20/8/1924 for Eastern Steamship.

1924 Chartered to Clyde. 1942-1946 War service. 1946 Chartered to Alcoa. FV 1/2/1946 New York-Bermuda. LV 19/4/1947 New York-Bermuda. 1948 Alaska Transportation Company. 1949 *Gascogne* (French Line). 1952 *Gascogne* (Messageries Maritimes). 1955 Scrapped at Hong Kong.

2 *Alcoa Cavalier* 1947-1960

Oregon Shipbuilding Corporation, Portland, Oregon, 1947.

8,481 gross tons; 455 × 62 ft (139 × 19 m); steam turbines; single screw; 16.5 knots; 98 first class passengers. Launched 22/9/1946.

MV 2/5/1947 New York-Caribbean. FV 1949 New Orleans-Caribbean. 1960 Withdrawn from service and laid up. 1963 Sold to Maritime Administration. 1968 Scrapped at New Orleans.

3 *Alcoa Clipper* 1947-1960

Oregon Shipbuilding Corporation, Portland, Oregon, 1947.

8,481 gross tons; 455 × 62 ft (139 × 19 m); steam turbines; single screw; 16.5 knots; 98 first class passengers. Launched 28/9/1946.

MV 23/5/1947 New Orleans-Caribbean. 1960 Withdrawn from service and laid up. 1963 Sold to Maritime Administration. 1969 Scrapped at Baltimore.

4 *Alcoa Corsair* 1947-1960

Oregon Shipbuilding Corporation, Portland, Oregon, 1947.

8,481 gross tons; 455 × 62 ft (139 × 19 m); steam turbines; single screw; 16.5 knots; 98 first class passengers. Launched 2/10/1946.

MV 3/6/1947 New Orleans-Caribbean. 22/10/1960 Collided with *Lorenzo Marcello* in the Mississippi River, ten killed. March 1961 *Alcoa* (American Bulk Carriers). 1963 *Rye* (American Bulk Carriers). Sept 1963 Scrapped in Japan.

American Banner Lines

(1957-1959)

Arnold Bernstein's ambition was to operate a passenger steamship service between the United States and Europe. During the summer of 1948 he chartered *Continental* for four round voyages from New York to Plymouth and Antwerp, but his ultimate goal was to run an economy passenger and cargo service from New York to Antwerp or Rotterdam. After a lull in the negotiations, which had begun in 1946, Bernstein acquired the 9,214-ton freighter *Badger Mariner* in 1957. During the $11 million refit, American Banner Lines was created to operate the new acquisition, which was renamed *Atlantic*. American Banner followed the pattern set by Holland-America's *Maasdam, Ryndam* and *Statendam* by devoting over 85 per cent of the interior space to tourist class; and again, like the Holland-America ships, *Atlantic* was

The tourist class ship, Atlantic (Frank O. Braynard Collection).

completely air-conditioned, and all her cabins had private facilities.

Atlantic left New York on 11 June 1958 on her first voyage to Zeebrugge and Amsterdam. In all, she undertook eleven round voyages in 1958 at a 40.3 per cent occupancy rate, and 15 voyages in 1959 at 51.9 per cent occupancy. This was not a profitable venture, and on *Atlantic*'s arrival in New York on 3 November 1959 she was withdrawn and sold to American Export Lines.

Shortly thereafter, Arnold Bernstein retired from the shipping business. He died on 6 March 1971 at the age of 83.

Atlantic 1957-1959

Sun Shipbuilding & Drydock Company, Chester, Pennsylvania, 1953.

14,138 gross tons; 564 × 76 ft (172 × 23 m); geared turbines; single screw; 20 knots; 40 first class, 860 tourist class passengers. Launched 1/7/1953 as C-4 freighter *Badger Mariner* at 9,214 tons.

1957 *Atlantic* (American Banner). Rebuilt at Ingalls Shipbuilding Corporation, Pascagoula. FV 11/6/1958 New York-Zeebrugge-Amsterdam. LV 25/10/1959 Amsterdam-New York. 1960 Sold to American Export (see page 50). 1971 *Universe Campus* (Orient Overseas). 1976 *Universe* (Orient Overseas).

American Canadian Line
(1966-1988)

American Canadian Caribbean Line
(1988 to date)

The pioneer who re-introduced cruising along America's inland waterways and coastline was Luther Blount, founder and President of American Canadian Line. He conceived this idea during the winter of 1965-6 and in May of the latter year he launched his first ship, *Canyon Flyer*, from his shipyard, Blount Marine Corporation, established in 1949.

The 65 ft (20 m) *Canyon Flyer* catered for 20 passengers and operated a series of week-long excursions from Warren, Rhode Island, through southern New England waters. Following her sale in 1970 to interests in the Virgin Islands, Blount launched his second vessel, *Mount Hope*. She was 110 ft (33 m) long, accommodated 40 passengers and had four unique features. The first was a bow ramp device which enabled the narrow-draught vessel to be brought right up on to the beach to disembark passengers in out-of-the-way places; secondly there were vista-view windows which wrapped around the bow of *Mount Hope* affording passengers a panoramic view while cruising. The third feature was her pilot-house, which was mounted on hydraulic pistons and could be lowered from 24 ft (7 m) to 15 ft (5 m), allowing clearance for low bridges. Fourthly, a stern ramp attached by hinges swung down practically to water level to provide a swimming platform — all these features were patented by Blount.

Mount Hope's cruising grounds were: from Warren to Chicago via rivers, canals and the Great Lakes; the Mississippi River; along the Atlantic intracoastal waterway to Warren; and New England cruises.

Sensing the need for larger tonnage, *New Shoreham* was launched in 1970. Among her many features were once again bow and stern ramps, vista-view windows and a retractable pilot-house. Capable of carrying 60 passengers in 30 staterooms, she operated a similar

itinerary to that of *Mount Hope* except that the Mississippi River and the southern states were excluded. After careful research and planning, including one cruise from Nassau in February 1975 by *New Shoreham* to introduce Bahamaian dignitaries to the ship and the idea, an agreement was reached between American Canadian and the Bahama Island government for the vessel to make cruises out of Nassau to the Bahama Out Islands. These cruises started in December 1975.

Mount Hope remained in service until she was sold in 1973. In the spring of 1979, *New Shoreham* was sold to Alaska Cruise Boat, leaving American Canadian with no summer services that year. In the autumn of that year, however, *New Shoreham II* was launched. She was American Canadian's largest vessel, with a length of 150 ft (46 m) and a complement of 72 passengers in 36 de luxe staterooms. The features of *New Shoreham II* followed that of her predecessors, with such added touches as bow and stern thrusters, underwater exhausts, soft-mounted machinery placed away from living spaces and sound insulation to ensure a quiet, restful atmosphere.

The first trip of *New Shoreham II* was a positioning voyage from Warren to West Palm Beach, Florida, sailing on 14 November 1979. She then made directly for Nassau where on 22 December she commenced her winter programme of eleven-day cruises to the Bahama Out Islands, becoming the largest US-registered, US-flagged passenger ship to sail from Nassau. On 1 June 1980 she began sailing from Warren on twelve-day Saguenay River cruises (Warren to Tadoussac via the Hudson River, Erie Canal and St Lawrence River).

After years of hard labour, intensive advertising and bookings by mail, dividends were finally being

Above left *The first ship in the Blount fleet was* Canyon Flyer (American Canadian Line).

Left *Mount Hope with a full load of passengers* (American Canadian Line).

Above New Shoreham *cruising an inland waterway* (American Canadian Line).

realized. Travel agents who at first declined to book Blount's cruises eventually accounted for 40 per cent of American Canadian business in 1980. In addition, non-union labour worked on the ships, as a result of a law that stated that non-union crews could be used on ships operating in coastal waters if they were under 100 gross registered tons.

To cope with the increased popularity of his cruises, Blount ordered and built his biggest ship. Christened on 25 October 1983 by John Gentles, director of tourism for Jamaica, the $4.5 million *Caribbean Prince* was completed in December. Like her running-mates, *Caribbean Prince* has all the patented Blount features, and, in addition, a bulbous bow.

American Canadian applied for and received a SOLAS (Safety of Life at Sea) Certificate which enabled it to carry passengers on short international sea voyages. In addition, the certificate also stated that the company's ships must always be within twenty miles of land. This certificate was required for the *Caribbean Prince* to make cruises out of Jamaica and, later, the Virgin Islands. All companies have to apply for this certificate annually for each of its ships that sails in America's inland waterways and then in international waters.

Caribbean Prince sailed from Rhode Island on 4 December 1983 for West Palm Beach, Florida where she embarked seven passengers. She then departed on her first cruise to Montego Bay, Jamaica, her winter base, whence she would sail on twelve-day cruises circumnavigating the island. Having wintered in the Caribbean, she sailed for Warren and thence to Detroit via many canals, making her the largest canal vessel in the world. On 17 June 1984 she started a series of twelve-day cruises between Detroit and Georgian Bay, Ontario, Canada.

The Jamaican cruises proved not to be successful, however, so *Caribbean Prince* was switched to twelve-day cruises out of St Thomas to the numerous Virgin Islands in December 1984. *New Shoreham II*

New Shoreham II *at a beach-head* (American Canadian Line).

continued on her winter seven-day Bahama Out Island cruises from Nassau, interrupted by a two-month stint in 1985 out of St Thomas and St Maarten.

Life aboard American Canadian ships is informal, with an emphasis on enjoying your ship's company and the scenery. There are no big bands, celebrities or cruise directors; instead, days are spent in secluded harbours or at beaches, while evenings are spent chatting, reading, playing cards or board games, listening to the piano or taking a stroll around the island, beach or town. Alcohol is not served on board American Canadian vessels, although passengers are at liberty to bring their own to be served by the company's on-board non-union staff.

In the spring of 1988, American Canadian changed its name to American Canadian Caribbean Line to reflect its Caribbean presence. Its President, Luther Blount, further announced that following a successful 12-day cruise in April 1988 by *New Shoreham II* from Cancun, Mexico, to Belize City, a series of ten 12-day cruises will be operated by the vessel from Cancun to Belize City, starting in January 1989. *Caribbean Prince* will continue to be based from a Caribbean port during the winter, while in the summers both ships cruise out of Warren on Saguenay River cruises and in the autumn on 'Fall Foliage' cruises. Per diem rates for an outside cabin with private facilities average around $100 (£63).

1 **Canyon Flyer** 1966-1970

Blount Marine Corporation, Warren, Rhode Island, 1966.

64 gross tons; 65 × 18 ft (20 × 5 m); General Motors V12; twin screw; 20 first class passengers.
1969 Sold to interests in the Virgin Islands.

2 **Mount Hope** 1969-1973

Blount Marine Corporation, Warren, Rhode Island, 1969.

99 gross tons; 110 × 21 ft (33 × 6 m); 2 General Motors V8; twin screw; 40 first class passengers.
1973 *Arkansas Traveller* (Arkansas River Charter Company). *Viking Explorer* (Paddleford Packet).

3 **New Shoreham** 1970-1979

Blount Marine Corporation, Warren, Rhode Island, 1970.

99 gross tons; 116 × 28 ft (35 × 9 m); General Electric diesels; twin screw; 12 knots; 60 first class passengers.
12/1975 Nassau-Bahama Out Islands. 1979 Sold to Alaska Cruise Boat. 1979 *Glacier Bay Explorer* (Glacier Bay Lodge Inc — charter). 1980 *Glacier Bay Explorer* (Exploration Holidays and Cruises) (see page 103).

4 **New Shoreham II** 1979

Blount Marine Corporation, Warren, Rhode Island, 1979

97 gross tons; 150 × 32 ft (46 × 10 m); General Electric diesels; twin screw; 10 knots; 72 first class passengers.

Position voyage 14/11/1979 Warren-West Palm Beach. MV 22/12/1979 Nassau-Bahama Out Islands. FV 1/6/1980 Warren-Saguenay River. FV 4/1988 Cancun-Belize City (1 cruise). 1/1989 Cancun-Belize City.

5 *Caribbean Prince* 1983

Blount Marine Corporation, Warren, Rhode Island, 1983.

100 gross tons; 165 × 35 ft (50 × 11 m); General Electric diesels; twin screw; 80 first class passengers. Launched 25/10/1983.

Positioning voyage, Rhode Island-West Palm Beach-Montego Bay. MV 12/83 West Palm Beach-Montego Bay. FV 6/1/1984 Montego Bay-round Jamaica. 6/1984 Warren-Detroit. 17/6/1984 Detroit-Georgian Bay cruises. FV 21/12/1984 St Thomas-Virgin Islands cruise. FV 9/6/1985 Warren-Saguenay River.

Below Caribbean Prince *is the largest canal vessel in the world* (American Canadian Line).

Bottom *The lounge on board* Caribbean Prince (American Canadian Line).

American Cruise Lines

(1974 to date)

One of the pioneers in the revival and expansion of passenger traffic on America's inland and coastal waterways was American Cruise Lines, an affiliate of the New England Steamship Company of Haddam, Connecticut, both initiated and owned by Charles A. Robertson.

The first vessel to slide down the ways for American was *American Eagle*. Built specifically for coastal cruising, she had a draught of only 7 ft and was 80 gross tons. An important factor which American Cruise Lines had to consider was staffing, and in order to be able to use American non-union crew the ship had by law to be under 100 gross registered tons, therefore all future American Cruise Lines ships had to fit that criterion. *American Eagle* had all outside staterooms, each with large picture windows and completely private facilities. There were several lounges, of which one was glass enclosed for use during inclement weather, and a pleasant dining room capable of sitting all 60 passengers at one sitting. *American Eagle* also carried an inboard/outboard fibreglass launch on stern davits enabling the 'mini-liner' to be independent of docking facilities at remote ports.

American Eagle undertook her maiden voyage from Haddam to Block Island, Cape Cod, Nantucket and Martha's Vineyard in September 1975. Later that autumn, she headed along America's coastline for Florida.

The popularity and heavy advance bookings for *American Eagle* led American Cruise Lines to place an order for another vessel. *Independence* was launched on 11 June 1976 and completed in August of that year. The two vessels were practically sister ships, but *Independence* was the largest inland cruise ship on the East Coast. Her amenities were a

duplicate of *American Eagle*, and she commenced her inaugural cruise on 4 August 1976 from Haddam, a ten-day affair visiting various New England Islands. After the New England season ended, *American Eagle* was laid up and *Independence* proceeded south, making cruises out of Annapolis to the Chesapeake Bay, and finally Florida, her winter home. Five-day cruises were made along the St John's River and ten-day cruises between Savannah, Georgia, and Fort Myers, Florida, via the intracoastal waterway using rivers, Lake Okeechobee and landcuts — one of the least travelled waterways in the world. In the spring, both ships saw service out of Annapolis before reaching their summer home of Haddam.

Capitalizing on their success, American introduced the 87-passenger *America* in 1982 and the 140-passenger *Savannah* in 1984, the latter being largest inland coastal cruise ship on the east coast at that time. The keys to the company's prosperity were the emphasis placed on ambience and good friendly service provided by a young non-union crew. In addition, itineraries were, and are, carefully planned with noted personalities on board, and with the cuisine tailored to offer a variety of local culinary specialities, continued patronage seemed assured. However, just as *Savannah* made her appearance, a depression hit the New England cruise market and *American Eagle* was sold to unidentified buyers.

Sensing the need for more competition on the mighty Mississippi River, American launched the newest and most luxurious riverboat, *New Orleans*,

Above right *American Cruise Lines' second vessel,* Independence (American Cruise Lines).

Right *The three-deck* America *docked at an American port* (American Cruise Lines).

on 21 December 1984, the first of three riverboats planned by the company for the Mississippi River trade. Her maiden cruise was a fourteen-day trip from Chesapeake, Maryland, to Fort Myers, Florida, on 22 June 1985. She left New Orleans on her first cruise up the Mississippi on 13 July and arrived at Memphis, Tennessee, seven days later.

On the East Coast, American Cruise Lines was adjusting its tonnage requirements. During the spring of 1985, *Independence* was sold to Great Pacific Cruise Line, leaving *America* and *Savannah* to carry out the New England sailings in the summer, the southern and northern intracoastal voyages in the spring and autumn, and the winter schedule out of Florida.

Tariffs for the 1985 season were competitive with the major cruise lines, starting at $1,190 (£930) for a seven-day cruise, $1,700 (£1,328) for ten days, $2,380 (£1,959) for fourteen days and $3,570 (£2,789) for a 21-day cruise from Florida to New England or vice versa, all per person, double occupancy.

With an eye on expansion into new markets (Pacific north-west, the Hawaiian islands and inter-island Caribbean cruising), American Cruise Lines went public on 9 July 1986 to raise capital, becoming the second major cruise line (Regency Cruises was the first) to offer stock to the public. Robertson, chairman and chief operating officer, bought 66 per cent of the shares, giving him the chance to control

Below *The sleek* Savannah (American Cruise Lines).

Bottom *The riverboat* New Orleans (American Cruise Lines).

Charleston *departing on another coastal voyage* (American Cruise Lines).

the company's affairs and elect its board of directors. Four million dollars was raised by selling 725,000 shares, and this enabled the company to pay for its fourth ship, the $8.8 million *Charleston*. In the autumn of 1986, *America* completed her New England cruises from Rockland, Maine, and was then withdrawn from service and offered for sale.

Charleston was launched on 4 October 1986, and commissioned on America's intracoastal waterways on 16 May 1987 with a cruise from Baltimore to Savannah. She then sailed north to Boston to commence a series of seven-day cruises along the Maine coast, following which she sailed south to Fort Myers to undertake her winter programme. *Savannah* spent the summer of 1987 on seven-day cruises from Haddam, then spent the winter sailing from Jacksonville, Florida. *New Orleans* had her 1987 summer itinerary diversified — she remained on the Mississippi River until June, then she was transferred to make cruises from Jacksonville. During the autumn she returned to the Mississippi, and from 16 November made cruises from either Fort Myers or Fort Pierce (both in Florida) to Lake Okeechobee. In the spring of 1988, the ships returned to their summer itineraries.

1   *American Eagle* 1975-1984

Harvey F. Gamage Shipyard, South Bristol, Maine, 1975.

80 gross tons; 155 × 29 ft (47 × 9 m); 2 General Motors diesels; twin screw; 13 knots; 60 first class passengers. Launched 21/6/1975.

MV 6/9/1975 Haddam-New England. 1984 Sold to unidentified buyers.

2   *Independence* 1976-1985

Eastern Shipbuilding Corporation, Boothbay Harbor, Maine, 1976.

94 gross tons; 180 × 38 ft (55 × 12 m); 2 Caterpillar diesels; twin screw; 15 knots; 87 first class passengers. Launched 11/6/1976.

MV 4/8/1976 Haddam-New England cruise. 1985 *Columbia* (Great Pacific Cruise Lines) (see page 124).

3 *America* 1982

Chesapeake Shipbuilding Inc, Salisbury, Maryland, 1982.

99 gross tons; 180 × 38 ft (55 × 12 m); 2 Caterpillar diesels; twin screw; 15 knots; 87 first class passengers. Launched 10/9/1981.

MV 10/4/1982 Baltimore-Chesapeake Bay cruise. 9/1986 Laid up.

4 *Savannah* 1984

Chesapeake Shipbuilding Inc, Salisbury, Maryland, 1984.

77 gross tons; 220 × 45 ft (67 × 14 m); 2 General Motors diesels; twin screw; 15 knots; 140 first class passengers. Launched 21/12/1984.

MV 14/4/84 Baltimore-Savannah.

5 *New Orleans* 1985

Chesapeake Shipbuilding Inc, Salisbury, Maryland, 1985.

90 gross tons; 220 × 49 ft (67 × 15 m); 2 General Motors diesels; twin screw; 15 knots; 140 first class passengers. Launched 21/12/1984.

MV 22/6/1985 Norfolk-Fort Myers. FV 13/7/1985 New Orleans-Memphis.

6 *Charleston* 1987

Chesapeake Shipbuilding Inc, Salisbury, Maryland, 1987.

77 gross tons; 215 × 42 ft (66 × 13 m); Detroit diesels; twin screw; 15 knots; 125 first class passengers. Launched 4/10/1986.

MV 16/5/1987 Baltimore-Savannah. FV 20/6/1987 Boston-Maine Coast.

A typically relaxed American Cruise Lines daily programme (American Cruise Lines).

An ample selection on a menu for one of the American Cruise Lines vessels (American Cruise Lines).

Welcome to American Cruise Lines
Today we will be arriving in historic Vicksburg, Mississippi

6:00 a.m. RIVERBOAT LOUNGE	**Early Riser** Coffee and Freshly Baked Pastries
7:30 — 9:00 a.m. DINING SALON	**Breakfast** is served (open seating)
8:00 a.m.	**Arrive** at City Landing, Vicksburg, MS
9:00 — 11:30 a.m.	**Welcome to Vicksburg** Historic tour of Vicksburg including **Vicksburg National Military Park** and **Cairo Museum**. Have mulled cider and cookies while visiting spectacular **Antebellum** homes and sample the famous treats at **Biedenharn Candy Company**.
10:00 a.m. RIVERBOAT LOUNGE	**Mid Morning Snacks** Relax and enjoy Quiche Lorraine or freshly baked cookies.
11:30 — 12:30 p.m. SKY LOUNGE	**Mint Julep Party** A refreshing drink at any time! Perfect when served in our fabulous Sky Lounge
12:30 p.m. DINING SALON	Lunch is served (open seating)
2:00 p.m.	**Afternoon tea** in Vicksburg at the **Grey Oak Mansion**. Re-live the drama of **Gone With The Wind** as you visit this elegant replica of Scarlett O'Hara's **Tara** OR **Tour Vicksburg** on your own! Visit the shops and attractions where you want to spend more time. Explore Vicksburg, it's quite a town!
5:00 p.m. SKY LOUNGE	**Dixieland Jazz Band**, sing along and have a wonderful time.
6:00 — 7:00 p.m. SKY LOUNGE	**Cocktail Hour** Socialize, relax and catch up on the day's activities with hot hors d'oeuvres and refreshments.
7:00 p.m. DINING SALON	**Dinner** is served (open seating)
8:30 p.m. NANTUCKET LOUNGE	**Feature Movie** Watch your favorite first run feature movie. We supply plenty of popcorn of course! OR **Guest Lecturer** You'll be fascinated by the "History of the Mississippi" as presented by he Army Corps of Engineers.
10:00 p.m.	**Late night snack** This event is not to be missed! Luscious ice cream sundaes will satisfy anyone's sweet tooth! And if ice cream doesn't do the trick, we'll tempt you with an assortment of snacks sure to appease.

American Cruise Lines'
Dinner Menu

APPETIZERS	French Onion Soup	Crayfish Bisque
	Oysters on the Half Shell	
SALADS	Caesar Salad	Tossed Garden Salad
	Spinach & Cauliflower Salad with Orange Dressing	
BREADS	Sesame	Pumpernickel	Corn Bread

ENTREES
Swordfish Steak with Maitre d'hotel Butter
Shrimp Creole
Filet Mignon with Bernaise Sauce
Veal Marsala

VEGETABLES Zucchini with Dill   Wild Rice   Parsley New Potatoes
Asparagus with Hollandaise Sauce

DESSERTS Cheesecake with Strawberries   Baked Alaska
Chocolate Truffle Cake   Southern Pecan Pie

American Export Lines

(1936-1968)

The Export Steamship Corporation Inc was founded in January 1919 under the laws of the State of New York and undertook its first Mediterranean sailing on 26 July 1919 by *Lake Festina*. Nine years later, a fleet of seventeen 'Hog Island' freighters were plying Export Steamship routes. After being awarded a ten-year mail contract in 1928, Mr Henry Herbermann, company president, announced that all ship names would begin with the prefix 'Ex', and passenger operations would commence in 1929 with converted freighters each carrying 37 passengers. In 1931, American Export placed in commission a quartet of combination liners — *Excalibur, Exochorda, Exeter* and *Excambion* — popularly known as the 'Four Aces'. During the 1930s, they provided a fortnightly service from Hoboken, New Jersey, to the Mediterranean.

The economic depression in the United States, however, made it an inopportune moment for Export to place the 'Four Aces' in service. In order to remain solvent, the United States Commerce Department demanded a complete reorganization of the company. Henry Herbermann resigned as president, and a year later the New York Shipbuilding Corporation, who had a controlling interest in the company, sold their interest to a syndicate which included Lehman Brothers and Thomas L. Chadbourne. They in turn formed American Export Lines in August 1936.

By the time the Second World War came to a close, practically every steamship company had lost tonnage, and American Export was no exception. The only survivor was *Exochorda*, and she was sold upon release in 1946 to Turkish Maritime Lines and renamed *Tarsus*.

To reactivate the Mediterranean service, the Italian motorship *Vulcania* was used to carry out American Export's first post-war sailing. She departed from New York in April 1946 and undertook six round voyages for American Export before being handed back to her Italian owners. Between May 1946 and the spring of 1949, 63 round trips were also made by 'C-4' steamers — *Marine Shark, Marine Carp, Marine Flasher, Marine Perch* and *Marine Jumper*. All were war-built troopships resembling tankers, with the bridge situated forward and engines and funnel placed aft. Space had been provided for 3,800 troops, but for these peacetime voyages the accommodation was reduced to cater for between 850 and 930 tourist class passengers in austere, mainly dormitory conditions. The passage fare to Italy in the spring of 1947 was a flat $225 (£56) with room/berth assignment made at embarkation.

American Export started a rebuilding programme by purchasing four redundant attack transports from the US Navy. After rebuilding, the first to be dispatched to the Mediterranean was *Excalibur* (II) which sailed on her first voyage on 24 September 1948. Next in succession was *Exochorda* (II) on 2 November 1948, *Exeter* (II) on 1 December 1948 and *Excambion* (II) two days later. The second 'Four Aces' all had first class accommodation for 125 passengers and they were claimed to be the first vessels in the world to be completely air-conditioned. They sailed from Pier B, Hoboken, New Jersey (across the Hudson River from New York City), and their routing, with minor revisions, was Cadiz, Barcelona, Marseilles, Naples, Beirut, Alexandria, Piraeus, Naples, Marseilles, Genoa, Leghorn and Barcelona. Istanbul was added to the itinerary in 1950, but deleted a year later. One-way fares to Italy per person, double occupancy during the summer season of 1959 ranged from $465 to $800 (£165 to £285). A round trip 'Deluxe Yankee Cruise' lasting 41-43 days ranged from $1,390 up to $2,400 (£495 to £854).

Marine Shark *was the second of fifteen C4-S-A3 ships, shown here in American Export colours* (Frank O. Braynard collection).

In late 1947, American Export announced that it was planning to build three 22-knot express liners for its New York-Naples and Genoa run. The proposed trio were to be 30,000 tons (displacement), 650 ft long, 89 ft wide, and steam 12,500 miles on 37,000 shaft horse power. In addition, each was to have adequate cargo space and cargo handling facilities and carry enough passengers (678) to meet demand and show a return on investment. Industrial designers and interior decorators, led by Henry Dryfuss, were consulted to work on the interior of the proposed trio.

American Export placed a $50 million order with the Bethlehem Shipbuilding Corporation, but only for two of the originally proposed trio. The keel of *Independence* was laid at the Fore River yard at Quincy on 19 March 1949, and four months later, 12 July, the keel of *Constitution* was laid.

Meanwhile, the former troopship *General W.P. Richardson* was chartered for two years and renamed *La Guardia* in honour of a mayor of New York. After an extensive $5 million refit, she emerged with accommodation for 157 first class and 452 tourist class passengers, and sailed on her first voyage from New York on 27 May 1949 for Naples and Genoa.

First class high season fares ranged from $385 (£96), without bath, to $830 (£206) for the ten-day voyage. When *Independence* and *Constitution* were firmly established in 1951, *La Guardia* was returned to Military Sea Transportation Service (MSTS) and laid up.

Independence sailed from New York on her maiden voyage on 11 February 1951 on a 51-day Mediterranean cruise as far as Bombay. On 12 April 1951 she departed from New York on her regular Mediterranean itinerary — Gibraltar, Naples and Genoa. *Independence* was followed on 25 June by her sister ship, *Constitution*. Both were named after two navy sailing vessels in the war of 1812, and at the time of their completion were the fastest American liners constructed in the United States, both exceeding 26 knots on their trials. Their conical funnels were a unique innovation, and they were completely air-conditioned, providing identical and comfortable accommodation for 1,000 passengers — 295 first, 375 cabin and 330 tourist class. Together they plied the route from New York (Pier 84, North River) to Gibraltar, Algeciras, Naples, Genoa and Cannes. During the 1960s, additional ports were added and the sailings were advertised as 'Sunlane Cruises' to the Mediterranean. Fares for a 21-day cruise on *Independence* departing 8 August 1967 ranged from $911 to $3,903 (£325 to £1,394) first class, two in a cabin, and from $696 to $872 (£249 to £311) cabin class per person based on two in a room. Tourist class passengers were not carried on 'Sunlane Cruises', but if one wished to do so he could book one way to Italy for as little as $33 (£12) per day.

Movie makers and celebrities regularly patronized American Export ships. During the early 'fifties, *Independence* was the ship chosen for the American television comedy series 'I Love Lucy'. On 4 April 1956, Grace Kelly set sail in *Constitution* across the Atlantic to marry Prince Rainier III of Monaco. Since the US Mail contract specified which ports were to be called at, American Export applied for and received a permit by a special act of Congress to enable *Constitution* to anchor in Monaco on 12 April to disembark Miss Kelly and her entourage. In 1957, 20th Century Fox's 'An Affair to Remember' starring

Below Marine Carp *docked at American Export's Pier 84 in Manhattan* (National Archives, Washington DC).

Bottom Marine Jumper *at Fort Mason, California, on 17 July 1946. Note the Moore-McCormack funnel colours* (National Archives, Washington DC).

Left Panama, *the former* Marine Jumper, *after her 1966 refit* (Ingalls Shipbuilding).

Below left Excalibur *painted black up to the superstructure* (Frank O. Braynard collection).

Cary Grant and Deborah Kerr was filmed aboard *Independence* and *Constitution*. Other notables of the 'jet set' of those days who experienced a crossing on American Export were Nancy and Ronald Reagan, Harry Truman, John Wayne, Glenn Ford, Mary Pickford, Peter Ustinov and Cecil B. de Mille.

Early in 1959, *Constitution* (January-March) and *Independence* (February-April) received extensive refits at Newport News. The wheel-house, bridge wings and navigation rooms were rolled forward by 21 ft and raised 8½ ft. A whole deck of cabins was added — 110 berths. Both ships resumed their regular itineraries after the refit, but *Constitution* collided with the Norwegian tanker *Jalanta* on 1 March 1959. Thirteen days later, however, she returned to service.

In 1960, American Export bought *Atlantic*, and on 16 May 1960 dispatched her on its Mediterranean service. Later, in October, the Isbrandtsen Company Inc of New York acquired a controlling interest in American Export Lines, and two years later, in October 1962, American Export and Isbradtsen Lines came into being. This was restyled a year later to American Export Isbrandtsen Lines Inc, with a new house-flag denoting the change of ownership.

The arrival of the jet aircraft signalled the end of transatlantic lines, and the first to suffer the decline in passenger numbers were the 'Four Aces'. *Exochorda* was withdrawn in 1958, *Excambion* in 1959 and then six years later *Excalibur* and *Exeter*. The introduction of the Italian twins, *Michelangelo* and *Raffaello*, the increasing competition from the airlines and trade

Excambion *steaming into New York. The black hull was moved one deck down a few months after the ship's commissioning* (Moran Towing & Transportation Company).

43

Above *The tourist liner* La Guardia (Frank O. Braynard collection).

union problems (American Export was affected by the 1965 labour strike) all but sealed the fate of American Export's passenger trade. *Atlantic* was converted into a single-class liner in 1965, but it was too late. She was withdrawn in 1967, and *Constitution* survived until August 1968. In a last ditch effort to capture the 'youth market', *Independence* was given a $3.5 million overhaul and painted in 'psychedelic' colours in the spring of 1968. Managed by Diners/Fugazy, she was sent on 'cruises' to the Mediterranean and West Indies, under a 'new' concept of paying for the ocean passage only and paying for extras such as meals on board. This was supposed to bring the cost down for the passengers, but needless to say the youth market did not espouse the new idea, and *Independence* was withdrawn and laid up on 26 October 1968. Happily, both *Independence* and *Constitution* are now sailing again under the American flag in Hawaiian waters.

The Isbrandtsen interest withdrew from American Export in 1973 and the company's title was again restyled American Export Lines Inc. Finally, on 28 March 1978, Farrell Lines of New York acquired the company.

1   *Vulcania* 1946 (c)

Cantiere Navale Triestino, Monfalcone, 1928.
24,469 gross tons; 632 × 80 ft (192 × 24 m); FIAT diesels; twin screw; 19 knots; 2,196 passengers (for Italian Line). Launched 18/12/1926 for Cosulich. 1941-45 War service. FV 29/3/1946 for American Export, New York-Naples-Alexandria. LV 4/10/1946 Alexandria-New York. 6 RV. 15/11/1946 Returned to Italian Line. 1965 *Caribia* (Siosa). 9/1973 Scrapped.

2   *Marine Shark* 1946-1948 (c)

Kaiser Company Inc, Vancouver, Washington, 1945.
12,420 gross tons; 523 × 71 ft (159 × 21 m); steam turbines; single screw; 16 knots; 930 tourist class passengers. Launched 4/4/1945 as troopship for US Maritime Commission.
FV 2/5/1946 for American Export, New York-Naples. LV 9/12/1948 New York-Naples-New York. 15 RV. 1949 US Lines (see page 211). 1968 *Charleston* (Litton). 1984 Laid up. 1985 Scrapped.

3   *Marine Carp* 1946-1949 (c)

Kaiser Company Inc, Vancouver, Washington, 1945.
12,420 gross tons; 523 × 71 ft (159 × 21 m); steam

Right Independence *before her 1959 refit sailing into New York* (courtesy of Peter M. Warner).

Independence *in her 'psychedelic' colours in 1968* (Author's collection).

turbines; single screw; 16 knots; 900 tourist class passengers. Launched 5/7/1945 as troopship for US Maritime Commission.

FV 22/7/1946 for American Export New York-Piraeus. LV 28/3/1949 New York-Haifa-Piraeus-Naples-New York. 22 RV. 1949 Laid up. 1952 Saw action in Korea. 1958-1967 Laid up. 1968 *Green Spring* (Central Gulf, US), 10,575 tons. 1979 Scrapped in Taiwan.

4   *Marine Flasher* 1946 (c)

Kaiser Company Inc, Vancouver, Washington, 1945.

12,420 gross tons; 523 × 71 ft (159 × 21 m); steam turbines; single screw; 16 knots; 914 tourist class passengers. Launched 16/5/1945 as troop-ship for US Maritime Commission.

FV 7/8/1946 for American Export New York-Naples. 1 RV. 1946 Returned to US Lines (see page 207). 1966 *Long Beach* (Litton), 17,814 tons, 684 ft (208 m). 1975 *Long Beach* (Reynolds Leasing). 1987 Scrapped in Taiwan.

5   *Marine Perch* 1946-1949 (c)

Kaiser Company Inc, Richmond, California, 1945.

12,420 gross tons; 523 × 71 ft (159 × 21 m); steam turbines; single screw; 16 knots; 901 tourist class

passengers. Launched 25/6/1945 as troopship for US Maritime Commission.

FV 26/9/1946 for American Export New York-Lisbon-Naples. 5/3/1949 LV New York-Genoa-Naples. 24 RV. 1949 Laid up. 1965 *Yellowstone* (Rio Grande Transport). 14/6/1978 Sank 77 miles SE of Gibraltar after collision with *Ibn Batouta* (Algerian).

6   *Marine Jumper* 1947-1948 (c)

Kaiser Company Inc, Vancouver, Washington, 1945.

12,420 gross tons; 523 × 71 ft (159 × 21 m); steam turbines; single screw; 16 knots; 850 tourist class passengers. Launched 30/5/1945 as troopship for US Maritime Commission.

FV 27/9/1947 for American Export New York-Beirut-Haifa-Alexandria-Piraeus-New York, arr 28/10. 1 RV. 1947 US Lines (see page 210). 1966 *Panama* (Litton), 17,184 gross tons, 684 ft (208 m). 1975 *Panama* (Reynolds). 1987 Scrapped in Taiwan.

7   *Excalibur* (II) 1948-1964

Bethlehem Shipbuilding Corporation, Sparrow's Point, Maryland, 1944.

Right Constitution *following her 1959 refit which saw the installation of an additional deck* (Moran Towing & Transportation Company).
Inset Constitution *departing from New York for another dash to the Mediterranean* (Moran Towing & Transportation Company).

Atlantic boasted the largest outdoor swimming pool of her day (Author's collection).

9,644 gross tons; 473 × 66 ft (144 × 20 m); steam turbines; single screw; 17 knots; 125 first class passengers. Launched 26/8/1944 as *Dutchess* (sic) (US Navy). 1947 *Excalibur.*
FV 24/9/1948 Jersey City (New York)-Mediterranean. 27/6/1950 Beached in New York after collision with *Colombia* (Danish). 7/7/1950 Refloated. 1953 Hoboken, NJ (New York)-Mediterranean. LV 11/4/1964 Hoboken, NJ (New York)-Mediterranean. 1965 *Oriental Jade* (Orient Overseas). 1972 Atlantic Far East Lines. 1974 Scrapped at Kaohsiung.

8 *Exochorda* (II) 1948-1958

Bethlehem Shipbuilding Corporation, Sparrow's Point, Maryland, 1945.
9,644 gross tons; 473 × 66 ft (144 × 20 m); steam turbines; single screw; 17 knots; 125 first class passengers. Launched 10/6/1944 as *Dauphin* (US Navy). 1947 *Exochorda.*
FV 2/11/1948 Jersey City (New York)-Mediterranean.

1953 Hoboken, NJ (New York)-Mediterranean. LV 21/2/1958 Hoboken, NJ (New York)-Mediterranean. 1958 Laid up. 1960 *Stevens* (Stevens Institute of Technology, New Jersey). 1975 Scrapped.

9 *Exeter* (II) 1948-1964

Bethlehem Shipbuilding Corporation, Sparrow's Point, Maryland, 1945.
9,644 gross tons; 473 × 66 ft (144 × 20 m); steam turbines; single screw; 17 knots; 125 first class passengers. Launched 25/10/1944 as *Shelby* (US Navy). 1947 *Exeter.*
FV 1/12/1948 Jersey City (New York)-Mediterranean. 1953 Hoboken, NJ (New York)-Mediterranean. LV 2/12/1964 Hoboken, NJ (New York)-Mediterranean. 1965 *Oriental Pearl* (Orient Overseas). 1972 Atlantic Far East Lines. 1974 Scrapped at Kaohsiung.

10 *Excambion* (II) 1948-1959

Bethlehem Shipbuilding Corporation, Sparrow's Point, Maryland, 1944.
9,644 gross tons; 473 × 66 ft (144 × 20 m); steam

turbines; single screw; 17 knots; 125 first class passengers. Launched 12/9/1944 as *Queens* (US Navy). 1947 *Excambion*.

FV 3/12/1948 Jersey City (New York)-Mediterranean. 1953 Hoboken, NJ (New York)-Mediterranean. LV 29/1/1959 Hoboken, NJ (New York)-Mediterranean. 1965 *Texas Clipper* (State of Texas) cadet training ship, Texas Aviation and Maritime University at Galveston.

11 *La Guardia* 1949-1951 (c)

Federal Shipbuilding Company, Kearny, New Jersey, 1944.

17,951 gross tons; 622 × 75 ft (188 × 23 m); steam turbines; twin screw; 19 knots; 157 first class, 452 tourist class passengers. Laid down as *General R. M. Blatchford*. Launched 6/8/1944 as *General W. P. Richardson* (US Navy troopship).

1949 *La Guardia*. FV 27/5/1949 New York-Naples-Genoa. 5 RV. 12/10/1949 FV New York-Haifa. LV 13/11/1951 New York-Haifa. Returned to MSTS, made four Orient voyages under the APL banner, then laid up. 1956 *Leilani* (Textron) (see page 127). 1960 *President Roosevelt* (American President) (see page 66). 1970 *Atlantis* (Chandris). 1972 *Emerald Seas* (Eastern Steamship). 1986 *Emerald Seas* (Admiral Cruises). 7/1986 Fire, 44 injured. Still sailing.

A crew menu from Atlantic. *This unusual item offers a fine selection — no wonder American companies went under!* (Author's collection).

A Captain's Dinner menu from Atlantic (Author's collection).

```
            C R E W   M E N U
                 Breakfast
  Prune or Grapefruit Juice    Stewed Mixed Fruit
            Boiled Hominy Grits
          Assorted Dry Cereals
          Broiled Kipper Herring
  Eggs:   Fried   Scrambled   Boiled   Poached
         Omelette with Onions
      Breakfast Sausages or Bacon
          Home Fried Potatoes
        Griddle Cake with Syrup
  Assorted Jams              Assorted Jellies
  Fresh Rolls      Sweet Buns         Toast
    Coffee                          Tea

                 Luncheon
  Carrot Sticks                      Radishes
         Minestrone Sicilienne
    Codfish Cake with Tomato Sauce
        Spaghetti and Meat Sauce
  Pork Chop Suey, Noodles and Rice
  Braised Brisket of Beef, Glazed Vegetables
  Fresh Garden Kale    Macedoine Vegetables
            Mashed Potatoes
             Dubarry Salad
  Peach Pie                      Custard
        Cheese with Crackers
    Coffee       Iced Tea        Tea

                  Dinner
  Mixed Olives              Indian Relish
           Cream of Tomato
  Broiled Halibut Steak, Parsley Butter
  Shell Macaroni a la Piemontaise
  Stuffed Roast Chicken, Pan Gravy, Dressing
  Emince of Beef, Stroganoff, Dill Pickles
  Buttered String Beans  Creamed White Onions
           Home Fried Potatoes
        Potato Salad with Mayonnaise
  Mocha Bars    Sherbet       Fresh Fruit
        Cheese and Crackers
    Coffee     Iced Coffee      Tea

  S. S. Atlantic          Saturday, July 6, 1963
                                Ce-10
```

```
           Captain's Dinner
                    ★
       CHILLED PINEAPPLE TIDBITS CUP
             LOBSTER COCKTAIL
  ICED CELERY                    QUEEN OLIVES
                    ★
      VELOUTE OF CHICKEN A LA REINE
                    ★
      FRESH DOVER SOLE, SAUTE MEUNIERE
                    ★
  ROCK CORNISH GAME HEN, WILD RICE, PERIGORD
   BAKED VIRGINIA HAM, CHAMPAGNE SAUCE
   BROILED SIRLOIN STEAK, MAITRE D'HOTEL
                    ★
  BUTTERED ASPARAGUS        GREEN PEAS, FRANCAISE
         FRENCH FRIED POTATOES
                    ★
  MOCHA BARS                 BOMBE ATLANTIQUE
                    ★
         SALAD "BELLE HELENA"
                    ★
         ASSORTED CHEESES
                    ★
  TUNIS DATES     MIXED NUTS      CLUSTER RAISINS
         CRYSTALLIZED GINGER
                    ★
            FRESH FRUIT
                    ★
              COFFEE
          AFTER DINNER MINTS

                           capt.-T-wb
```

12   *Independence* 1951-1968

Bethlehem Shipbuilding Corporation, Quincy, Massachusetts, 1951.

23,719 (B 30,293) gross tons; 682 × 89 ft (208 × 27 m); steam turbines; twin screw; 23 knots; 295 first class, 375 cabin class, 333 tourist class passengers. Launched 3/6/1950.

MV 11/2/1951 New York-Mediterranean cruise. FV 12/4/1951 New York-Naples-Genoa. 2-4/1959 refit, deck added, 110 first class berths added, 504 first class, 330 cabin class, 254 tourist class, tonnage 23,754. 18/4/1959 Resumed service. 1967 20,251 gross tons. 1968 Operated by Fugazy Travel, single class. LV 21/9/1968 New York-Mediterranean. Laid-up in Baltimore. 1974 *Oceanic Independence* (Orient Overseas). 1975 Cruising from Cape Town. 1976 Laid up at Hong Kong. 11/1976 *Sea Luck I.* 1978 *Oceanic Independence* (American Hawaii Cruises) (see page 55). 1983 *Independence* (American Hawaii Cruises).

13   *Constitution* 1951-1968

Bethlehem Shipbuilding Corporation, Quincy, Massachusetts, 1951.

23,754 (B 30,293) gross tons; 682 × 89 ft (208 × 27 m); steam turbines; twin screw; 23 knots; 295 first class, 375 cabin class, 33 tourist class passengers. Launched 16/9/1950.

MV 25/6/1951 New York-Naples-Genoa. 1-3/1959 Refit, deck added, 110 first class berths added, 504 first class, 330 cabin class, 254 tourist class, 23,754 gross tons. 1/3/1959 Collided with *Jalanta* (Norwegian tanker) in NY. 13/3/1959 Resumed Mediterranean service. 1967 20,269 gross tons. 1968 single class only. LV 10/8/1968 New York-Mediterranean. Laid up at Jacksonville. 1974 Sold to Atlantic Far East Lines (C.Y. Tung) *Oceanic Constitution.* 4/8/1974 Arrived at Hong Kong and laid up. 1981 Transferred to American Hawaii Cruises (see page 55). 1982 *Constitution* (American Global Line).

14   *Atlantic* 1960-1967

Sun Shipbuilding & Drydock Company, Chester, Pennsylvania, 1953.

14,138 (B 18,100) gross tons; 564 × 76 ft (172 × 23 m); steam turbines; single screw; 20 knots; 40 first class, 860 tourist class passengers. Launched 1/7/1953 as C-4 cargo vessel *Badger Mariner*, 9,214 tons. 1957 *Atlantic* (American Banner) (see page 28). 1960 Purchased by American Export.

FV 16/5/1960 New York-Mediterranean. 1965 single class, 840. LV 15/9/1967 New York-Mediterranean. Laid up in Brooklyn, NY. 3/1949 Transferred to Baltimore. 1971 *Universe Campus* (Orient Overseas). 1976 *Universe* (Orient Overseas).

American Global Cruises

(1980-1981)

American Global Cruises was based in San Francisco, and in 1980 signed a lease-purchase agreement with Investment Mortgage Leasing Co of Portland, Oregon, to operate Investment's new acquisition, *Aquamarine*, which had formerly been named *Princesa Isabel* (1962-69) and *Marco Polo* (1969-78). The plan was to operate the ship on 14-day sailings from Hong Kong and Kobe beginning on 29 April 1981. However, *Aquamarine* had serious mechanical difficulties, forcing American Global to charter *Melody*, a rather shabby, rebuilt cruise ship owned by Cambridge Shipping (a London-based company with Greek interests). *Melody* was originally the French vessel *Djebel Dira*, built in 1948.

Schedules were revised to allow a 27 May start for the renamed *Marco Polo*. A brochure was issued describing the attributes of this 'royal legend in travel' and the exciting itinerary that awaited the lucky few. Rates started at $1,950 (£848) (airfare additional) for an inside double cabin with facilities. Ports of call northbound from Hong Kong were Amoy, Shanghai, Tientsin and Kobe.

The *Marco Polo* sailings never materialized, however, because she failed to receive a certificate of seaworthiness. American Global was unable to find a suitable hull for their operation and so had to cancel its summer programme. Other hoped-for acquisitions fell through, and by the end of 1981 American Global faded away.

American Hawaii Cruises

(1979 to date)

In an attempt to enter the United States cruise scene, Chinese-born Mr C.Y. Tung spearheaded the creation of American Global Lines, New York, in 1978 along with other US investors interested in restoring an all-passenger cruise service under the American flag. Heading the company was Tung's American-born daughter-in-law, Harriet Tung. In that year, American Global purchased *Oceanic Independence* from the C.Y. Tung Group of Hong Kong and asked for approval from the Federal Government to recommission the 30,000-ton liner as an American-flagged vessel, a clever manoeuvre possible because the ship would be sailing for an American company headed by an American. The bill that Mr Tung and his associates lobbied hard for was unanimously approved by the US Senate and House of Representatives, and signed into law in November 1979. American Hawaii Cruises was created as a subsidiary of American Global Lines, with headquarters in San Francisco, and *Oceanic Independence* was renovated into a cruise liner for service out of Honolulu.

With the American flag flying on her mast and stern, *Oceanic Independence* departed from Honolulu on 7 June 1980, visiting Hilo, Kona, Kahului and Nawiliwili, taking seven leisurely days to complete the cruise with fares starting at $645 (£280) per person for double occupancy. The emphasis was on an 'all-American' crew and staff providing a new way to see the Hawaiian islands without the otherwise constant problems of inter-island flying and checking into and out of hotels.

The early success of the Hawaiian cruise programme led to the purchase of *Constitution*, sister ship of *Oceanic Independence*, from C.Y. Tung. Both liners were former transatlantic vessels belonging to American Export Lines. Again, a bill was signed into law in February 1982 by President Reagan which allowed *Constitution* to be restored to her American-flag status.

Constitution underwent a complete restyling and redecoration for her Hawaii cruise debut. To launch the ship into service, Her Serene Highness Princess Grace of Monaco, who was a frequent traveller in the ship during its American Export days, christened *Constitution* in May 1982 at the China Ship Building Corporation dock in Kaohsiung, Taiwan; she became the only American ship to be christened by royalty. In her honour, American Hawaii renamed the writing room the Princess Grace Room. *Constitution* departed from Taiwan on 12 May and left Honolulu on 6 June on her inaugural cruise to Nawiliwili, Kona, Hilo and Kahului. Because of insufficient bookings in the Hawaiian market, American Hawaii laid up *Oceanic Independence* for five months during the winter of 1983. Before returning to service, she received minor alterations resulting in reduced passenger capacity, and her name was shortened to *Independence*.

After a thirteen-year absence, a passenger cruise service was offered from Honolulu to California. The first sailing was undertaken by *Independence* when she departed Honolulu on 6 August 1983 for Los Angeles. After a layover for drydock maintenance, *Independence* sailed from San Francisco on 29 August with actor Cary Grant renewing an old acquaintance and bandleader Alvino Rey and his musicians leading the featured 'big band' entertainment. Meanwhile, *Constitution* took leave of her Hawaii service for a transpacific voyage that departed from Honolulu on 3 December 1983, arriving at Los Angeles on 8 December and San Francisco the following day. After her annual overhaul, she sailed on 12 December and was back in Honolulu on 24 December.

Following these successful transpacific cruises, American Hawaii repeated the sailing in 1984. *Independence* left Honolulu on 30 June with the Russ Morgan Orchestra aboard and arrived at Los Angeles on 7 July and San Francisco a day later. The next day she departed from San Francisco and arrived back at Honolulu on 16 July. On 12 December 1984 *Constitution* once more returned to San Francisco, and, after a few days in port, left again on 15 December, and, after a call at Los Angeles, arrived back in Honolulu on 22 December. Seven days later, *Independence* sailed from Honolulu arriving in Los Angeles on 4 January 1985 and San Diego on the 5th. Eastbound entertainment was the 'big band' sound while the westbound trip featured nostalgic music for which passengers were requested to bring their zoot suits, bowlers and cigarette holders for a voyage down Memory Lane! Further calls were made at San Diego, Los Angeles and San Francisco, before reaching Honolulu again on 26 January. Later, *Constitution* departed Honolulu on 30 November and returned on 21 December with calls at San Francisco, Los Angeles and San Diego.

In a bold move, William Jesse, president and chief executive of American Hawaii, announced in April 1984 his company's decision to enter the Polynesian market with its new acquisition, *Liberté*, leased from Banstead Shipping Ltd, one of Tung's shipping subsidiaries. She was the former *Volendam* of Holland-America and *Brasil* of Moore-McCormack, and, unlike her Hawaiian running consorts, *Liberté* was placed under the Panamanian flag. After a $25 million refit at Sasebo, Japan, she was positioned at Papeete, Tahiti, whence she departed on 21 December 1985 on her first seven-day cruises to Rangiroa Atoll, Huahine, Raitea, Tahaa, Bora Bora and Moorea. Rates for this Polynesian cruise ranged from $1,195 to $2,495 (£934 to £1,949), with air transportation provided by a 747 jet chartered from Transamerican

Independence in American Hawaii colours (American Hawaii Cruises).

53

Left Constitution *arriving at Honolulu* (American Hawaii Cruises).
Below left Liberté *anchored off a South Pacific isle* (William H. Miller Jr).

Airlines. The twice weekly flights which departed on Wednesdays and Saturdays from Los Angeles to Papeete were designed to accommodate passengers opting for American Hawaii's pre-cruise and post-cruise packages in Tahiti at a supplement of $299 (£234) (West Coast) or $399 (£312) (East Coast), whether or not a package was involved.

In January 1987, Peter C.R. Huang, former head of the City Investing Company of New York, succeeded in taking over American Global Lines from the Tung family for some $20 million. Mr Huang became president and chief executive officer of American Hawaii Cruises, and shortly after taking over announced that American Hawaii was withdrawing *Liberté* from service. He said that 'logistical problems associated with operating *Liberté* in the area resulted in an unacceptable return on the assets employed'. In short, high operating costs (everything, including food, had to be shipped in and was heavily taxed), a sagging US dollar and an embarkation point 4,000 miles from the American mainland created financial and promotional problems necessitating the withdrawal of the ship. *Liberté*, which was in San Francisco for her annual overhaul at the time, was returned to her owner, Banstead Shipping. A spokesperson for the line stated that 'while the decision to withdraw from Tahiti had been made with considerable regret, we enter 1987 with renewed confidence that the proven demand for our Hawaii cruises will allow us to continue to operate successfully'.

1 *Oceanic Independence* 1980-1982
   Independence 1983

Bethlehem Shipbuilding Corporation, Quincy, Massachusetts, 1951.

20,220 (B 30,090) gross tons; 682 × 89 ft (207 × 27 m); steam turbines; twin screw; 20 knots; 750 first class passengers. Launched 3/6/1950 for American Export (see page 50).

1974 *Oceanic Independence* (C.Y. Tung). 1976 *Sea Luck I.* 1978 *Oceanic Independence* (American Hawaii). FV 7/6/1980 Honolulu-Hawaiian Islands. 12/1982-5/1983 Laid up. 1983 Refit, 798 passengers. 1983 *Independence.* FV 6/8/1983 Honolulu-Los Angeles-San Francisco-Honolulu.

2 *Constitution* 1982

Bethlehem Shipbuilding Corporation, Quincy, Massachusetts, 1951.

20,269 (B 30,090) gross tons; 682 × 89 ft (207 × 27 m); steam turbines; twin screw; 20 knots; 798 first class passengers. Launched 16/9/1950 for American Export (see page 50).

1974 Sold to C.Y. Tung. *Oceanic Constitution* 1982 Sold to American Hawaii. FV 6/6/1982 Honolulu-Hawaii. FV 3/12/1983 Honolulu-San Francisco-Honolulu.

3 *Liberté* 1985-1986 (c)

Ingalls Shipbuilding Corporation, Pascagoula, Mississippi, 1958.

23,500 gross tons; 617 × 86 ft (188 × 26 m); geared turbines; twin screw; 21 knots; 715 first class passengers. Launched 16/12/1958 as *Brasil* (Moore-McCormack) (see page 145).

1972 *Volendam* (Holland-America). 1975 *Monarch Sun* (Monarch Cruises). 1979 *Volendam* (Holland-America). 1984 *Island Sun* (C.Y. Tung). 1985 *Liberté* (American Hawaii). FV 21/12/1985 Tahiti-South Pacific islands. LV 14/12/1986 Tahiti-South Pacific. 12/1986 Sailed to San Francisco for overhaul. 1/1987 Laid up. 1987 *Canada Star* (Bermuda Star Line). 1988 *Queen of Bermuda* (Bermuda Star Line).

American President Lines

(1938-1973)

At the instigation of the US government and to prevent Dollar Line from going into bankruptcy, the company's board of directors voted on 28 October 1938 to change formally the name of Dollar Line to American President Lines. Along with this change came the decision to alter the fleet's well-known funnel marking from the distinctive dollar sign to a white eagle on a red field.

At the conclusion of the war in 1945, APL was obliged to start off with an almost entirely new fleet. The only vessels returned to APL were *President Monroe* and *President Polk*, built in 1940 and 1941 for round-the-world service. *President Polk* resumed sailing in August 1946, and *President Monroe* in November. Each ship had space for 96 first class passengers, all but one cabin being accommodated outside with private facilities. During their 100-day circumnavigation, the passengers could enjoy the well-appointed lounge with a bar, read in the library, swim in the outdoor pool and dine in the intimate dining salon at a cost of $2,716 to $3,201 (£970 to £1,143) in 1950 and $3,185 to $4,190 (£1,138 to £1,496) in 1961.

Faced with the problem of being the principal ship operator in the Pacific with only two vessels, APL temporarily chartered government-owned military transports. *General W.H. Gordon, General M.C. Meigs, Marine Adder, Marine Lynx* and *Marine Swallow* were all pressed into service as passenger ships. Accommodation was austere, with all cabins priced the same, but the large capacity of these ships enabled the company to take care of the urgent demands of transporting business people, missionaries, and so on back and forth across the Pacific.

Meanwhile, under the presidency of George Killion, who served from 1947 to 1966, APL entered a period of expansion. Killion's objectives were simple: to provide the finest transpacific service in the history of the line and to make the APL fleet the most efficient United States flag carrier afloat. He therefore proceeded to make arrangements to replace the troop-ships, and the company took over the construction and design of two troop-ships still on the stocks and had them refitted as passenger liners. Originally, the United States Maritime Commission, in consultation with APL, had wanted to build and operate a pair of 29-knot ships with a displacement of 37,500 tons and a passenger capacity of 1,000; these had been designated PXE in 1945. A year later, the Maritime Commission had initiated another proposed design for operation by APL of two twin-funnelled liners with the designation P5-S2-E1 to operate on the round-the-world service. They were to have had an overall length of 942 ft and carry 1,248 passengers. However, neither proposal came to fruition as both projects became victims of President Truman's budget cuts that year.

As a result, APL made do with the two troop-ships being redesigned as passenger liners. Both were owned by the US Government and chartered to APL, and emerged from the shipyard as *President Cleveland* and *President Wilson*. *President Cleveland* sailed from San Francisco on 15 December 1947 for the Orient, followed on 27 April 1948 by *President Wilson*. Ports of call were Honolulu, Yokohama, Hong Kong and Manila. Shanghai was also included until 1949. Accommodation was provided for 326 first class and 506 third class passengers. Practically all the first class cabins had private facilities, and amenities included a Cleveland/Wilson room, writing room, library, games room, cocktail lounge, marine veranda with dance floor and projection room, outdoor swimming pool and dining room. For third class there was a main lounge, veranda lounge, outdoor pool and dining room. Accommodation was in cabins with two, three, four and six berths, and two dormitories for 30 and 32 passengers respectively. Ownership of the vessels was passed from the Government to APL in 1954. In a 1963 remodelling, third was renamed economy class and the dormitories were removed. For smoother sailing, stabilizers were installed.

It is interesting to take a look at the passenger tariffs in dollars (pounds) for this particular route over a twenty-year period, based on double occupancy of

a first class cabin during high season for *President Cleveland* and *President Wilson*, sailing from San Francisco to:

Honolulu — *5 days*

	1950	1961	1972
min	140 (50)	–	350 (135)
max	600 (214)	–	1,050 (403)

Yokohama — *14 days*

	1950	1961	1972
min	490 (175)	510 (182)	600 (230)
max	1,490 (532)	1,695 (605)	2,625 (1,010)

Manila — *18 days*

	1950	1961	1972
min	580 (207)	715 (255)	880 (338)
max	1,660 (593)	2,075 (741)	3,850 (1,481)

Hong Kong — *22 days*

	1950	1961	1972
min	600 (214)	675 (241)	840 (323)
max	1,800 (643)	2,075 (741)	3,675 (1,413)

Below Marine Adder *was the first vessel to commence postwar sailings for American President* (Frank O. Braynard collection).

Bottom General W.H. Gordon *as a Navy transport* (National Archives, Washington DC).

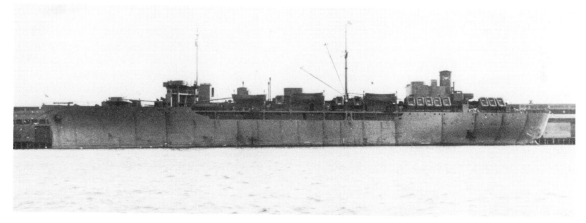

General M.C. Meigs *steaming under the Golden Gate Bridge in San Francisco* (Al Palmer collection, courtesy of American President Lines Archives).

In 1951, APL was to take delivery of three 13,000-ton vessels to be *President Jackson, President Adams* and *President Hayes*, but during construction the ships were taken over by the US Navy and completed as troop-transports. Renamed *Barrett* (T-AP 196), *Geiger* (T-AP 197), and *Upshur* (T-AP 198) respectively, they served in the Korean War. *Barrett* went on to become *Empire State V* and *Upshur* became *State of Maine*, both maritime training schools. *Geiger* was laid up in 1971.

An article in the *New York Times* of 1 January 1952 stated that the government had assigned the liner *La Guardia* to APL to operate for the Military Sea Transport Service, carrying only military personnel, their dependents and supplies to bases in the Orient. Her first sailing with APL funnel colours was in February 1952 and she made three subsequent voyages before being laid up.

In the same year, back at APL headquarters, an agreement was reached between the United States government and certain former stockholders in which the controlling interest of the Company was sold to APL Associates Inc for $18,360,000. APL Associates was organized by Ralph K. Davies, President of the American Independent Oil Company (based in Texas). Within two years APL had purchased a two-thirds interest in American Mail Line, while

another two years later, the Natomas Company, whose business was oil, acquired 49% of the outstanding stock of American President Lines.

With the increasing demand for passage across the Pacific, APL purchased *Panama* in 1957 from Panama Railroad Company. She was renamed *President Hoover*, and, after an extensive refit, was placed on the San Francisco-Orient service with *President Cleveland* and *President Wilson*. Her 202 passengers enjoyed the use of a cocktail lounge, a double-decked 'outdoor veranda café', an upper deck called the 'upper lounge' and an outdoor pool. Below was a full width dining room. APL made attempts during the late 'fifties to resurrect the P5-S2-E1 project with one ship tentatively named *President Washington*, but by this time the government was mute on the subject, and eventually APL gave up.

The final addition to the APL fleet was made in 1962 with the purchase of the laid-up *Leilani*, previously chartered as *La Guardia*. She was renamed *President Roosevelt* and was taken into Puget Sound Bridge and Drydock where she received a $10 million refit. In charge of the decorative theme were the designers Anshen and Allen and their choice was 'space'. All staterooms, including the many single cabins and suites, were provided with private baths; air-conditioning was installed throughout; lounges for relaxation included the Pacific, Cocktail and Games Room; the Starlight Room had a band and a dance floor that looked out to the swimming pool and stern; and three decks down on main was the

Presidential Dining Room. For added passenger comfort, stabilizers were installed. *President Roosevelt* was completed in April, and after a series of shakedown cruises, she left San Francisco on 10 May 1962 for Yokohama and ports east.

Two years later, American President started slowly to withdraw its passenger ships from service, beginning in 1964 with the sale of *President Hoover* to Chandris Cruises. The next year saw *President Polk* and *President Monroe* sold to foreign buyers, and as passengers and freight took to the air, APL began to switch its ships to different routes. *President Roosevelt* undertook annual round-the-world cruises during

the early 1960s, while *President Cleveland* and *President Wilson* were sent cruising to Alaska, Hawaii, the South Pacific and the Mediterranean.

By 1970, the transpacific passenger service was quickly dying. To curtail operating losses, APL sold *President Roosevelt* in 1970 to Chandris Lines, who again spent another $10 million reconditioning her. Now there were only two passenger ships left and a fleet of freighters that were being converted into container carriers.

In 1973, *President Cleveland* and *President Wilson* came to the end of their twenty-five year government contract. With no government subsidy, high opera-

Below *APL's round-the-world liner,* President Polk (Henri Van Wandelen, courtesy of American President Lines Archives).

Bottom President Cleveland *departing from San Francisco* (Al Palmer collection, courtesy of American President Lines Archives).

tion and labour costs, low passenger and freight bookings and stiff completion from the airlines, APL had no choice but to withdraw the two ships, *President Cleveland* in February 1973 and *President Wilson* upon the completion of her 'Presidential World Cruise' in April.

During the mid-1970s, APL withdrew from world-wide freighter operations and concentrated its efforts on consolidating its Pacific trade routes. A further development occurred in September 1983 when APL, which had become wholly owned by the Natomas Company in 1979, became independent from its parent corporation. Today, American President Lines Ltd, listed on the New York Stock Exchange, is one of the largest US container ship companies and has a healthy balance sheet.

1 *President Monroe* 1941-1965

Newport News Shipbuilding & Drydock Company, Newport News, Virginia, 1941.

9,255 gross tons; 492 × 70 ft (150 × 21 m); steam turbines; single screw; 16.5 knots; 96 first class passengers. Launched 7/8/1940.

MV 17/1/1941 Around the world from San Francisco. 1/1942 Transport for War Shipping Administration. 1943 USS *President Monroe* (US Navy). FV 11/1946 Around the world from San Francisco. 1965 *Marianana V* (John S. Latis, Greece). 1969 Broken up at Hong Kong.

2 *President Polk* 1946-1965

Newport News Shipbuilding & Drydock Company, Newport News, Virginia, 1941.

9,256 gross tons; 492 × 67 ft (150 × 20 m); steam turbines; single screw; 17 knots; 96 first class passengers. Launched 28/6/1941.

MV 6/11/1941 New York-San Francisco. 12/1941 Taken over by the War Shipping Administration as a troop-ship. 10/1943 USS *President Polk* (US Navy). 1946 Returned to service. FV 23/8/1946 Around the world from San Francisco. LV 1/3/1965 Around the world from New York. 1965 *Gaucho Martin Fierro* (Ganaderos del Mar). 1966 *Minotauros*. 1970 Scrapped at Kaohsiung, Taiwan.

President Monroe *docking in New York* (Moran Towing & Transportation Company).

Left Oriental President *laid up at Hong Kong* (James L. Shaw).

Below left *The launch of* President Wilson *on 24 November 1946* (Frank O. Braynard collection).

3 *Marine Adder* 1945-1947 (c)

Kaiser Company, Richmond, California, 1945.

12,420 gross tons; 523 × 71 ft (159 × 21 m); steam turbines; single screw; 16 knots; more than 900 passengers. Launched 16/5/1945 as troop-transport. MV 11/1945 San Francisco-Orient. 1947 Laid up. 1950 *T-AP 193* (US Navy). 1957 Laid up. 1967 *Transcolorado* (Machine & Foundry Co). 1968 Refitted as car transporter.

Right *Economy class deck plan of* President Cleveland *and* President Wilson. *Note the dormitories on C-Deck* (Author's collection).

Below President Wilson (Frank O. Braynard collection).

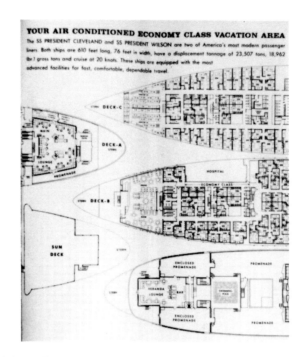

YOUR AIR CONDITIONED ECONOMY CLASS VACATION AREA

The SS PRESIDENT CLEVELAND and SS PRESIDENT WILSON are two of America's most modern passenger liners. Both ships are 610 feet long, 76 feet in width, have a displacement tonnage of 23,507 tons, 18,962 (by) gross tons and cruise at 20 knots. These ships are equipped with the most advanced facilities for fast, comfortable, dependable travel.

4 *Marine Swallow* 1945-1947 (c)

Kaiser Company, Richmond, California, 1945.

12,420 gross tons; 523 × 71 ft (159 × 21 m); steam turbines; single screw; 16 knots; 850 passengers. Launched 21/6/1945 as troop-transport.

FV 23/12/1945 San Francisco-Orient. 1947 Laid up. 1948 United States Lines (see page 211). 1948 Laid up. 1965 *Missouri* (Meadowbrook Transport). 1974 *Ogden Missouri* (Ogden Missouri, Panama). *Linnet* (Linnet Shipping). 1978 Scrapped.

5 *General W.H. Gordon* 1946-1950 (c)

Federal Shipbuilding & Drydock Company, Kearny, New Jersey, 1944.

17,833 gross tons; 622 × 75 ft (188 × 23 m); steam turbines; twin screw; 20 knots; 900 tourist class passengers. Launched 7/5/1944 as Navy Transport. 1946 Chartered to APL. FV 10/7/1946 San Francisco-Shanghai. 11/1950 Laid up at Suisun Bay, California. 1951 Reactivated by military. 1958 Laid up. 1961 Again reactivated. 1970 Laid up at James River, Virginia.

6 *General M.C. Meigs* 1946-1950 (c)

Federal Shipbuilding & Drydock Company, Kearny, New Jersey, 1944.

17,707 gross tons; 622 × 75 ft (188 × 23 m); steam turbines; twin screw; 20 knots; approx 950 passengers; Launched 13/3/1944 for US Navy.

MV 10/7/1944 Newport News-Naples. 1946 Chartered to APL. FV 1946 San Francisco-Orient.

Top left President Cleveland *arriving,* President Wilson *docked* (Frank O. Braynard collection).

Middle left President Hoover *discharging cargo* (Al Palmer, courtesy of American President Lines Archives).

Left *A rare photograph of* La Guardia *under APL funnel colours during her charter to them in 1952* (James L. Shaw collection).

Above President Roosevelt *arriving in San Francisco* (Al Palmer collection, courtesy of American President Lines Archives).

Right *Deck plan of* President Roosevelt (Author's collection).

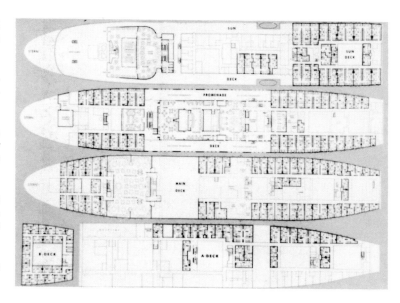

1950 *T-AP 116* (Military Sea Transportation Service). 1958 Laid up. 9/1/1972 While being towed to California, tow-line parted, ship drifted ashore at Cape Flattery and broke in two.

7   *Marine Lynx* 1947 (c)

Kaiser Company, Vancouver, Canada, 1945.

12,420 gross tons; 523 × 71 ft (159 × 21 m); steam turbines; single screw; 16 knots; over 900 passengers. Launched 17/7/1945 as troop transport.

1947 Chartered to APL. FV 27/6/1947 Around the world from San Francisco (1 RV). 1947 Laid up at Suisun Bay. 1950 *T-AP 194* (US Navy). 1958 Laid up. 1967 *Transcolumbia* (Machine & Foundry Co). 1968 Refitted as car carrier. 1985 Laid up at San Francisco.

8   *President Cleveland* 1947-1973 (c 1947-1953)

Bethlehem Shipbuilding Corporation, Alameda, California, 1947.

15,359 gross tons; 609 × 75 ft (185 × 23 m); turbo-electric; twin screw; 20 knots; 326 first class, 506 third class passengers. 1944 Laid down as transport USS *Admiral D.W. Taylor*. Chartered to APL and completed as passenger liner. Launched 23/6/1946.

MV 15/12/1947 San Francisco-Hong Kong. 1954 Purchased from Government. 1963 Modernized; 14,456 tons, 379 first class, 380 economy class passengers. 1973 *Oriental President* (C.Y. Tung Group). 1974 Scrapped at Kaohsiung.

9   *President Wilson* 1948-1974 (c 1948-1953)

Bethlehem Shipbuilding Corporation, Alameda, California, 1948.

15,359 gross tons; 609 × 75 ft (185 × 23 m); turbo-electric; twin screw; 20 knots; 326 first class, 506 third class passengers. 1944 Laid down as transport USS *Admiral R.B. Upham*. Chartered to APL and completed as passenger liner. Launched 24/11/1946.

MV 27/4/1948 San Francisco-Hong Kong. 1954 Purchased from Government. 1963 Modernized; 14,446 tons, 379 first class, 380 economy class passengers. 1973 *Oriental Empress* (Orient Overseas Line — C.Y. Tung Group). 1975 Laid up at Hong Kong. 1984 Scrapped at Taiwan.

10   *President Hoover* 1957-1964

Bethlehem Shipbuilding Corporation, Quincy, Massachusetts, 1939.

10,603 gross tons; 493 × 64 ft (150 × 19 m); steam turbines; twin screw; 17 knots; 204 first class passengers. Launched 27/4/1939 as *Panama* (Panama Railroad).

1941 *James Parker* (Army transport). 1946 *Panama* (Panama Railroad) (see page 155). 1957 *President Hoover* (APL). FV 11/2/1957 San Francisco-Hong Kong. 1965 *Regina* (Chandris Cruises). 1973 *Regina Prima* (Chandris Cruises). 1979 Laid up at Piraeus. 1986 Scrapped.

11   *President Roosevelt* 1962-1970

Federal Shipbuilding & Drydock Company, Kearny, New Jersey, 1944.

18,920 tons; 622 × 75 ft (188 × 23 m); steam turbines; twin screw; 19 knots; 456 first class passengers. Launched 6/8/1944 as *General W.P. Richardson* (US Navy).

1948 *La Guardia* (American Export) (see page 49) 1951 Returned to MSTS. Made four Orient voyages under APL banner then laid up. 1956 *Leilani* (Hawaiian Steamship) (see page 127). 12/1958 Laid up. 1960 *President Roosevelt* (APL). FV 10/5/1962 San Francisco-Yokohama. 1970 *Atlantis* (Chandris Lines). 1972 *Emerald Seas* (Eastern Steamship). 1986 *Emerald Seas* (Admiral Cruises). 7/1986 Fire, 44 injured. Still sailing.

American Scantic Line

(1932-1948)

The Moore & McCormack Company purchased American Scantic Line in 1918 and operated the company as a subsidiary, with vessels purchased from the United States Shipping Board to carry out freight sailings to Scandinavia. On 12 September 1927, American Scantic Line was incorporated, and five years later the company converted four 'Hog Islanders' to carry 40 passengers each and dispatched them to the Baltic. Due to the efforts of American Scantic Line and its parent, Moore & McCormack, Gdynia was developed as a Polish seaport and the movement of Czech and other European exports was encouraged via Gdynia, in competition with German ports. This provocative behaviour on the part of Poland and Czechoslovakia in developing Gdynia at the expense of German ports had a decisive bearing on Hitler's decision to speed up the invasion of those two countries in 1939.

In anticipation of new tonnage, American Scantic sold the 'Hog Islanders' in 1939, with the result that the company entered the war and saw its conclusion with no passenger ships.

Freighter services were resumed between Philadelphia and Scandinavia in 1945. Because demand for passage across the Atlantic was so high, the War Shipping Administration assigned three ships, former troopers, to American Scantic to operate on passenger sailings. Each ship was able to carry over 850 passengers, albeit in austere, cramped conditions. The first departure from New York was made on 29 April 1946 by *Marine Perch*. After four voyages, she was transferred to American Export Lines; her replacement was *Marine Jumper*, which started joint services with US Lines in June 1947. The third vessel, *Ernie Pyle*, joined the 'fleet' for two voyages in 1947. By 1948, the established transatlantic lines were back

on the ocean, and American Scantic concluded passenger services in August 1948.

Although plans were considered for building a pair of steamers with accommodation for 160 passengers, nothing ever materialized. American Scantic decided to concentrate on its freighters, which carried only twelve passengers. Declining revenues led Moore & McCormack to absorb American Scantic in 1965, and as a result all its ships were withdrawn from service, bringing an end to another carrier of the American flag.

1   *Marine Perch* 1946 (c)

Kaiser Company Inc, Richmond, California, 1945.
12,420 gross tons; 523 × 71 ft (159 × 21 m); steam turbines; single screw ; 16 knots; 901 tourist class passengers. Launched 25/6/1945 as troop-ship. FV 29/4/1946 New York-Oslo-Gothenburg. LV 5/8/1946 New York-Bermen-Oslo-Gothenburg-New York, 4 RV. 1946 American Export (see page 46). 1965 *Yellowstone* (Rio Grande Transport). 14/6/1978 Sank after colliding with *Ibn Batouta*.

2   *Marine Jumper* 1947-1948 (c)

Kaiser Company Inc, Vancouver, Washington, 1945.
12,420 gross tons; 523 × 71 ft (159 × 21 m); steam turbines; single screw; 16 knots; 850 tourist class passengers. Launched 30/5/1945 as troop transport. FV 6/6/1947 New York-Le Havre-Copenhagen-Oslo-Gdynia. 27/9/1947 One voyage for American Export. LV 11/8/1948 New York-Copenhagen-Oslo-Gdynia, 5 RV. 1948 US Lines (see page 210). 1966 *Panama* (Litton), 17,184 GRT, 684 ft (208 m). 1975 *Panama* (Reynolds). 1987 Scrapped in Taiwan.

3 *Ernie Pyle* 1947 (c)

Kaiser Company Inc, Vancouver, Washington, 1945.
12,420 gross tons; 523 × 71 ft (159 × 21 m); steam
turbines; single screw; 16 knots; 869 tourist class passengers. Launched 25/6/1945 as troop transport.

FV 26/9/1949 New York-Le Havre-Copenhagen-
Oslo-Gdynia. LV 9/12/1947 New York-Le Havre-
Copenhagen-Oslo-Gdynia, 2 RV. 1947 US Lines (see
page 208); 1965 *Green Lake* (Central Gulf Steamship
Company). 1978 Scrapped at Kaohsiung.

Arnold Bernstein Line

(1948)

Arnold Bernstein was born in Germany, and in 1933 founded the shipping line that bore his name. Two years later he acquired Red Star Line, but was arrested by the Nazis in 1937 and sentenced to two and a half years in gaol. He was released in 1939 and headed for New York where he founded the Arnold Bernstein Shipping Company in 1938 and, after he became a naturalized US citizen in 1940, his company became the general agents for Compañia Trasatlantica (Spanish Line).

Bernstein's dream was to operate a weekly passenger service between New York and Antwerp or Rotterdam, and to this end he submitted his applications to the US Maritime Commission in 1946. While waiting for a decision, he chartered the 47-year-old *Tidewater*, the former *Ancon*, which had

Arnold Bernstein's Continental *as* Ancon *passing through the Panama Canal* (Frank O. Braynard collection).

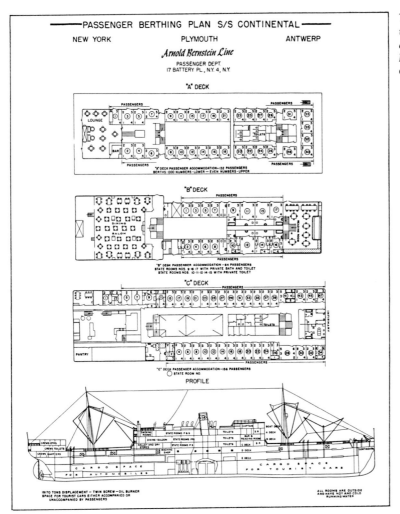

The deck plan of Continental *was unusual. Note that the cabins on A-Deck and B-Deck open out on to the Promenade Deck* (Frank O. Braynard collection).

been the first ocean-going ship to make a ceremonial passage through the Panama Canal from the Atlantic to the Pacific in 1914.

Tidewater was overhauled, given space for 350 single-class passengers and renamed *Continental*. She sailed from New York on 3 June 1948 for Plymouth and Antwerp. After four round trips she was withdrawn from service and returned to Tidewater Commercial Company, a Panamanian company.

Bernstein continued his negotiations with the Maritime Commission and his dream was partially fulfilled when he acquired *Atlantic*, which sailed under the trade name of American Banner Lines.

Continental 1948 (c)

Maryland Steel Company, Sparrow, Maryland, 1901. 10,005 gross tons; 505 × 58 ft (154 × 18 m); triple expansion engines; twin screw; 13 knots; 352 single class passengers. Launched 19/12/1901 as *Shawmut* (Boston Steamship Co).

1909 *Ancon* (Panama Railroad Company). 1940 *Exancon* (US). 1941 *Ancon* (US). 1941 *Permanente* (US). 1946 *Tidewater* (Tidewater Commercial Co). 1948 Chartered to Arnold Bernstein. FV 3/6/1948 New York-Plymouth-Antwerp. LV 13/9/1948 New York-Plymouth-Antwerp, 4 RV. 1950 Scrapped at Genoa.

A.H. Bull & Company

(1923-1953)

Archibald Bull was instrumental in establishing the New York and Porto Rico Steamship Company in 1885, and a firm bearing his name, A.H. Bull & Company, in 1902. The latter firm operated a fleet of cargo vessels from the US mainland to the island of Puerto Rico. In 1923 A.H. Bull commenced a passenger service with the introduction of *Catherine* sailing on overnight trips between San Juan and St Thomas. This service was supplemented in 1930 by *Barbara* on the Baltimore-San Juan route.

The Second World War disrupted all passenger services, and A.H. Bull & Company lost its *Barbara*, and although *Catherine* survived she was immediately sold to British buyers, who later sold her to French interests.

Intent upon re-entering the passenger business, A.H. Bull & Company purchased Porto Rico Line's flagship *Boriquen*, refurbished her and dispatched her on the New York-San Juan run as *Puerto Rico* in 1949. Ports of call were San Juan, Ciudad Trujillo, back to San Juan and then New York, the circuit being completed in eleven days.

In March 1953, Mr E. Myron Bull stated that 'the operation of the ship has been successful in terms of service and satisfaction to passengers who travelled in her... but costs have continued to increase at such a level that the losses are no longer tolerable'. Hence, after only four years of service, *Puerto Rico* was withdrawn from service and laid up. The company was subsequently purchased by several others, with the name Bull Line being phased out by 1966.

Puerto Rico 1949-1953

Bethlehem Shipbuilding Corporation, Quincy, Massachusetts, 1931.

7,114 gross tons; 466 × 60 ft (142 × 18 m); steam turbines; single screw; 16.5 knots; 200 first class passengers. Launched 24/9/1930 as *Boriquen* (New York & Porto Rico Steamship Company) (see page 147).

1949 *Puerto Rico* (A.H. Bull). FV 18/8/1949 New York-San Juan. LV 19/3/1949 New York-San Juan. 3/1953 Laid up. 1954 *Arosa Star* (Arosa Line). 1959 *Bahama Star* (Eastern Steamship) (see page 97). 1969 *La Jenelle* (Western Steamship Co). 13/4/1970 Destroyed in a gale off California while under tow on her way to being converted to a floating hotel.

Bull Line's Puerto Rico *departing from New York* (Henry W. Uhle/SSHSA Collection).

Bahama Cruise Line

(1968-1978)

The American public firm of United States Freight Company formed Bahama Cruise Line in 1968 with headquarters in Miami, Florida. The company was to concentrate on short two-day and three-day cruises from Miami to the Bahamas.

Their first ship was the 10,488-ton Panamanian registered *Freeport I*. Amenities for 812 single class passengers distributed through seven decks included private baths for all cabins, full air-conditioning, one dining room, four lounges and an outdoor swimming pool. In addition, there was garage space for 144 cars. *Freeport I* commenced her maiden voyage, a two-day cruise to Freeport, with minimum rates starting at $25 (£10) for the round trip. During her first year of operation, she alternated between two-day and three-day cruises to Freeport. Then, during 1969, her registry was switched to Liberia, and Nassau was added to her three-day itinerary, so that she did two back-to-back three-day Bahamas cruises, then a three-day Freeport cruise, followed by an overnight voyage to Freeport.

In 1973, *Freeport I* was sold to Birka Line AB, a Finnish company. She was replaced by the chartered *Ariadne*. Renamed *Freeport II*, she commenced three-day cruises from Miami to Nassau during the spring of 1973. She sailed for one year then was returned to Eastern and subsequently sold to Chandris Cruises. Her place was to have been taken by *Theodor Herzl*, a vessel purchased from the Israelis and chartered by Bahama Cruise Line. Her name was changed to Freeport and she was to have made her debut in June 1974, but because of conversion delays Bahama Cruise Line was forced to charter *Cunard Ambassador* for a series of New Orleans-Mexico cruises (a new cruising field), and then Miami-Bahama sailings. However, during *Cunard Ambassador*'s positioning voyage to New Orleans on 12 September 1974, a ruptured fuel tank caused a fire. The ship was towed to Key West, Florida, and declared a total loss.

Bahama Cruise Line turned next to Epirotiki Line, chartering their newly-refitted *Atlas*, laid up due to the Middle East oil situation. Retaining her Greek colours and name, she commenced operations for Bahama Cruise Line on 2 November 1974 out of New Orleans. She made six seven-day cruises to Tampico and Veracruz, then in December was positioned out of Miami, and made her first departure for Nassau and Freeport on 18 December. Her three-day cruises departed on Fridays and her four-day trips left on Sundays. *Atlas* was returned to Epirotiki in April 1975.

Finally, in September 1975, the new *Freeport* was delivered by Italian shipbuilders. There were 375 air-conditioned cabins for 880 passengers — a bit tight, but economy rates were the rule — and seven days ranged from $299.50 for an inside upper and lower cabin to $499.50 for a suite. Her first cruise departed from New Orleans on 13 September and called at Veracruz and Yucatan, both in Mexico. Within a year of her delivery, she was renamed *Veracruz I*. From December 1976 to September 1977, and again from November 1978 to May 1979, she operated under the banner of Strand Cruises on sailings to Alaska and Caribbean.

In 1978, Bahama Cruise Line was acquired by the British firm of Common Brothers. Eight years later

Above right *Bahama Cruise Line's first ship,* Freeport (Author's collection).

Right Freeport II *shown here as Eastern's* Ariadne *after her 1970 refit* (Author's collection).

Veracruz I *also sailed briefly as* Freeport (Author's collection).

the company changed its name to Bermuda Star Line and went public, being listed on the American Stock Exchange. Today it operates *Veracruz I, Bermuda Star and Queen of Bermuda* on cruises from New York, Montreal and Florida.

1 *Freeport I* 1968-1973

LMG, Orenstein Kopel & Lubecker Maschinenbau AG, Lubeck, 1968.

10,488 gross tons; 441 × 70 ft (134 × 21 m); Pielstick diesels; twin screw; 20 knots; 812 first class passengers. Launched 20/4/1968.

MV 15/12/1968 Miami-Freeport. 1973 *Freeport* (Birka Line AB). 1974 *Svea Star* (Stockholm Rederi AB). 1976 *Caribe* (Bremer Schiffahrts-Gesellschaft). Chartered by Commodore Cruise Lines (see page 92). 1981 *Caribe Bremen*. 1981 *Scandinavian Sun* (DFDS Seaways).

2 *Freeport II* 1973-1974 (c)

Swan, Hunter, & Wigham Richardson Ltd, Newcastle, 1951.

6,644 gross tons; 454 × 58 ft (138 × 18 m); steam turbines; single screw; 18 knots; 239 first class passengers. Launched 8/11/1950 as *Patricia* (Swedish Lloyd).

1957 *Ariadne* (Hamburg-America). 1961 *Ariadne* (Eastern Steamship) (see page 97). 1963 Refitted.

1973 *Freeport II* (chartered to Bahama Cruise Line on Miami-Bahamas islands service). 1974 *Bon Vivant* (Chandris). 1978 *Ariadne* (Chandris). 1980 *Saronic Sea* (Saronic Cruises SA, Piraeus).

3 *Atlas* 1974-1975 (c)

Wilton-Fijenoord Dok-en Werf Maats NV, Schiedam, 1951.

9,114 gross tons; 502 × 69 ft (153 × 21 m); geared turbines; single screw; 15 knots; 575 first class passengers. Laid down as freighter *Dinteldyk*, launched 19/12/1950 as *Ryndam* (Holland-America Line).

1968 *Waterman* (NV Mij Transocean). 1968 *Ryndam* (Holland-America Line). 1972 *Atlas* (Epirotiki Line). 1974 Chartered to Bahama Cruise Line. FV 2/11/1974 New Orleans-Mexico. FV 18/12/1974 Miami-Bahama. 4/1975 Returned to Epirotiki as cruise ship.

4 *Freeport* 1975-1976 (c)
Veracruz I 1976 (c)

Deutsche Werft, Hamburg, 1957.

10,596 gross tons; 487 × 64 ft (148 × 19 m); steam turbines; twin screw; 18 knots; 880 single class passengers. Launched 1/10/1956 as *Theodor Herzl* (Zim Israel Navigation).

1969 *Carnivale* (New Horizons Shipping). 1974 *Freeport* (Bahama Cruise Line). FV 13/9/1975 New Orleans-Mexico. 1976 *Veracruz I* (Bahama Cruise Line). 1986 *Veracruz I* (Bermuda Star Line).

Caribbean Atlantic Steamship Company

(1954-1955)

Caribbean Atlantic was formed in 1954 with headquarters at Southern Building, Washington, DC. The company acquired Alaska Steamship's *Aleutian*, reconditioned her, painted her white, registered her in Liberia and renamed her *Tradewind*. A brochure issued by the company described her as '...your delightful cruise liner', and went on to entice potential passengers with the information that *Tradewind* provided a ballroom, a forward observation room and an intimate club lounge with private bar. An expansive Lido Sun Deck, wide promenades, swimming pool and shuffleboard courts completed the amenities, all of which could only lead to 'a full programme of enterainment featuring dancing, sports, games, parties, activities for young and old alike'.

Tradewind departed in January 1955 on her first series of cruises out of Miami to the Caribbean. Late spring, summer and early autumn saw her undertaking seven-day and nine-day cruises out of Washington, DC, Savannah and Richmond to Bermuda, Nassau and/or Havana. Seven-day cruises began at

A bon voyage crowd of 8,000 wishes Tradewind *well as she departs from Richmond, Virginia, on 25 September 1955 (Everett E. Viez/SSHSA Collection).*

$110 (£39) and nine-day cruises at $150 (£54). All staterooms were outside, but only the best had private facilities. When *Tradewind* departed on a ten-day cruise on 25 September, a crowd of 8,000 came down to bid *bon voyage* to the first ocean-going vessel to depart from Richmond.

On 25 November 1955, *Tradewind* left Washington for Ensenada, sailing west via the Panama Canal. Passengers completed their 'cruise' to Los Angeles by complimentary transportation provided by Caribbean Cruise Lines. By disembarking her passengers at a foreign port so close to the American mainland, Caribbean Atlantic circumvented the Jones Act of 1920, an act that prohibited foreign-flagged vessels from engaging in the coastal trade. *Tradewind* then made her way to San Diego, whence she departed for a thirteen-day cruise to Acapulco at fares from $295 (£105). Upon her return to San Diego on 3 January, *Tradewind* continued, without passengers, to San Francisco, whence she departed on 7 January for Havana. Again, complimentary transportation to Miami was provided by Caribbean Cruise Lines.

Although a series of five-day cruises from Miami to Havana and Nassau was planned for February and March 1956, together with a summer programme out of Washington, *Tradewind* never carried them out.

According to a recent issue of 'Steamboat Bill', *Tradewind* was due to sail from California on 7 January but was impounded there for outstanding debts totalling $550,000. She was apparently subsequently sold at auction to Boston Metals, and later in 1956 was resold to Belgian shipbreakers.

Tradewind 1954-1955

William Cramp & Sons Shipbuilding Company, Philadelphia, Pennsylvania, 1906.

6,361 gross tons; 416 × 50 ft (127 × 15 m); triple expansion engines; twin screw; 17 knots; approximately 240 passengers. Launched 21/3/1906 as *Mexico* (New York & Cuba Mail).

1929 *Aleutian* (Alaska Steamship) (se page 22). 1953 Chartered to Hawaiian-Pacific (see page 125). 1954 *Tradewind* (Caribbean Atlantic Line). FV 1/1955 Miami-Caribbean. FV 4/6/1955 Washington, DC-Bermuda and Nassau. FV 25/9/1955 Richmond-Havana and Nassau. FV 25/11/1955 Washington, DC-Ensenada. FV 21/12/1955 San Diego-Acapulco-San Diego, arriving 3/1/1955. 7/1/1956 San Francisco-Havana, arriving 29/1. 1956 Scrapped in Belgium.

Caribbean Cruise Lines

(c 1960-1964)

Headquartered in Washington, DC, Caribbean Cruise Lines never owned a single vessel, but instead this American firm chartered its ships.

In 1964 the company advertised a series of cruises as 'unforgettable vacations at prices you can afford'. When passengers arrived at the pier in New York, the cruise liner they saw was the 37-year-old *Evangeline*, dubbed *Yarmouth Castle* for this series of 'unforgettable vacations'. *Yarmouth Castle* sailed from New York on 26 June on her first charter cruise to Nassau. She limped in and out of New York on four such cruises, usually nine to fifteen hours late. Finally, after her 24 July arrival, *Yarmouth Castle* was placed in drydock at the Erie Basin in Brooklyn. Charges were brought against the ship's owner, Chedade, because the ship did not maintain her 15 knot speed; Chedade counter-charged CCL with wrongfully revoking the charter agreement. *Yarmouth Castle* posted bond and quietly slipped south, and CCL went bankrupt due to the adverse publicity.

Yarmouth Castle 1964 (c)

William Cramp & Sons Shipbuilding Company, Philadelphia, Pennsylvania, 1927.

5,002 gross tons; 380 × 56 ft (116 × 17 m); steam turbines; twin screw; 18 knots; 350 first class passengers. Launched 12/2/1927 as *Evangeline* (Eastern Steamship Lines) (see page 93).

1954 *Evangeline* (Eastern — F.L. Fraser) (see page 97). 1964 *Yarmouth Castle* (Yarmouth Steamship Co) (see page 218). 6/1964 Chartered to CCL. FV 26/6/1964 New York-Nassau (4 RV). 7/1964 Returned to Yarmouth. 13/11/1965 Burned and sank in the Caribbean with the loss of 87 lives.

Carnival Cruise Lines

(1972 to date)

It took one decade for Carnival Cruise Lines to evolve from an insignificant one-ship operation to the leader and trend-setter of the 1980s. The man responsible for this is Ted Arison, a man with shipping in his blood.

Ted acquired his maritime interest from his father, who owned the largest shipping firm in Israel. When Ted was 28 years old, he left Israel and moved to the United States, settling in Miami. He became an American citizen and embarked on many enterprises before entering shipping.

Miami in the late 'sixties and early 'seventies was fast becoming the Mecca for the cruise industry. Ted Arison created Arison Shipping Company, which in 1967 briefly operated the liner *Miami*. He also attempted to operate the Israeli car ferries *Bilu* and *Nili* during the late 1960s. When that fell through, he teamed up with Knut Kloster, founder of Norwegian Caribbean Lines, and after that partnership broke up he turned to Meshulam Riklis, a long-time friend and president of the Rapid-American Corporation. Arison still hoped to capitalize on this growing cruise market and with Riklis' financial backing, he was able to negotiate a $6.5 million financing deal with American International Travel Service Inc (AITS) of Boston for the purchase of *Empress of Canada* from Canadian Pacific. Carnival Cruise Lines was established in early 1972 as a wholly owned subsidiary of AITS to operate the new ship, which was renamed *Mardi Gras*, given a new coat of paint and the distinctive half moon funnel livery (an economic expedient, for Canadian Pacific had the same shape) of red, white and blue. She was then immediately dispatched from Tilbury to Miami.

Unfortunately, the hasty preparations led to a courtship with catastrophe. *Mardi Gras* departed from Miami on her first seven-day Caribbean cruise on 11 March 1972 with 300 travel agents aboard, as well as passengers paying from $175 to $450 (£67 to £173) each. Shortly after sailing, the liner ran aground harmlessly outside Miami. She was refloated and the cruise continued while competitors joked that the drink of the day was 'Mardi Gras on the Rocks'. The service was also questionable, a fact which the departing travel agents never forgot.

During the next two years, Carnival pulled out all the stops to improve its image and its product. This included a stem to stern facelift for *Mardi Gras* which began at sea and was completed during a 50-day dry-docking. However, by 1974 Carnival was faced with near bankruptcy and AITS wanted to part company. For $1 cash and Arison's assumption of Carnival's $5 million debt, AITS sold him full ownership of the line and its precarious future.

Maybe fate took a hand, but within months of the sale berths on *Mardi Gras* started to fill, thanks no doubt to the introduction of on-board casino gaming, and she operated during 1975 at an occupancy rate of over 100 per cent. The 'Fun Ship' concept was in its infancy but taking hold; gone were the rigid class distinctions and pretensions to formality, and instead Carnival turned its attention to making the shipboard experience vibrant, with the focus on activities for the young (25-40) age group. By the end of 1975, Carnival had made another purchase, from Greece, *Queen Anna Maria*, the former *Empress of Britain* of Canadian Pacific.

Above right *Carnival's first ship was* Mardi Gras (Carnival Cruise Lines).
Right *'Fun Ship'* Carnivale (Carnival Cruise Lines).

Carnival's Festivale (Carnival Cruise Lines).

Newly renamed *Carnivale,* she had few interior or exterior alterations. With some new furniture and paint, she sailed on her first seven-day Caribbean cruise on 7 February 1976, with fares ranging from $365 to $750 (£209 to £428) for off-season double occupancy. For that year, *Carnivale's* occupancy rate was over 95 per cent, approaching that of *Mardi Gras.*

Quickly following up his success, Arison purchased the 32,697 ton South African liner, *SA Vaal* in the autumn of 1977. She sailed to Japan for a $20 million reconstruction at Kawasaki Heavy Industries, emerging as *Festivale* and billed 'the ship of the 'eighties'. At 38,175 tons and with a capacity of 1,432 passengers, *Festivale* featured 15 public rooms in a variety of decors including the Gaslight Club (a casino/saloon), Fanta Z (a discotheque replete with an illuminated dance floor), Le Cabaret (a night-club) and the Copacabana Lounge. *Festivale* arrived in Miami in October 1978 and sailed on her first cruise to San Juan, St Thomas and St Maarten on 28 October. Season rates began at $465 (£254) for inside upper and lower accommodation, rising to $1,060 (£579) for an outside suite with veranda. Carnival Cruise Lines now had the largest and fastest vessel

sailing from Miami to the Caribbean.

With aggressive marketing and offering an affordable alternative to land-based vacations and other cruises, such as the 'Fly Aweigh Cruises' (air/sea all-inclusive package tours, inaugurated by Carnival), the 'Fun Ships' *Festivale, Mardi Gras* and *Carnivale* were heavily booked. As a result, in the autumn of 1978 Ted Arison surprised everyone by announcing that Carnival would build a brand new ship.

Contracts were signed and the keel laid. During construction, Carnival invited its sales representatives, travel agents, operations department and advertising agents to come up with a name for the new ship. Among the suggestions were *Jubilee, Frolic, Holiday, Melody, Whoopee, Celebration, Fandango* and *Fantasy; Fiesta, Carousel* and *Tropicale* were given serious consideration. In the end, *Tropicale* was selected by Carnival and four years after conception the 'ship of the 'nineties' sailed from the Aalborg Shipyard in Denmark for Miami. At 36,647 tons, she was the first ship designed and built by and for Carnival.

Among the unique features to enthral *Tropicale's* 1,422 passengers were that every stateroom had closed circuit colour television capable of picking up shoreside programmes via the ship's satellite navigational system, piped music and telephones.

Twenty-two cabins were designed to accommodate the handicapped and stateroom doors used a slim keycard instead of a conventional keys. In the public areas, the dining room was, unusually, built within the hull instead of in the superstructure, and the Tropicana Lounge was arranged on three tiers, the Paradise Club Casino, the Exta-Z Discotheque and a unique room called the Boiler Room, a lido/bar restaurant with colour-coded exposed pipes.

Tropicale sailed on her maiden voyage on 16 January 1982 to the Western Caribbean ports of Ocho Rios, Grand Cayman and Cozumel. Rates started at $760 (£425) for inside upper and lower accommodation and rose to $1,445 (£807) for a veranda suite (low season per person with airfare extra). *Mardi Gras* was switched to the same itinerary in January 1982, but visiting the ports in reverse order. In May 1982, *Tropicale* headed for the West Coast to take up her new home ports of Vancouver in summer and Los Angeles in winter. Under the marketing direction of

Below *The first of Carnival's new generation of cruise ships was* Tropicale (Carnival Cruise Lines).

Bottom Holiday *heads out to sea for the first time* (Carnival Cruise Lines).

Jubilee *in Miami* (Carnival Cruise Lines).

Westours, a subsidiary of Holland America Cruises, *Tropicale* departed from Vancouver on her first seven-day cruise on 5 June 1982. After the Alaska season, she sailed down to Los Angeles to open up Carnival's new market, seven-day cruises to Mexico, which she commenced on 19 September.

Everything Carnival touched seemed to turn to gold. All the ships were sailing full: in 1980, Carnival occupancy rate totalled 112 per cent. In 1981 it was 113.6 per cent and in 1982, with expansion into new markets — the western Caribbean and West Coast — 109 per cent. Clearly the 'Fun Ships' were pleasing the cruising public and establishing themselves as pace-setters.

Emulating *Tropicale*'s new concepts of spaciousness and efficiency, Carnival embarked on a $1 billion construction programme. Contracts were signed at Aalborg Shipyard for a 45,000-ton liner, and at Kockums Shipyard for two 48,000-ton vessels. To pave the way for their arrival, in the spring of 1984 Carnival switched *Carnivale* to three-day and four-day cruises from Miami to the Bahamas, and in December 1985 repositioned *Mardi Gras* on three-day and four-day cruises to the Bahamas from Port Everglades.

All this activity led to speculation about Carnival's future plans. In the company's *Cruise News* release, dated 1984, Carnival was examining the prospects of cruising the South Pacific waters, with attention centred on Australia and New Zealand, but with an eye also on Japan and China. Bob Dickinson, Senior Vice President of Sales and Marketing, emphasized, however, that any potential repositioning was for the long term, and that the primary commitment would continue to be in the North American market-place.

To reassure the maritime and travel industry, Carnival's first super-liner, *Holiday*, arrived in Miami in July 1985. After a series of gala parties and mini-cruises to nowhere, *Holiday* set out on her maiden voyage on 13 July with a full complement paying from $995 to $1,795 (£780 to £1,402) each, including complimentary air fare from many eastern and mid-western cities, for St Maarten, St Thomas and Nassau.

The Swedish-built *Jubilee* was completed in June and sailed for New York in June 1986 for a mini 'coming-out' party. After hosting thousands of travel agents, she sailed for Miami for more pre-maiden voyage festivities. When all was over, *Jubilee* departed on her maiden voyage on 6 July for Cozumel, Grand Cayman and Ocho Rio. Fares ranged from $1,045 (£706) for inside upper and lower accommodation to $1,995 (£1,348) for a veranda suite, including free connecting air travel. On 7 December, *Jubilee*'s itinerary was changed to Nassau, San Juan and St Thomas.

On 26 October 1986, to pave the way for *Celebration*, *Festivale*'s home base was switched from Miami to San Juan, and ports of call to St Thomas, St Maarten, Barbados and Martinique. Her in-season fares were the same as those of *Jubilee* and included free air travel connection. *Celebration* arrived at Miami in March 1987 and commenced her seven-day San Juan-St Thomas-St Maarten programme on 14 March. Like *Tropicale,* all staterooms in the *Holiday, Jubilee* and *Celebration* are more or less standard (180 sq ft) and possess private facilities, piped music, closed circuit colour television and individually controlled air-conditioning. A different decor is tastefully executed in each of the ships' public rooms. Though the names of Carnival's ships may not be maritime 'classics', they do play upon Carnival's theme of 'We've Got The Fun'.

The construction of Celebration *and* Jubilee *(Carnival Cruise Lines).*

Carnival Cruise Lines is a Panamanian corporation, and all its ships are registered there except for *Tropicale, Jubilee* and *Celebration,* which are registered in Liberia. In addition, all ships are staffed by Italian officers and an international crew, mainly from Central America and the West Indies. The foreign registry and foreign crew both help keep operational costs down in terms of taxes and low wages, and, as a foreign-registered company, Carnival pays no US taxes yet all the profits ($97.7 million in 1986) go to Ted Arison, an American.

In February 1987, Carnival signed a contract with Wärtsilä Marine for the construction of the world's most expensive cruise ship, the $200 million *Fantasy.* According to Bob Dickinson, 'A vacation aboard this vessel will be just as the name implies — a Fantasy'. She is to be about 70,000 tons with 1,025 cabins with

Top *Carnival's* Celebration *arriving, with* Jubilee *docked, at Miami* (Carnival Cruise Lines).

Above Celebration *sailing off to the Caribbean* (Carnival Cruise Lines).

a capacity of 2,600 passengers. There will be fourteen lifts to transport passengers between her fourteen decks, twelve bars and lounges, two dining rooms, a full casino, a jogging track and a seven-decks-high atrium, the largest at sea. The person in charge of the decoration will be Joe Farcus, creator of Carnival's awesome trio.

Carnival anticipates a continued increase in patronage to justify the new ship. In 1985 the line carried 317,569 passengers and in 1986 that number increased 40 per cent to 443,132 (that is one in five of all North American cruise passengers), thanks no doubt to the success of *Holiday* and the introduction of *Jubilee*. The 1987 target projections are for 545,000 passengers, and Carnival is so confident those figures will be reached that in June 1987 Ted Arison, sole owner of Carnival, announced that his company would go public and offer 23.6 million shares of common stock on the American Stock Exchange. According to documents that he filed with the Securities and Exchange Commission, Arison would own 75 to 82 per cent of the common stock, six per cent would be in a family trust and approximately three-quarters of one per cent would be owned by each of Arison's two children, Micky Arison and Sharon Arison Sueiras. The sale would raise around $401 million which would pay off the company's entire debt, including the cost of *Fantasy*, as well as partially finance two sister ships.

Carnival's other successful operations include Carnival Tours, which handles air travel and post-cruise trips for the line; Seachest Associates, a wholly-owned subsidiary handling food and beverage operations on the Carnival ships; and Carnival Leisure Industries which manage the Crystal Palace Resort and Casino property in Nassau.

In the autumn of 1987, Carnival exploded a bomb-shell. They signed a letter of agreement with Wärtsilä Marine Industries for two additional ships, at $200 million apiece, similar in design to the currently-building *Fantasy*. Not even the Stock Market crash of Monday 19 October 1987 put dampers on the spirits at CCL headquarters. As Arison reiterated Carnival's views that the cruise market is only in its infancy, there seems to be no stopping the feverish expansion plans of Carnival to capture that other 96 per cent.

Then, on 5 January 1988, Carnival's board launched 'Project Tiffany'. According to an article in *Travel Weekly*, the purpose of 'Project Tiffany' is to announce Carnival's formal entry into the 'upscale' market. Carnival hopes to have a fleet of three all-suite liners in operation by 1991, and possible cruising areas include Alaska, the Mediterranean,

Carnival's newest 'super-liner' will be Fantasy *(Carnival Cruise Lines).*

trans-canal, Caribbean and Mexican Riviera, with minimum per diems of around $350 (£250).

1 *Mardi Gras* 1972

Vickers-Armstrong Shipbuilding Ltd, Newcastle, 1961.
18,261 (B 27,284) gross tons; 650 × 86 ft (198 × 26 m); steam turbines; twin screw; 20 knots; 1,240 first class passengers. Launched 10/5/1960 as *Empress of Canada* (Canadian Pacific).

1972 *Mardi Gras* (Carnival). FV 11/3/1972 Miami-Caribbean. FV 16/4/1978 Miami-Los Angeles. 4/5/1978 Los Angeles-Mexico-Los Angeles. 11/5/1978 Los Angeles-Miami. 5/1978 Miami-Caribbean. FV 22/12/1985 Port Everglades-Bahamas.

2 *Carnivale* 1975

Fairfield Shipbuilding & Engineering Company Ltd, Govan, 1956.

18,952 (B 27,250) gross tons; 640 × 85 ft (195 × 26 m); steam turbines; twin screw; 20 knots; 1,350 first class passengers. Launched 22/6/1955 as *Empress of Britain* (Canadian Pacific). 1964 *Queen Anna Maria* (Greek Line). 1/1975 Laid up. 12/1975 Sold to

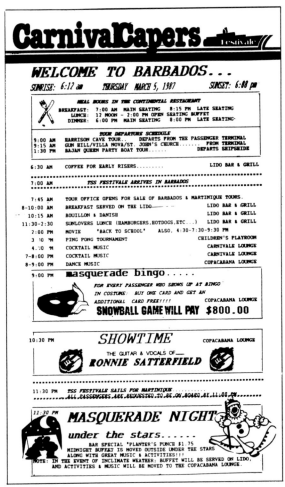

Daily programme for Festivale. *Compare Carnival's activities to those of American Cruise Lines (page 38)* (Carnival Cruise Lines).

Carnival. 1975 *Carnivale*. FV 7/2/1976 Miami-Caribbean. FV 26/5/1984 Miami-Bahamas.

3 *Festivale* 1977

John Brown & Company (Clydebank), Glasgow, 1961.
26,632 (B 38,175) gross tons; 760 × 90 ft (232 × 27 m); steam turbines; twin screw; 22.5 knots; 1,432 first class passengers. Launched 17/1/1961 as *Transvaal Castle* (Union Castle).
1966 *S.A. Vaal* (Safmarine). 1967 30,212 tons. 1969 Registered at Cape Town. 1977 *Festivale* (Carnival). 1977 Reconditioned at Kawasaki Heavy Industries,

Kobe. FV 28/10/1978 Miami-Caribbean. LV 12/10/86 Miami-Caribbean. FV 2/11/86 San Juan-Caribbean.

4 *Tropicale* 1981

Aalborg Vaerft A/S, Aalborg, 1981.
22,919 (B 36,647) gross tons; 672 × 86 ft (205 × 26 m); Sulzer diesels; twin screw; 19.5 knots; 1,422 first class passengers. Launched 31/10/1980.
MV 16/1/1982 Miami-Caribbean. FV 5/6/1982 Vancouver-Alaska. FV 19/9/1982 Los Angeles-Mexico.

5 *Holiday* 1985

Aalborg Vaerft A/S, Aalborg, 1985.
46,052 gross tons; 727 × 92 ft (221 × 28 m); Sulzer diesels; twin screw; 21 knots; 1,794 first class passengers. Launched 10/12/1984.
7/1985 Positioning voyage, Aalborg-Miami. MV 13/7/1985 Miami-Caribbean.

6 *Jubilee* 1986

Kockums AB, Malmö, 1986.
47,262 gross tons; 750 × 94 ft (229 × 29 m); Sulzer diesels; twin screw; 21.5 knots; 1,896 first class passengers. Launched 25/10/1985.
6/1986 Positioning voyage, Malmö-New York. MV 6/7/1986 Miami-Caribbean.

7 *Celebration* 1987

Kockums AB, Malmö, 1987.
48,000 gross tons; 750 × 94 ft (229 × 29 m); Sulzer diesels; twin screw; 21.5 knots; 1,896 first class passengers. Launched 8/5/1986.
MV 14/3/1987 Miami-Caribbean.

8 *Fantasy* 1989 (proposed)

Wärtsilä Marine Shipyard, Helsinki, 1989.
70,000 gross tons; 865 × 105 ft (264 × 32 m); diesel-electric engines; twin screw; 21 knots; 2,600 first class passengers.

9 *Ecstasy* 1990

70,000 gross tons; 2,025 first class passengers.

10 *Sensation* 1991

70,000 gross tons; 2,025 first class passengers.

Clipper Cruise Line

(1982 to date)

Foreseeing the potential of the coastal cruising market, Windsor Corporation of St Louis, Missouri, created Clipper Cruise Line who then commissioned Jeffboat Inc, of Jeffersonville, to construct three 'ultra yachts'. In order that these yachts should be able to operate the coastal waterways with non-union crews, each had to measure no more than 100 gross registered tons, enabling them to be classified as class 'D' vessels which are not subject to the bureaucratic regulations and, most importantly, the union rules, which have been the death knell of practically all the major American passenger firms. However, in actuality the ships are larger due to an aberration in the measurement rules with space normally included — passenger cabins, companionways, wheelhouse and galley — not included for the overall gross tonnage measurement.

Clipper Cruise Line fused the best elements of cruising America's scenic East Coast and the Virgin Islands with the luxury and manoeuvrability of multi-million-dollar yachts, each of which was specifically constructed with a shallow draught of only 7½ ft (2 m), permitting it to enter and berth at yacht marinas.

At a cost of $9 million, and named after one of the world's foremost yachting centres, Clipper took delivery of its first ultra-yacht, *Newport Clipper*, for a christening ceremony on 13 September 1983. Preceding the christening was the contract signing of its second vessel, *Nantucket Clipper*.

Following delivery at Louisville, Kentucky, *Newport*

Clipper's Newport Clipper *and* Nantucket Clipper (Clipper Cruise Line).

Clipper sailed on her positioning voyage to Savannah, Georgia, whence she commenced her maiden cruise on 1 October 1983. Following an autumn schedule from Savannah, she sailed to St Thomas for her seven-day winter programme which started on 25 December 1983. Like American Canadian, Clipper had to apply for a SOLAS Certificate to operate *Newport Clipper* out of the Virgin Islands. Spring saw her cruising northward along the Georgia and Chesapeake Bay coasts, and the summer of 1984 sailing out of New England ports.

Nantucket Clipper was christened on 9 December 1984 and joined her sister ship in the Caribbean on 23 December when she departed from St Thomas on her maiden seven-day Caribbean cruise to various Virgin Islands.

A unique sailing was undertaken by *Newport Clipper* on 18 May 1985 when she departed from Fort Lauderdale on a 29-day, 22-port 'Great American Odyssey' to Boston. Billed as a 'bonanza of Americana', passengers were treated to regional specialities in the dining room and entertained and educated by 13 lecturers whose topics ranged from ecology, flora and fauna to space exploration, American history and culture. This type of cruise is repeated each spring northbound and autumn southbound. *Per diem* rates for all cruises in 1987 started at $227 (£152) per person.

Clipper Cruise Lines capitalized on its success by introducing the 'ultra yacht' *Yorktown Clipper* in 1988 She departed from Savannah on her maiden voyage on 9 April, and shortly thereafter sailed north to her summer port of Boston.

Nantucket Clipper and *Yorktown Clipper* follow the schedule of *Newport Clipper*: winters in the warm Caribbean waters, springs sailing north along the southern and mid-eastern states, summers from New England and autumns heading south again via the scenic waterways and inlets of America's eastern seaboard.

All three ships are practically identical in size and furnishings. *Newport* and *Nantucket* have 51 outside staterooms, while the slightly larger *Yorktown* has 69. All have twin lower beds and private facilities, with the majority possessing large picture windows. Extensive use of light-toned maple and ash together with pastel colours and fabrics give all the public areas and the cabins a warm, contemporary, luxurious look.

1 *Newport Clipper* 1983

Jeffboat Shipyard, Jeffersonville, Indiana, 1983.
99.5 gross tons; 207 × 37 ft (63 × 11 m); Detroit diesels; twin screw; 10 knots; 102 first class passengers. Launched 16/7/83. Christened 13/9/1983.
MV 1/10/1983 Savannah-Colonial South cruise. FV 25/12/1983 St Thomas-Caribbean cruise. FV 16/6/1984 Boston-New England cruise.

2 *Nantucket Clipper* 1984

Jeffboat Shipyard, Jeffersonville, Indiana, 1984.
99.5 gross tons; 207 × 37 ft (63 × 11 m); Detroit diesels; twin screw; 10 knots; 102 first class passengers. Christened 9/12/1984.
MV 23/12/1984 St Thomas-Caribbean cruise. FV 13/4/1985 Savannah-Colonial South cruise. FV 23/6/1985 Boston-New England cruise.

3 *Yorktown Clipper* 1988

Jeffboat Shipyard, Jeffersonville, Indiana, 1987.
99.5 gross tons; 257 × 37 ft (78 × 11 m); Detroit diesels; twin screw; 10 knots; 138 first class passengers. Launched 24/12/1987. Christened 8/4/1988.
MV 30/4/1988 Savannah-East Coast-Savannah. FV 11/6/1988 Boston-New England cruise.

Coastwise Cruise Line

(1984-1985)

Hyannis Harbor Tours of Massachusetts created a subsidiary, Coastwise Cruise Line, in 1984 to operate a trio of intracoastal ships. However, unlike the sleek, clean-cut lines of other modern intracoastal ships, the Coastwise trio were to resemble the coastal steamers that operated from the 1880s to the 1920s. Dubbed 'Steamer Class', cruising along America's East Coast was to be like it was at the turn of the century — majestic, elegant and sophisticated, yet leisurely and relaxed.

Coastwise first 'steamer' was *Pilgrim Belle*, built by Bender Shipbuilding of Mobile, Alabama. Catering for only 110 passengers in 49 de luxe outside cabins, the 192-ft ship was furnished with authentic period reproductions. However, she also boasted modern amenities like private facilities in all the cabins, a lift, two lounges, a Mariners' Pub and a dining room.

Pilgrim Belle inaugurated the Coastwise service on 12 December 1984 when she departed from

Pilgrim Belle *introduced 'Steamer Class' cruising to America's intercoastal waterways (Coastline Cruise Line).*

89

Savannah, Georgia, for a nine-day cruise to West Palm Beach. The rest of the winter was spent along Florida's east coast between Fort Pierce and Jacksonville. During the spring of 1985, a few cruises were made from Savannah and Alexandria before the vessel headed for her premier summer season out of Hyannis for a series of seven-day cruises to the New England ports of Plymouth, Provincetown, Newport, Block Island, Martha's Vineyard and Nantucket.

Unfortunately, tragedy befell Coastwise on 28 July 1985 when *Pilgrim Belle* ran aground while being steered by an unsupervised stewardess who was in training to be a deck officer. After four weeks of repairs, *Pilgrim Belle* resumed sailing, but the adverse publicity led to lost bookings which forced CCL to sell its only vessel in September 1985 to Exploration Cruises.

Pilgrim Belle 1984-1985

Bender Shipbuilding & Repair Company Inc, Mobile, Alabama, 1984.

92 gross tons; 192 × 40 ft (58 × 12 m); Caterpillar diesels; twin screw; 13 knots; 110 first class passengers. Launched 8/9/1984.

MV 12/12/1984 Savannah-West Palm Beach. FV 8/6/1985 Hyannis-New England cruise. 28/7/1985 Ran aground off Cuttyhunk Island, Mass. 24/8/1985 Resumed service after repairs. 9/1985 *Colonial Explorer* (Exploration Cruises) (see page 106).

Commodore Cruise Line

(1966-1981)

In 1966, Sanford Chobol, a Miami hotelier, founded Commodore Cruise Line. He ordered a ship from a yard in Finland, and that vessel, *Boheme*, was delivered in December 1968. She was able to accommodate 460 first class passengers and featured several lounges, the Rodolfo, Marcello, Café des Artistes, Place Montmartre, Le Club Mimi, as well as two dining rooms, an outdoor pool, gymnasium and cinema. Her itinerary was simple: leave Miami every Saturday at 3.30 pm for Freeport, San Juan and St Thomas. Her maiden voyage took place on 7 December 1968, and except for the deletion or addition of a port, her itinerary was constant throughout her life with Commodore. She flew the West German flag, her officers were German and the crew was international.

After spending the summer sailing between Portland, Maine, and Yarmouth, Canada, a Norwegian vessel, *Bolero*, was chartered by Commodore and sailed south to join *Boheme*. *Bolero* was specifically built as a car ferry for North Sea service, and as such offered cruising possibilities to other destinations. Mr Chobol decided to place his new acquisition on the Miami-Mexico route, calling at Cozumel, Puerto Morelos, Cozumel, Veracruz and Key West; the service started on 13 October 1973 from Miami. For a seven-day voyage, fares ranged from $235 to $450 (£92 to £176), while charges for vehicles depended on their size. The service was not economically viable and alterations were made — instead of calling at three Mexican ports, Cozumel only would be visited, with Montego Bay and Port-au-Prince added to provide a 'cruise' voyage. This new service became effective on 9 November 1974 and lasted continuously until June 1976, after which she returned to the Portland-Yarmouth run for the summer, then

back to the North Sea.

To replace her, Commodore chartered *Caribe* from the Germans. She sailed on her first voyage from Miami on 20 November 1976 and headed south-east calling at Montego Bay, Port-au-Prince, Puerto Plata (Dominican Republic) and Freeport. Her season lasted until April, when she sailed north for a summer season of Portland-Yarmouth sailings. She returned to Miami every November. In December 1978, her itinerary was altered to Freeport, St Thomas, San Juan and Puerto Plata.

Caribe concluded her 1980-81 season in April, and left Miami never to return. Later that year, Commodore was acquired by the Finnish maritime consortium of Sally Line, but today still trades in the Caribbean with *Caribe I*.

1 *Boheme* 1968-1986

Wärtsilä, Turku, 1968.

10,328 gross tons; 441 × 68 ft (134 × 21 m); Sulzer diesels; twin screw; 21 knots; 460 first class passengers. Launched 12/2/1968.
MV 7/12/1968 Miami-Freeport-San Juan-St Thomas. 23/10/1974 Collided with container-ship *Swift Arrow* in San Juan. 1986 Sold to International Association of Scientologists.

2 *Bolero* 1973-1976 (c)

Dubigeon-Normandie SA, Nantes, 1973.

11,344 gross tons; 466 × 71 ft (142 × 22 m); Pielstick geared turbines; twin screw; 21 knots; 967 single class passengers. Launched 13/6/1972 for Fred Olsen. 1973 Chartered to Commodore. FV 13/10/1973 Miami-Mexico. 1976 Back to North Sea service. 1978

Scandinavica (chartered by Stena Line AB). 1982 *Bolero* (Fred Olsen).

3 *Caribe* 1976-1981 (c)

LMG, Orenstein Kopel & Lubecker Maschinenbau AG, Lubeck, 1968.

10,488 gross tons; 441 × 70 ft (134 × 21 m); Pielstick diesels; twin screw; 20 knots; 812 first class passengers. Launched 20/4/1968 as *Freeport 1* (Bahama Cruise Line) (see page 74).

1973 *Freeport* (Birka Line AB). 1974 *Svea Star* (Stockholm Rederi AB). 1976 *Caribe* (Bremer Schiffahrts-Gesellschaft). 1976 Chartered by Commodore. FV 20/11/1976 Miami-Caribbean. 1981 *Caribe Bremen* (Bremer SG). 1981 *Scandinavian Sun* (DFDS Seaways).

A brochure advertising the 'Happy Ships' Caribe *and* Boheme *(Author's collection).*

Eastern Steamship Company

(1901-1954)

In 1901, Charles Wyman Morse merged together the Boston & Bangor Steamship Company, the Portland Steam Packet Company, the International Steamship Company, and several local lines on the Maine coast to form the Eastern Steamship Company. Because of the financial dealings of Mr Morse, and the competition Eastern gave the Fall River Line which was owned by the New Haven Railroad and backed by J.P. Morgan, a 'bankers' war' ensued between the two empire builders. Morse was eventually indicted in 1907 for conspiracy and the New Haven Railroad temporarily gained a controlling interest in Eastern. Increasing its strength Eastern merged in 1911 with the Metropolitan Steamship Company and the Maine Steamship Company, but was forced to declare bankruptcy in 1914. Three years later it re-emerged, reorganized as Eastern Steamship Lines, with the Yarmouth Line included. In 1925, Eastern acquired the Old Dominion Line (with services from New York to Norfolk) and the New York and Richmond Steamship Company.

Between 1925 and 1941 Eastern had services from as far south as Norfolk, Virginia, to its northernmost point, St Johns, New Brunswick, with intermediate stops *en route* to embark and disembark both freight and passengers. The Depression, and the intense competition from the railroads and the motor car, led Eastern to introduce 'cruises' to entice passengers to its ships. At the outbreak of the Second World War, Eastern had a fleet of eight sea-going ships, together with dozens of smaller vessels on trips lasting from a few minutes to a couple of hours. The only survivors to be returned to Eastern were *Yarmouth* and *Evangeline*, both 'hurricane deck'-type vessels. Both were restored and placed on Eastern's only surviving route, the Boston-Yarmouth line. This service was maintained during the summer months, with the liners being switched to cruising out of Miami during the winter. The Yarmouth line was practically profitless, and eager to withdraw the ships, so the Nova Scotia government stepped in and subsidized *Yarmouth* and *Evangeline* for the 1954 season until its own vessel, *Bluenose*, was ready. Finally, on 9 November 1954, *Evangeline* undertook the last of Eastern's sailings from Boston.

The two vessels continued to operate under different owners until the 1960s, while the name Eastern survived until the 1980s.

1 *Yarmouth* 1927-1954

William Cramp & Sons Shipbuilding Company, Philadelphia, Pennsylvania, 1927.

5,002 gross tons; 380 × 56 ft (116 × 17 m); steam turbines; twin screw; 18 knots; 589 first class, 162 second class passengers. Launched 6/11/1926.

MV 9/7/1927 Boston-Yarmouth. 12/7/1936 Collided with freighter *Losmar* in Boston harbour. 1942 Army transport. 28/2/1947 Returned to service, New York-Nassau. 29/5/1947 Boston-Yarmouth. 1954 *Yarmouth Castle* (Eastern — F.L. Fraser) (see page 96). 1955 *Queen of Nassau* (Eastern — F.L. Fraser) (see page 96). 1956 *Yarmouth Castle* (Eastern — F.L. Fraser) (see page 96). 1958 *Yarmouth* (Eastern — F.L. Fraser) (see page 96). 1961 *Yarmouth* (Yarmouth Steamship Co) (see page 217). 1966 *San Andres* (Yarmouth). 1967 *Elizabeth A* (Hellenic International Line). 1979 Scrapped.

2 *Evangeline* 1927-1954

William Cramp & Sons Shipbuilding Company, Philadelphia, Pennsylvania, 1927.

5,002 gross tons; 380 × 56 ft (116 × 17 m); steam turbines; twin screw; 18 knots; 589 first class, 162 second class passengers. Launched 12/2/1927.

Chartered to Clyde Line. 1928 Returned to Eastern. FV 21/6/1928 New York-Yarmouth. 29/6/1928 Rammed and sank steamer *Grecian*. 1941 Chartered to Alcoa. 1/1942 Army transport. 1946 Returned to Eastern, refitted to carry 306 first class passengers. FV 8/6/1947 Boston-Yarmouth. LV 9/11/1954

Boston-New York. 1954 *Evangeline* (Eastern — F.L. Leslie) (see page 97). 1964 *Yarmouth Castle* (Yarmouth Steamship Co) (see page 218). 13/11/1965 Burned and sank in the Caribbean.

Below Evangeline *photographed on 14 August 1932* (R. Loren Graham/SSHSA Collection).

Bottom Yarmouth *in Eastern colours in 1934* (R. Loren Graham/SSHSA Collection).

Eastern Steamship Company

(F.L. Fraser) (1954-1970)

Jamaican-born F. Leslie Fraser purchased the name Eastern Steamship Company (see previous entry) along with *Yarmouth* for $500,000 in 1954. Under the Panamanian flag, with operators listed as McCormick Shipping Corporation and then Eastern Shipping Corporation, *Yarmouth* was renamed *Yarmouth Castle* and immediately dispatched out of Miami on 28 June 1954 to the Caribbean. Her owners claimed that she was the 'ex *Yarmouth* fitted like a castle'. On which castle they were basing *Yarmouth Castle*'s interiors was unknown; all that could be said was that little change took place during 'refitting'.

Fraser next acquired *Evangeline* in the autumn of 1954 and sent her to the shipyard for interior work. She was fitted with a small swimming pool aft, and air-conditioning was installed in all her public rooms and in 50 per cent of her cabins. Limited to 350 guests, *Evangeline* commenced a series of ten-day cruises out of Miami on 22 December 1954. In 1957, a cruise to Port Antonio, Kingston, Ciudad Trujillo and St Thomas cost from $190 (£68).

During the autumn of 1954, the government of Nassau and Eastern Shipping concluded negotiations which made *Yarmouth Castle* Nassau's contract ship, one of the provisions being that she be renamed *Queen of Nassau*. This was done and during 1955 and 1956 the *Queen* sailed from Miami on three-day and four-day cruises. When the contract expired, her name reverted to *Yarmouth Castle* and she reported to the shipyard for some modernization. A swimming pool was fitted, air-conditioning was installed in her public rooms and she was refurbished. She then saw service out of New Orleans and Washington, DC, on cruises to the West Indies. In 1958 Eastern returned to New England with cruises out of Boston to Yarmouth on *Yarmouth Castle*, now renamed *Yarmouth*. That year Eastern made *Yarmouth* on a par with *Evangeline* by making her completely air-conditioned and reducing her capacity to 365.

In 1959, Eastern acquired *Arosa Star* through the McCormick Shipping Corporation for approximately $510,000. She was renamed *Bahama Star* and after a refit was placed on the Miami-Nassau run. Two years later, the company purchased the tiny *Ariadne* from Hamburg-America. She was placed on luxury cruises to the Caribbean, and to enhance her appeal, she was completely redecorated, refurnished and air-conditioned in 1963.

Ownership of Eastern changed hands again in 1962 when W.R. Lovett of Jacksonville purchased the company. This accounted for the white 'L' on the blue diamond which appeared on the funnels during Lovett's ownership. Gone were *Yarmouth* and *Evangeline*, *Ariadne* was put on three-day, four-day and seven-day cruises, and *Bahama Star* remained on the Nassau service. A seven-day cruise aboard *Ariadne* during the summer of 1965 ranged from $160 (£57) for inside accommodation without facilities to $425 (£152) for the owner's suite. A four-day cruise in *Bahama Star* ranged from $95 to $160 (£34 to £37), and a three-day cruise from $80 to $130 (£29 to £46). For the next seven years the itinerary of the ships did not alter. With the acquisition of Zim Line's *Jerusalem*, renamed *New Bahama Star*, in 1969, *Bahama Star* was sold to Pacific interests and finally lost in a hurricane.

The end of American ownership of Eastern Steamship came in 1970 when the Norwegian shipping firm of Gotaas-Larsen purchased the line. In 1981 the company was restyled Eastern Cruises, and later in 1983 amalgamated with Western Cruise Lines and Sundance Cruises to form Admiral Cruises.

1 *Yarmouth Castle* 1954-1955
 Queen of Nassau 1955-1956
 Yarmouth Castle 1956-1958
 Yarmouth 1958-1961

William Cramp & Sons Shipbuilding Company, Philadelphia, Pennsylvania, 1927.
5,002 gross tons; 380 × 56 ft (116 × 17 m); steam turbines; twin screw; 18 knots; 500 first class

passengers. Launched 6/11/1926 as *Yarmouth* (Eastern Steamship Lines) (see page 93).
1954 *Yarmouth Castle* (Eastern Steamship — F.L.

Below Bahama Star *when she was owned by F. Leslie Fraser — note the 'F' on the funnel* (Everett E. Viez/SSHSA Collection).
Bottom Ariadne *of Eastern Steamship under the ownership of W.R. Lovett* (Author's collection).

Fraser). FV 28/6/1954 Miami-Caribbean. 1955 *Queen of Nassau* (Eastern — F.L. Fraser). FV 1955 Miami-Nassau. LV 1956. 1956 *Yarmouth Castle* (Eastern — F.L. Fraser). FV 7/9/1957 Washington-Caribbean. 1958 *Yarmouth* (Eastern — F.L. Fraser). 1959 Refit, 365 passengers. 1961 *Yarmouth* (Yarmouth Steamship Co) (see page 217). 1966 *San Andres* (Yarmouth Steamship Co). 1967 *Elizabeth A* (Hellenic International Line). 1979 Scrapped.

2 *Evangeline* 1954-1963

William Cramp & Sons Shipbuilding Company, Philadelphia, Pennsylvania, 1927.

5,002 gross tons; 380 × 56 ft (116 × 17 m); steam turbines; twin screw; 18 knots; 350 first class passengers. Launched 12/2/1927 for Eastern Steamship Lines.

1954 *Evangeline* (Eastern — F.L. Fraser), refitted. FV 22/12/1954 Miami-Caribbean. 7/1963 Laid up. 1964 *Yarmouth Castle* (Yarmouth Steamship Co). 13/11/1965 Burned and sank in the Caribbean with the loss of 87 lives.

3 *Bahama Star* 1959-1969

Bethlehem Shipbuilding Corporation, Quincy, Massachusetts, 1931.

7,114 gross tons; 466 × 60 ft (142 × 18 m); steam turbines; single screw; 16.5 knots; 735 first class passengers. Launched 24/9/1930 as *Borinquen* (New York & Porto Rico) (see page 147).

1949 *Puerto Rico* (A.H. Bull) (see page 71). 1954 *Arosa Star* (Arosa). 1959 *Bahama Star* (Eastern Steamship). 1969 *La Jenelle* (Western Steamship Co). 13/4/1970 Ran aground during hurricane off Californian coast.

4 *Ariadne* 1961-1972

Swan, Hunter, & Wigham Richardson Ltd, Newcastle, 1951.

6,644 gross tons; 454 × 58 ft (138 × 18 m); steam turbines; single screw; 18 knots; 239 first class passengers. Launched 8/11/1950 as *Patricia* (Swedish Lloyd).

1957 *Ariadne* (Hamburg-America). 1961 *Ariadne* (Eastern Steamship). 1963 Refitted. 1973 *Freeport II* (Bahama Cruise Line) (see page 74). 1974 *Bon*

Daily programme aboard Ariadne (Author's collection).

Vivant (Chandris). 1978 *Ariadne* (Chandris). 1980 *Saronic Sea* (Saronic Cruises SA, Piraeus).

5 *New Bahama Star* 1969-1970

Deutsche Werft AG, Hamburg, 1958.

9,900 gross tons; 488 × 65 ft (149 × 20 m); steam turbines; twin screw; 19.5 knots; 566 first class passengers. Launched 9/5/1957 as *Jerusalem* (Zim Lines).

1966 Chartered to Peninsular and Occidental (see page 159). 1968 Returned to Zim Lines. 1969 *New Bahama Star* (Eastern Steamship). FV 10/3/1969 Miami-Nassau. 1972 *Bahama Star* (Eastern Steamship). 1975 *Bonaire Star* (Venzolana de Cruceros del Caribe), laid up at Mobile, never sailed. 1979 Sold for scrap. 3/10/1979 Sank in Pacific while under tow.

Exploration Holidays and Cruises
(1980-1985)
Exploration Cruise Lines
(1985 to date)

In 1971, Alaska Tour and Marketing Services, under the ownership of Robert Giersdorf, began operating tour programmes from Seattle and Vancouver to out-of-the-way Alaskan destinations. The most popular spot was Glacier Bay, Alaska, where the company's ship, *Thunder Bay*, operated by Glacier Bay Lodge Inc, made one-day cruises. Determined to capitalize on *Thunder Bay*'s success, Glacier Bay chartered *New Shoreham* from the Alaska Cruise Boat Company. The vessel, with a listed length of 125 ft, was renamed *Glacier Bay Explorer* and dispatched on 8 June 1979 on two-day cruises between Glacier Bay Lodge near Juneau and Glacier Bay. Following her last seasonal sailing on 13 September, she made cruises from Seattle to the American and Canadian Gulf Islands and to Victoria, BC. The tiny *Thunder Bay* was laid up for the winter, returning to service during the warm summer months.

In 1980, Robert Giersdorf, and other members of his family founded Exploration Holidays and Cruises. The new company immediately purchased *Glacier Bay Explorer*, and in June replaced her on two-day summer cruises within Glacier Bay, which she has maintained to this date.

During that first year, Robert Giersdorf decided to stake his company's future on small vessels that offered a special intimacy and were able to make bow-in landings near Alaskan glaciers and on palm-shaded reefs circling the South Sea island lagoons. The first such vessel completed for Exploration was *Pacific Northwest Explorer* in 1981. Her maiden voyage began on 25 April 1981 from Portland, Oregon, up the Columbia and Snake Rivers to the state of Idaho. After three such cruises, she sailed from 18 May until September on three-day to six-day cruises from Seattle to the Canadian and Pacific North-west. In

1982 Exploration took delivery of *Majestic Explorer* and *Great Rivers Explorer*.

Majestic Explorer was commissioned on 2 March 1982 for four-day round-trip cruises from San Francisco up the San Jaoquin River to Stockton and Sacramento, California. On 30 May she commenced seven-day cruises from Ketchikan, Alaska, to Skagway. The appropriately named *Great Rivers Explorer* arrived at Portland, Oregon, in May and started her maiden voyage on the 15th, undertaking seven-day cruises up the Columbia and Snake Rivers to Idaho. The rates for this unusual journey ranged from $1,197 to $1,799 (£669 to £1,005).

Exploration led the way with unusual cruise destinations by positioning its *Majestic Explorer* on four-day and five-night cruises out of Tahiti to the South Pacific islands during the winter months. Her first cruise departed Papeete on 9 November 1982 and called at Huahine, Bora Bora, Tahaa, Raiatea and Moorea. Five enchanting nights cost from $899 (£502), while a four-night cruise, with no stop at Huahine, ranged from $749 to $1,098 (£418 to £613). This winter programme (November to May) was repeated every year by the 'Majestic' until, starting in October 1986, it became a year-round operation.

Except for the repositioning of ships, the basic summer pattern of cruises from Ketchikan, Portland and Seattle was maintained in 1983 and 1984. In keeping with the theme 'Exploration', the company

Above right *Exploration's first overnight cruise vessel,* Glacier Bay Explorer *(Exploration Cruise Lines).*

Right *A feature of Exploration is bow landings at unusual places, such as here at John Hopkins Inlet, Glacier Bay National Park, Alaska (Exploration Cruise Lines).*

embarked on Panama Canal cruises during the autumn of 1984, either from Panama City for a five-day transit through the Canal to Colon, or from Colon to Panama City. Prices started at $699 (£507) and included a few selected shore excursions. The first cruise was undertaken by *Great Rivers Explorer,* leaving Panama City on 8 November.

Glacier Bay Explorer has two passenger decks and the other three 'Explorer's have four. Each 'mini-liner' features all outside cabins with private facilities, while comfortable and modern decorated public rooms include the 'Vista View' lounge with a small bar located forward and the 'Explorer' dining room with large picture windows accommodating all passengers at one sitting. Special construction features include a low profile, bow thrusters and a bow ramp for disembarking at glaciers and remote beaches at the various places visited. Each ship is crewed by non-union American personnel, and in the case of *Majestic Explorer,* a few Polynesians as well.

In 1985, Exploration chartered the Norwegian liner *North Star.* This vessel was built in 1966 as *Marburg,* a fish factory stern trawler. She was converted into a cruise ship in 1983 and operated by North Star Line, and when she joined Exploration's fleet she was its largest vessel at 3,095 gross tons with accommodation for 158 passengers on six decks. She departed from Vancouver on her first Alaskan cruise on 11 May, while subsequent seven-day cruises departed from Prince Rupert, BC, to Skagway and back. Keeping her company in those northern waters were *Great Rivers Explorer* and *Majestic Explorer* operating from Ketchikan, while *Pacific Northwest Explorer* cruised the Columbia and Snake Rivers. That winter, *North Star* and *Great Rivers Explorer* were sent cruising through the Panama Canal, and *Pacific Northwest Explorer* was laid up.

In August 1985, Exploration sold a controlling interest to the Busch Entertainment Corporation, a division of Anheuser Busch Companies. This purchase brought a change of name to Exploration Cruise Lines, as well as an infusion of capital, sales personnel, and, most importantly, the potential for quality entertainment aboard the ships, since Busch

A bow landing at the luxurious Club Bali Hai on Cook's Bay, island of Moorea (Exploration Cruise Lines).

100

North Star, *Tracy Arm's Sawyer Glacier, Alaska* (Exploration Cruise Lines).

Entertainment employs some of the finest American entertainers in its theme parks. A month later, Exploration announced the purchase of *Pilgrim Belle* from Coastwise Cruise Line. She was renamed *Colonial Explorer* and made her first voyage from St Thomas to the 'unspoiled' US and British Virgin Islands on 13 December 1985. In May 1986, she returned to the mainland and starting from Jacksonville, Florida, on the 7th, made intra-coastal cruises northwards to Boston, whence she commenced a seven-day summer programme throughout colonial New England.

The four-deck catamaran *Executive Explorer*, privately owned by Mr Giersdorf and manned by Exploration Cruise Line, and the 1,800-ton *Explorer Starship* joined Exploration's fleet in 1986. On 24 June, *Executive* sailed on her maiden voyage from Seattle north to Juneau where she was based for her summer series of two-day and five-day cruises, joining *Glacier Bay Explorer*, *Majestic Explorer* and

North Star in Alaskan waters. On 4 October, *Executive Explorer* started her seven-day winter Hawaiian programme from Honolulu. The four-decks-high vessel has 25 staterooms for 49 passengers, a 'Vista View' lounge and an 'Explorer' dining room. The 1,800-ton *Starship* was completed in 1974 as the 'ro-ro' *Bogonia*. She was purchased by North Star Line in 1985, chartered to Exploration and completely rebuilt to its specifications by Lloyd Werft, Bremerhaven, at a cost of $20 million into an 'ultra-deluxe vessel'. She commenced her first seven-day cruise on 3 August 1986 from San Juan to Barbados while the reverse itinerary called at different ports. Fares for an outside cabin with de-luxe tiled bathroom including a built-in hairdryer, stocked refrigerator, closed-circuit colour television, individual video-cassette playback unit, telephone, radio and extra-secure card-key door locks ranged from $2,195 to $3,395 (£1,483 to £2,294).

Misfortune struck Exploration on 8 August 1986 when *North Star* ran aground sustaining serious damage. All the passengers were safely disembarked and the vessel was drydocked at Vancouver for repairs affording the company an opportunity to bring her more into line with the luxurious *Explorer Starship*. *North Star* re-entered service on 9 May 1987 from Seattle to Alaska.

In the summer of 1987, Exploration served Alaska with *Glacier Bay Explorer, North Star, Great Rivers Explorer, Pacific Northwest Explorer* and *Explorer Starship*. *Colonial Explorer* was used in the Columbia and Snake Rivers during the summer. In the winter *Glacier Bay Explorer* and *Pacific Northwest Explorer* cruise Mexican waters; *Explorer Starship* sails the Caribbean; *Colonial Explorer* visits secluded inlets in the Virgin Islands; *Great Rivers Explorer* transits the Panama Canal; *North Star* sails between La Paz, Mexico, and Acapulco; and a year-round service is maintained out of Tahiti by *Majestic Explorer*.

In May 1988, Exploration repurchased its shares from Busch Entertainment Corporation, giving full ownership of the company back to the Giersdorf family.

1 *Glacier Bay Explorer* 1980

Blount Marine Corporation, Warren, Rhode Island, 1970.

99 gross tons; 125 × 28 ft (38 × 9 m); General Electric diesels; twin screw; 12 knots; 64 passengers. Launched 28/2/1971 as *New Shoreham* (American Canadian) (see page 32).

1979 Sold to Alaska Cruise Boat, then chartered to Glacier Bay Lodge. FV 8/6/1979 Juneau-Glacier Bay. 1980 Sold to Exploration.

2 *Pacific Northwest Explorer* 1981

Blount Marine Corporation, Warren, Rhode Island, 1981.

100 gross tons; 143 × 28 ft (43 × 9 m); Deutz diesels; twin screw; 12 knots; 80 passengers. Launched 1/10/1980.

MV 25/4/1981 Portland-Idaho. FV 18/5/1981 Seattle-Princess Louisa Inlet. FV 5/10/1983 San Francisco-Stockton-Sacramento.

3 *Majestic Exporer* 1982

Nichols Bros Boat Builders, Freeland, Washington, 1982.

100 gross tons; 152 × 31 ft (46 × 9 m); Deutz diesels; twin screw; 12 knots; 88 passengers. Launched 18/12/1981.

Colonial Explorer arriving in St Thomas, her winter cruise port (Exploration Cruise Lines).

RAIATEA ISLAND   DAY TWO

C O C O N U T   R A D I O
****

Early in the morning the Majestic Explorer will enter the lagoon of
Raiatea, Polynesia's sacred island. Today will serve as our introduction
to the beautiful motus (low, coral islands) and their great snorkeling
opportunities, as well as our first exposure to some of the traditional
music of the Tahitians. Our port of call this afternoon will be Uturoa,
the second largest town in French Polynesia.

7:00 am	Join your Cruise Director to learn about our anchorage sight, and some facts about Raiatea.	FOREDECK
7:30 am	BREAKFAST IS SERVED. Good Morning!	DINING ROOM
8:00 am	SNORKEL GEAR CHECK-OUT - Please meet your Cruise Director to check out for snorkel equipment for the week. Take this opportunity to view the undersea world of Tahiti.	200 LEVEL AFT
8:30 am	ARRIVAL TO MOTU NAO NAO - We will make our first bowlanding to this remote island for a morning of swimming, snorkeling, sunbathing, and exploring the motu. The ship will remain in place throughout the morning. Careful with the sun!	
9:00 am	SNORKELING LESSONS - Class begins in the water directly in front of the ship. Refresh your snorkeling skills, or learn a new sport that will acquaint you with the underwater world.	ON THE BEACH
11:00 am	CRAFT DEMONSTRATION - On a shady spot on the beach, we will show you some of the native skills still used by the Polynesians today.	ON THE BEACH
12:00 pm	BEACH BARBEQUE - EXPLORER STYLE! Taste the best hamburgers and hotdogs south of the equator.	ON THE BEACH
1:30 pm	ALL PASSENGERS ABOARD PLEASE.	
1:45 pm	SHIP DEPARTS MOTU NAO NAO - Our destination is the northern tip of the island, to the town of Uturoa. Enjoy the beautiful scenery as we cruise the lagoon of Raiatea.	
2:30 pm	CULTURAL TALK.- Join your Cruise Directors for an informal discussion of culture and the way of life in French Polynesia.	BRIDGE DECK
3:15 pm	ARRIVAL AT UTUROA - Here we can take time to browse through the Mama's Craft Bazaar and explore the town before our afternoon tour.	200 LEVEL AFT
4:00 pm	AFTERNOON TOUR BEGINS - Meet Le Truck at the ship for a visit to a local vanilla plantation as well as the highlight of the tour, the delightful children's dance presentation held at the Hotel Bali Hai.	GANGWAY
5:15 pm	TAXI RETURN TO SHIP - At the end of the performance, complimentary taxi service will begin returning you to the Majestic Explorer.	HOTEL BALI HAI
5:45 pm	LAST TAXI DEPARTS THE HOTEL BALI HAI	HOTEL BALI HAI
6:00 pm	COCKTAIL HOUR - Join us for cocktails, appetizers, and music performed by the Bali Hai Big Kids! Perhaps our Bartender can interest you in the Special Drink of the Day!	BRIDGE DECK
7:00 pm	DINNER IS SERVED - Bon Appetit!	DINING ROOM
After Dinner	The fun and entertainment continues; more music by the Bali Hai Big Kids, a pareo demonstration, and a special evening farewell!	BRIDGE DECK
11:00 pm	THE BAR IS CLOSED FOR THE NIGHT	BRIDGE DECK
2:30 am	ALL PASSENGERS ABOARD PLEASE. (Did you check in on the status board?)	
3:00 am	MAJESTIC EXPLORER DEPARTS UTUROA for an open ocean crossing to the island of Bora Bora. Please remember to secure you cabins before turning in for the night.	

Bonne Nuit! Good Night!

****

BAR HOURS

10:00 am - 1:00 pm	BEACH MOTU BAR	
1:00 pm - 4:00 pm	LOUNGE	
5:00 pm - 10:00 pm	BRIDGE DECK	
10:00 pm - 11:00 pm	LOUNGE	

GIFT SHOP

Our gift shop is open after Breakfast today.

MV 2/3/1982 San Francisco-Stockton-Sacramento. FV 30/5/1982 Ketchikan-Skagway-Ketchikan. 11/9/1982 Ran into shoal while on charter to Special Expeditions of New York, with the loss of one life. Refloated and repaired. FV 9/11/1982 Papeete-South Pacific Islands cruise.

4 *Great Rivers Explorer* 1982

Nichols Bros Boat Builders, Freeland, Washington, 1982. 100 gross tons; 152 × 31 ft (46 × 9 m); Deutz diesels; twin screw; 12 knots; 92 passengers. Launched 5/1982.

MV 15/5/1982 Portland-Columbia and Snake Rivers. FV 8/11/1984 Panama City-Colon.

5 *North Star* 1985-1986 (c)

AG Weser, Bremerhaven, 1966.

3,095 gross tons; 295 × 46 ft (90 × 14 m); diesel engines; single screw; 13.5 knots; 158 passengers. Launched 26/2/66 as *Marburg*, factory stern trawler. 1982 *Lindmar*. 1983 *North Star* (North Star Line AS — Fearnley & Eger AS, Oslo). 1985 Chartered by Exploration. FV 11/5/1985 Vancouver-Alaska. FV 12/10/1985 San Diego-Acapulco-Panama Canal. 8/8/1986 Ran aground during Alaskan cruise. 1986-87 Repaired and reconditioned. 9/5/1987 Returned to service, Prince Rupert-Alaska.

6 *Colonial Explorer* 1985

Bender Shipbuilding & Repair Company Inc, Mobile, Alabama, 1984.

96 gross tons; 192 × 40 ft (58 × 12 m); Caterpillar diesels; twin screw; 13 knots; 102 first class passengers. Launched 8/9/1984 as *Pilgrim Belle* (Coastwise Cruise Line) (see page 90).

1985 *Colonial Explorer* (Exploration). FV 13/12/1985 St Thomas-Caribbean. 21/6/1986 Boston-New England.

7 *Executive Explorer* 1986

Nichols Bros Boat Builders, Whidbey Island, Washington, 1986.

93 gross tons; 104 × 37 ft (32 × 11 m); Deutz diesels; single screw; 22 knots; 49 first class passengers. Built privately for Robert Giersdorf.

MV 24/6/1986 Seattle-Juneau. FV 4/10/1986

EXPLORATION® CRUISE LINES
ONE OF THE ANHEUSER-BUSCH COMPANIES
1500 METROPOLITAN PARK BUILDING
SEATTLE, WASHINGTON 98101 206/625-9600 TELEX #32-9636
RESERVATIONS 800-426-0600

THURSDAY'S MENU

Breakfast

Explorer Quiche
Assorted Pastries
Ham
Fresh Fruit

Lunch
TAMAARAA
TRADITIONAL TAHITIAN FEAST

Poisson Cru
Roast Suckling Pig
Roast Chicken
Fafa, Taro, Sweet Potatoes
Fruit Poi
Fresh Fruit
Huahine Coffee with Vanilla and Coconut Milk

Dinner

Sesame Seed Rolls
Green Salad
Broccoli
Seasoned Rice Pilaf

Lamb Brochettes
with Bell Peppers, Tomatoes, Onions and Pineapple

OR

Fresh Jackfish

Pound Cake wqith Pineapple Sauce

A typical menu offered on Exploration's Polynesian voyages (Author's collection).

Honolulu-Hawaiian Islands. Autumn 1987 Returned to Giersdorf. Operates under the firm of Catamaran Cruises.

8 *Explorer Starship* 1986 (c)

Kristiansands MV AS, Kristiansand, 1974.

1,800 gross tons; 407 × 52 ft (124 × 16 m); Wickmann diesel engines; twin screw; 16 knots; 250 first class passengers. 1974 Launched as *Fernhill*. 1974 'Ro-ro' *Bogonia* (NV Stoomvaart-Maatschappij Oostzee). 1985 Sold to North Star Line AS — Fearnley & Eger AS, Oslo). 1985 *Explorer Starship* (chartered to Exploration). FV 3/8/1986 San Juan-Barbados. FV 24/5/1987 Prince Rupert-Anchorage.

Farrell Lines

(1948-1959)

The predecessor of Farrell Lines was American-South African Line, a company created in 1922 by the United States Shipping Board and managed by John J. and James A. Farrell. Their father, Captain John Guy Farrell, was a master mariner in Ireland who emigrated to America in 1858. American-South African Line started operations with the freighter *West Isleta* in 1926, and in 1930 the company took delivery of the passenger ship *City of New York*. The Depression cancelled two planned sister ships, and the war interrupted delivery of three PC-3 passenger-cargo liners.

Under the re-organization plan of 1948, American-South African Line was restyled Farrell Lines Incorporated, and with memories of *City of New York*'s success still fresh in the management's minds, Farrell decided in 1948 to re-enter the passenger business. The company went looking for two passenger ships similar to *City of New York* and found two derelict vessels lying in the reserve fleet. The Maritime Commission sold the hulls for $100,000 apiece with the provision that Farrell pay for the re-conditioning, and granted Farrell a construction-differential subsidy to cover the extra domestic cost of the reconstruction. The vessels, the former Delta liners *Delargentino* (Army transport *J.W. McAndrew*) and *Delbrasil* (Army transport *George F. Elliot*), were renamed *African Enterprise* and *Africa Endeavor*. They were towed to Gulf Shipbuilding at Mobile in December 1948 and each given a $2.25 million refit (£2.1 million). In charge of the conversion was the firms of Gibbs & Cox.

Passenger accommodation was arranged for 82 passengers. Staterooms, each with its own private facilities, were located on two decks. Passengers had the use of a swimming pool, lounge, smoking room and dining room; decorations in the two latter rooms featured paintings of animals and foliage indigenous to South Africa.

In July 1949, *African Enterprise* arrived in New York, and after a series of celebratory Farrell dinners, departed on her first voyage on 30 July 1949. A month later, on 31 August, *Endeavor* commenced her first voyage. Ports of call were Cape Town, Port Elizabeth, Durban and Maputo (Lourenco Marques). In 1952, an eight-day voyage to Cape Town cost $750 (£268), fourteen days to Durban $805 (£288) and nineteen days to Maputo $820 (£293) per person, based on two in a cabin.

For the next decade, the two ships, along with Farrell's fleet of fourteen freighters, plied the North and South Atlantic Oceans. Freight bookings were prospering, but not so the passenger trade. As a result, in 1959 the passenger accommodation of *Enterprise* and *Endeavor* was sealed up, and the two continued to sail as freighters, carrying only twelve passengers. In the mid-1970s, Farrell ceased carrying any passengers at all on its freighters and committed itself to cargo only.

Today, Farrell has freight and container services to West Africa, Australia and New Zealand (inaugurated in 1965), and the Mediterranean (inaugurated in 1978 with the purchase of American Export Lines).

1 *African Enterprise* 1949-1959

Bethlehem Steel Co & Shipbuilding Division, Sparrows Point, Maryland, 1940

7,922 gross tons; 491 × 66 ft (150 × 20 m); steam turbines; single screw; 16.5 knots; 82 first class passengers. Launched 13/7/1940 as *Delargentino* (Delta).

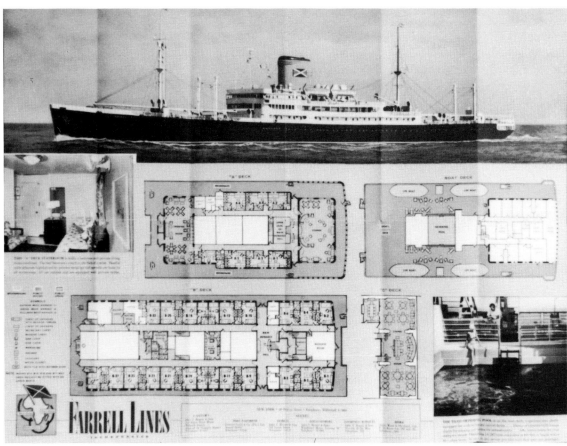

Left African Enterprise *sailing from Cape Town, South Africa* (Frank O. Braynard collection).

Below left *Deck plan of* African Enterprise *and* Africa Endeavor (Author's collection).

1942 USS *J.W. McAndrew* (Navy transport). 1947 Laid up. 1948 *African Enterprise* (Farrell). FV 30/7/1949 New York-Cape Town-Lourenco Marques. 8/1959 Laid up at James River. 1969 Scrapped by Boston Metals, Baltimore.

2 *Africa Endeavor* 1949-1959

Bethlehem Steel Co & Shipbuilding Division, Sparrows Point, Maryland, 1940.

7,922 gross tons; 491 × 66 ft (150 × 20 m); steam turbines; single screw; 16.5 knots; 82 first class passengers. Launched 16/12/1940 as *Delbrasil* (Delta).

1942 USS *George F. Elliot* (Navy transport). 1947 Laid up. 1948 *Africa Endeavor* (Farrell). FV 31/8/1949 New York-Cape Town-Lourenco Marques. 2/1959 Laid up at James River. 1969 Scrapped by Boston Metals, Baltimore.

Grace Line (Prudential-Grace Line)

(1913-1974)

William Russell Grace made his fortune in the marine goods business in Peru before emigrating to New York in 1865 for health reasons. In New York, he rented space at the edge of Hanover Square and began a trading route linking the United States, Peru and Europe. Grace left his prospering firm for eight years (1880-1888) to run New York as its mayor, then on his death in 1904, management of Grace passed to his brothers, and later to the son of one of them, Joseph P. Grace.

It was under Jospeh P. Grace that Grace Line developed its passenger fleet. The first 'passenger' ship sailing under the familiar green smoke funnel with the white band and black top was *Santa Cruz* in 1913, Grace Line's first ship to fly the American flag. Between 1914 and 1940, Grace Line owned and operated 17 passenger ships from the East Coast to the West Coast, Caribbean and South America.

During this period with Joseph P. Grace in control, the parent company of Grace Line, W.R. Grace, branched out into other activities. Business shifted from international trading to industrial activity in South America: building new cotton mills and sugar refineries, entering the woollen manufacturing business, vegetable oil production and electrical equipment manufacturing. All the necessary equipment, supplies and products were carried on Grace Line ships. In 1928, Panagra-Pan American Grace Airways was established, and this airline soared over the Andes where the Grace brothers had struggled to complete a railroad half a century earlier. The airline went on to develop an extensive South American network, and is today's giant Pan American World Airways.

The Second World War prompted the US Navy to purchase five of Grace Line's ships, then, in 7 December 1941, the rest of Grace Line's fleet was requisitioned by the Government. The only survivors to sail once more under Grace Line colours were *Santa Rosa* and *Santa Paula*.

As a result, a construction programme of nine 52-passenger cargo liners was initiated. At the helm of W.R. Grace was Joseph's son, J. Peter Grace Jr, who took over the reins of power in September 1945 after his father stepped down.

On 25 June 1946, the first of the nine, *Santa Barbara*, left New York on her maiden voyage to Valparaiso. In quick succession followed *Santa Cecilia, Santa Margarita, Santa Maria, Santa Luisa, Santa Isabel, Santa Monica,* and *Santa Clara.* All were delivered in 1946 by North Carolina Shipbuilding, with passenger accommodation amidships. The last of the nine was *Santa Sofia,* completed in the South American service, often switching their southern termini (Valparaiso, Cartagena or Puerto Cabello, Venezuela) as cargo bookings dictated.

Santa Rosa and *Santa Paula* were two of the quartet ordered by Jospeh P. Grace, and delivered in 1932 and 1933. Each was 9,135 tons, 508 ft long and 72 ft wide, and originated the sampan or winged funnel designed by Francis Gibbs. Accommodation was provided for 225 first class and 65 third class passengers, with space below for 7,000 tons of cargo. A unique feature was a dining room situated on the Promenade Deck between the twin funnels with a roll-back ceiling, allowing passengers to sample the novelty of dining under the stars in the Tropics. Another distinction of the original quartet was the use of waitresses instead of waiters in the dining room. Grace

Santa Rosa *departing from her New York pier* (Courtesy Peter M. Warner).

GRACE LINE (PRUDENTIAL-GRACE LINE)

Left Santa Rosa *outbound passing the Statue of Liberty* (Courtesy Peter M. Warner).

Below left Athinai, *the former* Santa Rosa, *starred in the film* Raise the Titanic (Antonio Scrimali).

Line reasoned that women were more pleasant and gracious to passengers than men, especially since American men made poor 'servants'. *Santa Rosa* was the first to resume sailing after the war on 7 February 1947, with *Santa Paula* returning to service on 2 May 1947, heading for the Caribbean.

During the 1950s, W.R. Grace's South American business grew and consisted of two large Peruvian sugar estates, seven cotton mills in Peru, Chile and Colombia, a paper mill and a bag and box plant in Peru, cement mills, flour mills, paint factories, a vegetable oil refinery, a tungsten and tin mine, and minority interests in a variety of other manufacturing enterprises. In the United States, concentration was on Grace Line, the Grace National Bank, the Naco Fertilizer Company, the export-import business, investments in the Panagra airline and a growing chemical division.

With all that capital, together with a generous operating differential subsidy contract entered into

with the Federal Maritime Board, it was time to replace the ageing *Santa Rosa* and *Santa Paula*. The new ships were identical twins built at Newport News, and were nothing more than a miniature version of the *United States*. Launched on 28 August 1957, *Santa Rosa* departed from New York on 26 June 1958 for her maiden voyage to the West Indies and South America. The old *Santa Rosa* was renamed *Santa Paula* and her sister ship laid up.

The new *Santa Paula* was launched on 9 January 1958 by the US Vice President's wife, Mrs Nixon, who failed to break the bottle of champagne on the bow during launching. The bottle was caught by a workman and smashed against the moving ship. *Santa Paula* left Newport News on 10 October 1958 and sailed for New York, but instead of docking at her New York City pier, she continued 112 miles up the Hudson River to Albany, New York, where she docked during the afternoon of 12 October, becoming the largest commercial vessel ever to call at Albany. The purpose of the visit was to salute the Empire State (New York), and that evening 400 officials and

Below *Heading for the West Indies are* Santa Isabel *on the left and* Santa Paula *on the right* (Courtesy Peter M. Warner).

113

their wives were invited aboard for a reception and buffet dinner. *Santa Paula* sailed the next morning for New York city, and again she became the first major passenger ship to make her 'maiden' entry at the Port of New York from the north. Her salute officially began at 4 pm when she steamed under the George Washington Bridge. One hour and ten minutes later she was docked at Pier 57. Once the 'coming out' parties were completed, *Santa Paula* departed on 17 October 1958 for the West Indies. The elder *Santa Paula* was laid up, and later both she and her sister were sold to Typaldos Lines of Greece.

The new *Santa Rosa* and *Santa Paula* had space for 300 first class passengers, all in outside staterooms with private facilities. Public rooms consisted of a Caribbean Lounge, a dining room amidships on Promenade Deck, Club Tropicana, Techo Bar, and the usual outdoor pool, children's playroom and shops. There were three grand suites on the aft portion of Sun Deck, each with its own balcony. A two-week cruise in one of these ships in 1966-67, high season, was $1,330 (£475) per person. Like the old quartet, the dining rooms were staffed by waitresses, with mainly Chinese tending the galleys.

In 1962, Grace Line withdrew *Santa Clara* from service and sold her to the Department of Commerce. She was followed in 1963 by *Santa Monica* and *Santa Sofia*, both of which were sold to Pacific Seafarers. *Santa Maria* was renamed *Santa Elena* in 1962, and the name was changed again in 1966 to *Santa Sofia*; *Santa Barbara* became *Santa Monica* in 1966.

The last ships built for Grace Line entered service in 1963. Designed by George Sharp, they were *Santa Magdalena, Santa Mariana, Santa Maria,* and *Santa Mercedes* — the Santa 'M' Class. They did not have traditional funnels, but instead possessed what their public relations manager, Fred Sands, called 'smoke stalks'. The maritime world had a good laugh at him and his employer, and, becoming increasingly self-conscious, Grace Line installed a traditional funnel on each ship at the first opportunity. The technique used for this installation was quite novel — the funnel was lowered into position by helicopter.

Each of the Santa 'Ms' carried 125 first class passengers in 49 outside cabins with private facilities. Passenger amenities included an outdoor pool on A Deck, dining room and Club on Promenade Deck, and a Passenger Lounge on Bridge Deck, with provision made to show films outdoors at night. Once a week, a Santa 'M' would depart from New York (Port Newark) for a 26-day trip to Callao, with definite stops at Santo Domingo or Kingston (every other sailing), Cartagena, Panama Canal Zone, Buenaventura and Guayaquil. The regular season fares for this voyage in 1967 ranged from $850 to $1,540 (£304 to £550) per person. By this time, the southern port for the 'Santa Barbara' Class was Cartagena.

Grace Line withdrew *Santa Isabel* from passenger

service in 1967 and renamed her *Santa Cristina*. In 1968 the rest of the 'Santa Barbara' Class was taken out of service and sold to various buyers. This left Grace Line with *Santa Rosa, Santa Paula* and the four Santa 'Ms'.

Grace Line was not immune to the labour troubles that plagued other US lines during the 1960s. It, too, was hurt by the devastating strike in June, July and August 1965 which saw its fleet tied up at various ports along the US eastern and Gulf coasts. In fact, the president of Grace Line had to quell rumours in August that Grace Line was not about to go out of business.

On 19 December 1969, J. Peter Grace, president of W.R. Grace and Spyros S. Skouras, president of Prudential Lines Inc, jointly announced the completion of the acquisition by Prudential of 100 per cent of the stock of Grace Line from W.R. Grace

Third of the series was Santa Margarita *(Courtesy Peter M. Warner).*

for the sum of $44.5 million. The assets and operations of both lines were combined to form Prudential-Grace Line Inc with a total of 27 ships. The 'Santas', whose funnels were painted in Prudential colours, continued to ply the sea lanes to the Caribbean and South America, but sadly the debts began to accumulate. Cargo revenue was down, strikes by the various unions caused delays and cancellations of sailings, jurisdictional disputes in Latin America, and newer, more economical cruise ships all played their part in Prudential-Grace's demise in 1971. *Santa Rosa* and *Santa Paula* were withdrawn from service and laid up, although the 'Santa Ms' continued to sail with their passenger quarters sealed up, giving Prudential-Grace the dubious honour of being the last American company to provide liner sailing from the eastern seaboard of the US to a foreign port.

On 27 June 1972, Prudential-Grace resumed passenger services with *Santa Mariana* out of Vancouver, Seattle, San Francisco and Los Angeles on voyages

Above left *The launching of* Santa Rosa *on 28 August 1957 at Newport News* (Courtesy Peter M. Warner).

Left *Fitting the funnel on to* Santa Rosa (Courtesy Peter M. Warner).

Above *The completed* Santa Rosa *engaged on thirteen-day Caribbean voyages* (Author's collection).

around South America. She was promptly followed by *Santa Maria* and *Santa Mercedes* in July and August respectively. All sailed under the Prudential-Grace banner until September 1974 when the company became known as Prudential Lines (see page 166). The following month, *Santa Magdalena* joined her sisters on the South America circuit.

Today, the firm of W.R. Grace & Company is a giant corporation in the chemical, consumer and natural resources spheres, with assets in 1986 of over $5.4 billion.

1 *Santa Rosa* 1932-1958
Santa Paula 1958

Federal Shipbuilding & Drydock Co, Kearny, New Jersey, 1932.

9,135 gross tons; 508 × 72 ft (155 × 22 m); steam turbines; twin screws; 19 knots; 225 first class, 65 third class passengers. Launched 24/3/1932.
MV 26/11/1932 New York-Los Angeles. FV 7/1/1938 New York-La Guaira. 1942 War Shipping Administration troopship. 2/7/1947 Resumed service from New York. 1958 *Santa Paula*. FV 7/3/1958. LV 9/1958. 1960 *Athinai* (Typaldos). 1967 Laid up. 1980 Chartered for film *Raise the Titanic*.

2 *Santa Paula* 1933-1958

Federal Shipbuilding & Drydock Co, Kearny, New Jersey, 1932.

9,135 gross tons; 508 × 72 ft (155 × 22 m); steam turbines; twin screws; 19 knots; 225 first class, 65 third class passengers. Launched 11/6/1932.
MV 7/1/1933 New York-Seattle. FV 14/1/1938 New York-La Guaira. 1942 War Shipping Administration troopship. 2/5/1947 Resumed service from New York. LV 6/1958 New York-La Guaira. 1958 Laid up. 1960 *Acropolis* (Typaldos). 1967 Laid up. 1977 Scrapped in Greece.

3 *Santa Barbara* 1946-1966
Santa Monica 1966-1968

North Carolina Shipbuilding Co, Wilmington, North Carolina, 1946.
8,357 gross tons; 459 × 63 ft (140 × 19 m); steam tubines; single screw; 16 knots; 52 first class passengers. Launched 24/1/1946.
MV 25/6/1946 New York-Valparaiso. 1966 *Santa Monica* (Grace). FV 23/12/1966 New York-Maracaibo. 1968 Sold to Baltimore shipbreaker. 1969 Resold to breakers in Spain.

4 *Santa Cecilia* 1946-1968

North Carolina Shipbuilding Co, Wilmington, North Carolina, 1946.
8,327 gross tons; 459 × 63 ft (140 × 19 m); steam turbines; single screw; 16 knots; 52 first class passengers. Launched 8/2/1946.
MV 19/7/1946 New York-Valparaiso. 1968 *Julia*

Above Santa Paula *entering Willenstad, Curacao* (Author's collection).

Above right *Fitting out* Santa Magdalena *(left) and* Santa Mariana *(right) at Bethlehem Shipbuilding* (Frank O. Braynard collection).

Right Santa Magdalena *passing the Empire State Building on a cold winter's day* (Moran Towing & Transportation Company).

(Anchor Shipping Corporation). 1970 Scrapped at Kaohsiung.

5 *Santa Margarita* 1946-1968

North Carolina Shipbuilding Co, Wilmington, North Carolina, 1946.
8,610 gross tons; 459 × 63 ft (140 × 19 m); steam turbines; single screw; 16 knots; 52 first class passengers. Launched 1/3/1946.
MV 13/8/1946 New York-Valparaiso. 1968 Scrapped at Bilbao.

Santa Mariana *on her maiden arrival in New York* (Frank O. Braynard collection).

6   *Santa Maria* 1946-1962
Santa Elena 1962-1966
Santa Sofia 1966-1968

North Carolina Shipbuilding Co, Wilmington, North Carolina, 1946.

8,327 gross tons; 459 × 63 ft (140 × 19 m); steam turbines; single screw; 16 knots; 52 first class passengers. Launched 15/3/1946.

MV 31/8/1946 New York-Valparaiso. 1962 *Santa Elena*. FV 28/9/1962 New York-Cristobal. 1966 *Santa Sofia*. FV 30/12/1966 New York-Santo Domingo-Puerto Cebello. 1969 *Sun* (Anchor Shipping Corporation). 1969 Scrapped at Kaohsiung.

7   *Santa Luisa* 1946-1968

North Carolina Shipbuilding Co, Wilmington, North Carolina, 1946.

8,327 gross tons; 459 × 63 ft (140 × 19 m); steam turbines; single screw; 16 knots; 52 first class passengers. Launched 2/4/1946.

MV 30/9/1946 New York-Valparaiso. 1968 *Luisa* (Central Gulf Steamship). 1969 Broken up.

8 *Santa Isabel* 1946-1967

North Carolina Shipbuilding Co, Wilmington, North Carolina, 1946.

8,327 gross tons; 459 × 63 ft (140 × 19 m); steam turbines; single screw; 16 knots; 52 first class passengers. Launched 16/4/1946.

MV 10/11/1946 New York-Valparaiso. 1967 *Santa Cristina*, no passengers. 1968 *Sofia* (Anchor Shipping

Corporation). 1970 Broken up at Kaohsiung.

9 *Santa Monica* 1946-1963

North Carolina Shipbuilding Co, Wilmington, North Carolina, 1946

8,327 gross tons; 459 × 63 ft (140 × 19 m); steam turbines; single screw; 16 knots; 52 first class pas-

Below Santa Mariana *with a proper funnel (Author's collection).*

Bottom Santa Maria *which briefly appeared with a black hull* (Moran Towing & Transportation Company).

sengers. Launched 12/7/1946.

MV 16/11/1946 New York-Curacao-La Guaira-Cartagena. 1963 *Maximus* (Cambridge Carriers). 1963 *A & J Mercury* (Pacific Seafarers Inc). 1964 *Santa Monica* (Grace), freight only. 1966 *Cosmos Trader* (Cosmos Navigation). 1969 Scrapped at Kaohsiung.

10   Santa Clara 1946-1962

North Carolina Shipbuilding Co, Wilmington, North Carolina, 1946.

8,610 gross tons; 459 × 63 ft (140 × 19 m); steam turbines; single screw; 16 knots; 52 first class passengers. Launched 29/8/1946.

MV 21/12/1946 New York-Cartagena. 1962 Sold to the Dept of Commerce. 1970 Scrapped at Castellon, Spain.

11   Santa Sofia 1947-1963

Federal Shipbuilding & Drydock Co, Kearny, New Jersey, 1947.

8,610 gross tons; 459 × 63 ft (140 × 19 m); steam turbines; single screw; 16 knots; 52 first class passengers. Launched 29/8/1946.

MV 30/1/1947 New York-Cartagena. 1963 *A & J Faith* (Pacific Seafarers Inc). 1964 *Santa Sofia* (Grace), freight only. 1966 *Cosmos Mariner* (Cosmos Steamship). 1970 Scrapped at Kaohsiung.

12   Santa Rosa 1958-1971

Newport News Shipbuilding & Drydock Co, Newport News, Virginia, 1958.

15,371 gross tons; 584 × 84 ft (178 × 25 m); steam

The forepart section of Santa Rosa after her collision with Valchem on 26 March 1959 (Frank O Braynard Collection).

turbines; twin screws; 20 knots; 300 first class passengers. Launched 28/8/1957.

MV 26/6/1958 New York-West Indies-Central America. 26/3/1959 Collided with US tanker *Valchem* 22 miles off Atlantic City. Forepart of *Santa Rosa* burned out. 1967 11,353 tons. 1970 Transferred to Prudential-Grace Lines. 22/1/1971 Laid up. 1975 To US Dept of Commerce. 1976 *Samos Sky* (Vintero Sales Corporation, NY), continued laid up.

13   Santa Paula 1958-1971

Newport News Shipbuilding & Drydock Co, Newport News, Virginia, 1958.

15,366 gross tons; 584 × 84 ft (178 × 25 m); steam turbines; twin screws; 20 knots; 300 first class passengers. Launched 9/1/1958.

MV 17/10/1958 New York-West Indies-Central America. 1967 11,353 tons. 1970 Transferred to Prudential-Grace Lines. 16/1/1971 Laid up. 1972 *Stella Polaris* (Sun Line). 1976 Became Kuwait Marriott hotel.

14   Santa Magdalena 1963-1974

Bethlehem Shipbuilding Corporation, Sparrow's Point, Maryland, 1963.

14,442 gross tons; 547 × 79 ft (167 × 24 m); steam turbines; single screw; 20 knots; 125 first class passengers. Launched 13/2/1962.

MV 15/2/1963 New York-Central America. 1966

Funnel added. 1967 11,219 tons. 1970 Transferred to Prudential-Grace Lines. 1971 Ceased carrying passengers. 10/1974 Returned to passenger service from West Coast. 1974 To Prudential Lines (see page 166). 1978 Chartered to Delta Line (see page 139). 1984 Laid up. 1985 *Santa Magdalena* (PSS Steamship Co Inc), laid up. 1988 Towed to Taiwan and scrapped.

15   *Santa Mariana* 1963-1974

Bethlehem Shipbuilding Corporation, Sparrow's Point, Maryland, 1963.

14,442 gross tons; 547 × 79 ft (167 × 24 m); steam turbines; single screw; 20 knots; 125 first class passengers. Launched 11/5/1962.

MV 28/6/1963 New York-Central America. 1966 Funnel added. 1967 11,188 tons. 1970 Transferred to Prudential-Grace Lines. 1971 Ceased carrying passengers. 1972 Returned to passenger service from West Coast. FV 27/6/1972 Vancouver-San Francisco-round South America. 1974 To Prudential Lines (see page 167). 1978 Chartered to Delta Line (see page 139). 1982 Laid up. 1985 *Santa Mariana* (PSS Steamship Co Inc), laid up. 1988 Towed to Taiwan and scrapped.

16   *Santa Maria* 1963-1974

Bethlehem Shipbuilding Corporation, Sparrow's Point, Maryland, 1963.

14,442 gross tons; 547 × 79 ft (167 × 24 m); steam turbines; single screw; 20 knots; 125 first class passengers. Launched 9/10/1962.

MV 4/10/1963 New York-Central America. 1966 Funnel added. 1967 11,188 tons. 1970 Transferred to Prudential-Grace Lines. 1971 Ceased carrying passengers. 1972 Resumed passenger service from West Coast. FV 21/7/1972 Vancouver-San Francisco-round South America. 1974 To Prudential Lines (see page 167). 1978 Chartered to Delta Line (see page 139). 1984 Laid up. 1985 Returned to Prudential, laid up. 1988 Towed to Taiwan and scrapped.

17   *Santa Mercedes* 1963-1974

Bethlehem Shipbuilding Corporation, Sparrow's Point, Maryland, 1964.

14,442 gross tons; 547 × 79 ft (167 × 24 m); steam turbines; single screw; 20 knots; 125 first class passengers. Launched 30/7/1963.

MV 17/4/1963 New York-Central America. 1966 Funnel added. 1967 11,188 tons. 1970 Transferred to Prudential-Grace Lines. 1971 Ceased carrying passengers. 1972 Resumed passenger service from West Coast. FV 13/8/1972 Vancouver-San Francisco-round South America. 1974 To Prudential Lines (see page 167). 1978 Chartered to Delta Line (see page 139). 1984 Laid up. 1984 *Patriot State* (Massachusetts Bay training ship).

Athinai, formerly Grace Line's Santa Rosa, starred in the film Raise the Titanic! — note the name on her bow (Antonio Scrimali).

Great Pacific Cruise Lines

(1985 to date)

Great Pacific Cruise Lines was created and incorporated in April 1985 by Charles A. Robertson, who also started American Cruise Lines, and James Navarre. The goal of the company was to capture the first class intracoastal cruise market of the West Coast, and its first and only ship, *Columbia*, was purchased from American Cruise Lines in the spring of 1985. After a general overhaul, she was pressed into service on 27 July 1985 from Seattle on seven-day cruises along the waterways of the Pacific Northwest. Ports of call were Port Townsend, Victoria, Salt Spring Island, Vancouver and Friday Harbor. Each summer since then she has made these cruises, and in the winter she undertakes two-day and three-day cruises from Seattle to Kirland, Port Townsend, Victoria and Friday Harbor.

In the spring of 1986, after *Columbia's* first season, she was given a major refit. Her passenger amenities

Great Pacific's intracoastal vessel Columbia *(Great Pacific Cruise Lines).*

were brought up to date and included all outside staterooms with private facilities and large cupboards, several lounges, of which the forward one has wrap-around windows at the bow, and a full service dining room capable of seating all the passengers at one sitting.

Due to her size, she is able to visit many small, colourful ports inaccessible to larger cruise ships, and, coupled with an initimate onboard atmosphere, *Columbia* is able to offer her passengers something a little different.

Columbia 1985

Eastern Shipbuilding Corporation, Boothbay Harbor, Maine, 1976.

150 gross tons; 180 × 38 ft (55 × 12 m); Caterpillar diesels; twin screw; 15 knots; 79 first class passengers). Launched 11/6/1976 as *Independence* (American Cruise Lines) (see page 37).

1985 *Columbia* (Great Pacific Cruise Lines). FV 27/7/1985 Seattle-Vancouver.

Hawaiian-Pacific Line

(1953)

Hawaiian-Pacific was hastily organized in 1953 to operate low-price travel to Hawaii from California against its chief competitor, Matson. The company chartered the 47-year-old *Aleutian* from Alaska Steamship, and the ship arrived in San Francisco on 28 November. The initial voyage was set to depart from San Francisco on 5 December, but inter-union squabbles broke out and it was cancelled. A new sailing date was announced, 21 December, with twelve more to follow at fares ranging from $125 to $310 (£45 to £111) one way and $220 to $560 (£79 to £200) for the round trip. This time, however, the squabbles ended in full-scale riots on the waterfront. Hawaiian-Pacific had no choice but to terminate the charter, and *Aleutian* left San Francisco on 17 December bound for Seattle. This ended the idea of low-cost travel to Hawaii, and the competition for Matson.

Aleutian 1953 (c)

William Cramp & Sons Shipbuilding Company, Philadelphia, Pennsylvania, 1906.

6,361 gross tons; 416 × 50 ft (127 × 15 m); triple expansion engines; twin screw; 17 knots; approximately 240 passengers. Launched 21/3/1906 as *Mexico* (New York & Cuba Mail).

1929 *Aleutian* (Alaska Steamship) (see page 22). Chartered to Hawaiian-Pacific. FV never sailed. 1954 *Tradewind* (Caribbean Atlantic) (see page 76). 1956 Scrapped in Belgium.

Hawaiian Steamship Company

(1956-1958)

The Textron Company, Providence, Rhode Island, purchased the laid-up *La Guardia*, the former *General W.P. Richardson*, from the Military Sea Transportation Service in 1956. She was sent to the New York Shipbuilding Corporation, Camden, for a $4 million refurbishment, and while she was being refitted, Textron formed the Hawaiian Steamship Company to operate her on California-Hawaii cruises in the hope of breaking Matson's stronghold.

Renamed *Leilani*, meaning 'lovely flower', the ship was given a pale green hull and had a revised gross tonnage of 18,298. Her superstructure was built up forward to supply additional cabin space, her promenade deck was partially enclosed and she was fitted with tourist class facilities for some 650 passengers. Hawaiian Steamship described her cabins

Leilani's first arrival in New York (Moran Towing & Transportation Company).

as 'nautical, comfortable and functional, not luxurious', which aptly described the rest of the ship.

Leilani's inaugural cruise was a 17-day positioning voyage from New York to Los Angeles that departed on 14 January 1957. *En route* everything that could go wrong went wrong. She encountered rough seas, her plumbing failed and many passengers suffered from food poisoning, all of which led to damaging publicity.

Leilani began her Hawaiian cruises from Los Angeles on 5 February. Thereafter, on a fortnightly basis she would alternate between Los Angeles and San Francisco. One-way rates for the five-day crossing ranged from $135 (£48) for an inside double cabin without facilities to $285 (£102) for an outside double on Sun Deck. Round trip fares were $245 to $515 (£88 to £184) for the same cabin categories.

Despite heavy advertising, passenger counts were not high. By 1958 the operation was deeply in the red, and Textron formed a new subsidiary, Hawaiian Textron Inc, to take over the ship, with Pacific Far East Line as operating agents. By the year's end,

unable to pay the mortgage, *Leilani* ended her Hawaiian service on arrival at San Francisco on 29 December 1958. She was handed back to MSTS, by then part of the US Maritime Commission, who laid her up.

Leilani 1956-1958

Federal Shipbuilding & Drydock Company, Kearny, New Jersey, 1944.

18,298 gross tons; 622 ×75 ft (188 ×23 m); steam turbines; twin screw; 19 knots; 650 tourist class passengers. Launched 6/8/1944 as *General W.P. Richardson* (US Navy troop-ship).

1949 *La Guardia* (America Export) (see page 49). 1951 Returned to MSTS and made four Orient voyages under APL colours (see page 66) then laid up. 1956 *Leilani* (Textron Company). FV 14/1/1957 New York-Los Angeles. FV 5/2/1957 Los Angeles-Honolulu. 1960 *President Roosevelt* (American President). 1970 *Atlantis* (Chandris). 1972 *Emerald Seas* (Eastern Steamship). 1986 *Emerald Seas* (Admiral Cruises).

Matson Navigation Company

(1908-1971)

William Matson was born in Lysekil, Sweden, on 18 October 1849. At the age of 12 he shipped out as a 'handy boy', landing in New York, then San Francisco where he made the acquaintance of the Spreckels family who had a thriving shipping business between Hawaii and the US mainland. Bill worked his way up the ranks to Captain and was given command of the Spreckels' yacht *Lurline*. Sensing the potential wealth to be made from the island trade, Captain Matson approached the Spreckels with a suggestion to open the port of Hilo, Hawaii, to more competition. Spreckels offered no resistance, and in fact helped Captain Matson to obtain his first ship, even furnishing him with an office. The ship Captain Matson purchased was the 195-ton schooner, *Emma Claudia*, of which he was one-quarter owner.

At the age of 32, Captain Matson sailed *Emma Claudia* out of San Francisco Bay, on 10 April 1882, heading for Hilo Bay, where he arrived on the 23rd. This was the beginning of his maritime empire. His shipping business was incorporated as the Matson Navigation Company, a Californian corporation capitalized on 9 February 1901, at $1.5 million, with Mastson as president and Walter D. K. Gibson as secretary. Within a few months, his wife, Lillian Low, had designed the flag for the company, a blue 'M' within a white circle surrounded by seven white stars on a red field.

Captain Matson was a bold man and in 1901 converted his steamer *Ehrenfels* from a coal burner to an oil burner. To make sure a steady supply of oil was available for his ships, he entered the oil-producing business. In 1907, 1909, 1913 and 1917, Matson took delivery of *Lurline, Wilhelmina, Matsonia* and *Maui* respectively; all had passenger accommodation and, most notably, engines aft.

During the 1920s and 1930s, Matson Navigation made a number of further acquisitions. In 1926 it purchased Oceanic Steamship Company for $1.5 million, a line that had maintained passenger services to Australia. Two years later, Matson bought Inter-Island Steam Navigation (Hawaiian inter-island trading) and Oceanic & Oriental Navigation Company, a freight concern to the South Pacific. Finally, on 1 January 1931, Matson acquired the Los Angeles Steamship Company. Non-nautical acquisitions included hotels in Waikiki and the Honolulu Oil Corporation.

Between 1927 and 1933, Matson took delivery of four passenger liners: *Malolo, Mariposa, Monterey,* and *Lurline*. *Malolo* and *Lurline* sailed on the San Francisco/Los Angeles-Hawaii service, while the other two vessels were engaged on Oceanic Steamship's antipodean service. All four vessels were requisitioned in 1942 by the US Government and served their country proudly, after which they were returned to Matson.

Before commenting on Matson's post-war recovery and subsequent passenger decline, it would be worth noting that the company was a pioneer in developing an air service to Hawaii, and thus one of the few steamship companies to help 'dig its own grave'. Matson was also instrumental in the early 1930s in starting Hawaiian Airlines as an inter-island air service to supplement its local steamship services between the islands. In the mid-30s, Matson made agreements with Pan American, then finally, on 5 July 1946, Matson started its own airline — Matson Lines

Above right Matsonia *after being rebuilt in 1938* (Matson Lines).

Right Lurline *entering Hawaii* (Matson Lines).

128

Free State Mariner (*left*) *and* Pine Tree Mariner *during lay-up* (Al Palmer collection, courtesy of Matson lines).

— between California and Hawaii. In trying to match its air fares with those of United and Pan American, Matson lost, and by 1947 Matson Navigation reluctantly suspended Matson Lines.

Returning to normal steamship operations after the Second World War proved to be one of the most difficult periods in the company's history. At issue were the age of its passenger ships and the cost of reconstruction. The oldest of the four was *Matsonia*, formerly *Malolo*, and the company decided to spend the least on her. She was returned to Matson in April 1946, given a $453,000 face-lift and placed on the Hawaii service on a fortnightly schedule from San Francisco and Los Angeles commencing on 22 May 1946. Her six-day passages cost, in February 1947, $115 (£29) for an inside cabin without facilities to $720 (£179) for the exclusive use of an air-conditioned Lanai suite for two.

Responding to urgent appeals from the Australian and New Zealand governments for an interim passenger service during this post-war adjustment period. The Oceanic Steamship Company, through Matson, chartered the C4-5-A3 troop-ship, *Marine*

130

Phoenix. Though designed to carry 3,000 troops, she was converted to carry only 520 passengers, but in spartan conditions. *Marine Phoenix's* initial voyage from San Francisco began on 13 December 1946. When the Canadian Australasian liner *Aorangi* returned to Vancouver, *Marine Phoenix* terminated her service with Matson when she arrived in San Francisco on 17 August 1948.

Attention now focused on rebuilding *Matsonia's* three sisters. After soliciting bids from Newport News, Bethlehem Steel and United Engineering (a Matson subsidiary), Matson chose United which, in 1945, estimated $6,881,500 per ship. *Monterey* was returned by the Government to Matson on 29 May 1946 and *Lurline* on 26 September 1946, and both proceeded to United Engineering's yard at Alameda. *Mariposa* was at Boston. An acute skilled labour shortage, inflation and cost of materials boosted the conversion costs in 1946 to $12 million and in 1947 to $16 million for each ship. On top of that there was an economic crisis in England which threatened potential passenger traffic between Australia and the United States, and United Airlines had won permission to operate to Hawaii with a fare of $135 (£34). Therefore Matson ceased conversion of *Monterey* and *Mariposa*; the former was sold to the US Maritime Commission and laid up at Suisun Bay while *Mariposa* was purchased by Home Lines in 1953 and renamed *Homeric*. This left *Lurline*. She was converted at a cost of $20 million and detailed to the California-Hawaii service, departing on 15 April 1948. On her

Mariposa arriving in port with her cargo booms ready to discharge freight (Matson Lines).

arrival, *Matsonia* was laid up, and later sold in 1949 to Home Lines.

On 28 October 1954, President Randolph Sevier announced that the Oceanic Steamship Company, the antipodean arm of Matson, planned to re-enter the New Zealand-Australia passenger trade. It was determined that it would be more economical and quicker to convert two existing hulls than to build two brand new ships, so in 1956 Matson purchased *Pine Tree Mariner* and *Free State Mariner* from the United States Maritime Administration for $19 million and sent them to Willamette Iron & Steel Company, Portland, for a $26,624,000 conversion.

Renamed *Mariposa* and *Monterey*, the 20-knot liners accommodated 365 passengers in air-conditioned comfort. On board were a dining room, Southern Cross Lounge, Polynesian Club, Outrigger Bar and a Pool Terrace. After being christened on 16 October by Miss Electa-Sevier, daughter of the president, *Mariposa* left San Francisco on 26 October 1956. Dignitaries from Matson and many well-wishers came to bid their farewells, including two 'boxing' kangaroos brought by a Matson guest. As the crowd witnessed the departure, one of the kangaroos threw a punch at one of the guests, throwing the pier into bedlam.

Monterey was christened by Mrs Clarence C. Morse, wife of the Federal Maritime Administrator, on 31 December 1956, then dispatched to the South Pacific on 9 January 1957. Ports of call included Los Angeles, Honolulu, Tahiti, Wellington and Sydney, returning via Auckland, Suva, Pago Pago and Honolulu, with fares ranging from $990 to $2,135 (£354 to £762) for the 42-day round trip voyage. In 1970 the rates

Above left Monterey *arriving at San Francisco* (Matson Lines).

Left *A 1967 sailing schedule for* Mariposa *and* Monterey (Author's collection).

Above *Matson's last vessel was* Matsonia (Moran Towing & Transportation Company).

ranged from $1,840 (£767) for a four-berth room to $6,480 (£2,700) for a Lanai suite.

Lurline was sailing in 1954 and 1955 at 97 per cent capacity. Matson hired the Stanford Research Institute to survey the prospects of increased passenger tonnage to Hawaii, and the Institute concluded there was room for another ship. In August 1956, Matson re-purchased the earlier *Monterey* from the Government for $2,556,000 and sailed her to Newport News for a $17,500,000 overhaul. Out went the B-deck promenade and in its place were staterooms and two Lanai suites. Polynesian decor and a graceful 'clipper' bow were also added, and she was renamed *Matsonia*.

The new *Matsonia* went to New York for a preview call then sailed on 22 May 1957 for Nassau, Port-

au-Prince, Kingston, Cartagena, Balboa and Acapulco before joining *Lurline* as running mate on the California-Hawaii service. *Matsonia's* first voyage left Los Angeles on 11 June 1957 with one-way fares starting from $145 (£52). Ten years later, one-way fares ranged from $230 (£82) for an inside triple to $785 (£280) for a Lanai suite. The round trip was priced from $437 to $1,492 (£156 to £533) for the same type of accommodation.

Ominous signs began to appear in 1959 with the selling of the company's hotel properties in Waikiki, then in 1960 came the disposal of Pacific National Life Assurance Company, Honolulu Oil Corporation, Pacific Intermountain Express Company and United Engineering. Two years later, losses from passenger vessel operations reached $2.2 million. Contributing to that figure were strikes that caused the cancellation of five voyages, disrupted schedules and resulted in the lay-up of *Matsonia* on 3 September 1962. On 3 February 1963, *Lurline's* port turbine failed as the ship was arriving in Los Angeles from Honolulu. When she docked, she was laid up and offered for sale 'as is, where is'. Not wanting to miss this unique opportunity to add to his fleet, Anthony Chandris

Lurline (Matson Lines).

quickly snapped up this bargain, renamed her *Ellinis*, repaired the engines, tripled her capacity and dispatched the 31-year-old lady on the exhausting Europe-Australia emigrant run.

Matsonia was steamed up to replace *Lurline* in February, and later that year, on 6 December 1963, she was rechristened *Lurline*.

Changes in Matson ownership occurred in 1964 and again in 1969. On 13 July, Alexander & Baldwin Inc, a firm incorporated in 1900 with large sugar interests in Maui and the co-developer of Wailea Resorts complex in Maui, purchased Matson stock held by Castle & Cooke (in pineapples and the purchaser of Standard Fruit), C. Brewer & Company, and American Factors. This brought A & B's ownership of Matson from 33.18 per cent to 73.85 per cent. This was increased to 95 per cent by the end of 1964 and 100 per cent by 1969, giving A & B sole ownership and making Matson its wholly-owned subsidiary.

To ensure passenger patronage, Matson began to reposition its ships in the 1960s. *Mariposa* was sent cruising to Alaska during the summers of 1968 and 1969, *Monterey* sailed to Alaska in 1970, *Lurline* was sent on a 45-day cruise to Expo '70 in Japan, and *Monterey* made two eleven-day 'Aloha Mexico' cruises in 1970, after which she sailed to South America on 23 May 1970. Scheduled for 1971 was a grand Mediterranean cruise for *Monterey* set for 16 April.

However, in 1970 Matson had an operating loss of $4,867,000. Consequently, it was no surprise, from a financial standpoint, when Matson announced on 27 May 1970 that *Lurline* would be withdrawn from service upon her arrival in San Francisco on 25 June 1970. Within five days, she too went to Chandris, was renamed *Britanis* and joined her former fleetmate as an Australian emigrant carrier.

The final straw was a 53-day maritime strike in 1970 together with spiralling operating and material costs of the twins. On 13 August 1970, Matson announced that it was pulling out of the passenger business. Two months later, on 1 October 1970, Pacific Far East Line concluded negotiations with Matson for the purchase of *Mariposa* and *Monterey* for $5.5 million each, along with two freighters and two container ships. The liners were handed over in January and February 1971.

Matson Navigation was one of the pioneers of

containerization in 1958, and today it operates a fleet of fast modern container vessels.

1 *Matsonia* 1946-1948

William Cramp & Sons Shipbuilding Company, Philadelphia, Pennsylvania, 1927.

17,226 gross tons; 582 × 83 ft (177 × 25 m); steam turbines; twin screw; 21 knots; 693 first class passengers. Launched 26/6/1926 as *Malolo* (Matson). 1938 *Matsonia* (Matson). 1941 Troopship for War Shipping Administration. 1946 Returned to Matson. FV 5/22/1946 San Francisco-Honolulu. 4/1948 Laid up. 1949 *Atlantic* (Home Lines). 1954 *Queen Frederica* (National Hellenic America Line). 1965 *Queen Frederica* (Chandris). 1971 Laid up. 5/1977 Sold for breaking up. 1/2/1978 Gutted by fire during scrapping.

2 *Marine Phoenix* 1946-1948 (c)

Kaiser Company, Vancouver, Washington, 1945.

12,420 gross tons; 523 × 71 ft (159 × 21 m); steam turbines; single screw; 16 knots; 520 passengers. Launched 9/8/1945 as troop transport.

1946 Chartered to Matson. FV 13/12/1946 San Francisco-Sydney. 12 RV. 8/1948 Returned to Maritime Commission and laid up. 1950 *T-AP 195* (US Navy), Korean War. 1958 Laid up. 1967 *Mohawk* (Mohawk Shipping, NY), freighter. 1979 Scrapped at Kaohsiung.

3 *Lurline* 1948-1963

Bethlehem Shipbuilding Corporation, Quincy, Massachusetts, 1932.

18,564 gross tons; 632 × 79 ft (193 ×24 m); steam turbines; twin screw; 20 knots; 760 first class passengers. Launched 18/7/1932.

MV 12/1/1933 New York-San Francisco. San Francisco-Honolulu service. 1941 Troop-ship for War Shipping Administration. 1946 Returned to Matson and refitted. FV 15/4/1948 San Francisco-Honolulu. 1963 *Ellinis* (Chandris). 1980 Laid up at Perama. 1986 Sold to Taiwan for scrap.

4 *Mariposa* 1956-1971

Bethlehem Shipbuilding Corporation, Quincy, Massachusetts, 1953.

14,812 gross tons; 563 × 76 ft (172 × 23 m); steam turbines; single screw; 20 knots; 365 first class passengers. Launched 7/11/1952 as *Pine Tree Mariner* for US Maritime Administration.

1956 *Mariposa* (Matson). Refitted as passenger liner. FV 26/10/1956 San Francisco-Sydney. LV 1/1971 San Francisco-Mexico cruise, arriving 21/1/1971. 1970 Sold to Pacific Far East Line (see page 152). 1979 Sold to World Airways. 1980 Sold to C.Y. Tung. 1983 *Jin Jiang* (China Ocean Shipping, Beijing). 1984 Transferred to Shanghai Jin Jiang Shipping.

5 *Monterey* 1957-1971

Bethlehem Shipbuilding Corporation, Sparrow Point, Maryland, 1952.

14,799 gross tons; 563 × 76 ft (172 × 23 m); steam turbines; single screw; 20 knots; 365 first class passengers. Launched 29/5/1952 as *Free State Mariner* for US Maritime Administration.

1956 *Monterey* (Matson). Refitted as passenger liner. FV 9/1/1957 San Francisco-Sydney. LV 9/1/1970 San Francisco-South Pacific, arriving San Francisco 15/2/1971. 1970 Sold to Pacific Far East Line (see page 152). 1979 Sold to World Airways. 1980 Sold to American Maritime Holdings, and laid up at San Francisco. 1987 *Monterey* (SS Monterey Limited Partnership Forecast) (see page 174).

6 *Matsonia* 1957-1963
Lurline 1963-1970

Bethlehem Shipbuilding Corporation, Quincy, Massachusetts, 1932.

18,655 gross tons; 641 × 79 ft (195 × 24 m); steam turbines; twin screw; 20 knots; 761 first class passengers. Launched 10/10/1931 as *Monterey* (Matson). MV 12/5/1932 New York-San Francisco. FV 5/1932 San Francisco-Honolulu-Sydney. 1941-1946 Troopship. 1946 Refit commenced then halted. 1952 Sold to US Government as transport. 1956 *Matsonia* (Matson). Extensively refitted and lengthened from 632 ft (193 m) to 641 ft (197 m). FV 11/6/1957 Los Angeles-Honolulu. 9/1962 Laid up. 2/1963 San Francisco-Honolulu. 1963 *Lurline* (Matson). FV 8/12/1963 San Francisco-Honolulu. LV 3/6/1970 Los Angeles-San Francisco-Honolulu-San Francisco, arriving 25/6/1970. 1970 *Britanis* (Chandris).

Mississippi Shipping Company

(1931-1972)
(1978-1984)

In an effort to carry the products of the South and the Mississippi Valley to the eastern coast of South America, and to receive the goods South America offered, a group of New Orleans businessmen saw that the time was ripe for a direct two-way service between New Orleans and Brazil. They included Thomas F. Cunningham, who was in the warehousing business; M.J. Sanders, the first manager of the Federal Barge Lines; R.S. Hecht, president of the Hibernia Bank; Theodore Brent, Traffic Manager of the Federal Barge Lines; and George G. Westfeldt, a New Orleans coffee merchant. Together they formed the Mississippi Shipping Company with capital of $50,000, under the presidency of Mr Sanders, and the doors were opened for business on 1 May 1919. Mr Brent was the gentleman who suggested the trade name 'Delta Lines', and it is under that name that the company has become known world-wide.

Delta's first ship was *Bound Brook*. After loading cargo at New Orleans and Pensacola, she departed the latter port on 12 August 1919 with 4,100 tons of freight for Rio de Janeiro and Santos. Delta entered the passenger business in 1931 with the departure of the 28-passenger steamer *Del Norte*, one of four such ships. In 1940 another trio of 63-passenger steamers was added.

During the war, all American ships were requisitioned by the US Government and pressed into various wartime roles. When peace returned, the trio of 1940 were returned to Delta, which laid them up. Two eventually sailed again under the banner of Farrell Lines, and one became a training ship in California in 1971.

To re-establish a passenger service from New Orleans and other Gulf of Mexico ports to Brazil, Uruguay and Argentina, the Mississippi Shipping

Company placed a $21 million order with Ingalls Shipbuilding for a trio of sleek passenger/cargo liners. First to sail from New Orleans was *Del Norte* on 29 November 1946. Next was *Del Sud* on 28 March 1947, followed by *Del Mar* on 13 June 1947. Designed by George Sharp, each ship was 10,073 gross tons and 494 ft (151 m) long, with a cargo capacity of 457,700 cu ft for general merchandise and 61,400 cu ft of refrigeration. A unique feature was their 'smoke-stack'. This aluminium structure was actually the living quarters for the radio officers, the radio rooms and an emergency generator. The real smoke-stacks were a pair of two tall, black-tipped pipes just behind the 'stack'. Other unusual features were the heavy use of aluminium and glass, and complete air-conditioning. The 'Del' trio could accommodate 120 passengers in their 41 outside staterooms, each with a fresh-water shower and toilet. They were also the first ships to eliminate the upper berth.

For the passengers' enjoyment there was a large outdoor swimming pool, sun decks, a grand salon, a library, a modern shopping centre, a café and a dining room reached by a semi-circular stairway. All this could be enjoyed for approximately 45 days in 1950, peak season, for as little as $940 (£336). One way to Rio, a fourteen-day voyage, was $400 (£143), and to Buenos Aires $500 (£179). In 1965, a 47-day cruise started at $1,296 (£463), with one way to Rio via San Juan and Bridgetown starting at $600 (£214).

Declining passenger traffic began to deplete the coffers of Delta, so in 1967 the 'Del' trio ceased to carry passengers and with reduced tonnages continued to ply the South American trade as freighters. Two years later, Holiday Inn, the hotel chain, acquired Delta.

In 1978, after an eleven-year absence, Delta re-entered the passenger shipping business. In May of that year the Maritime Commission approved Delta Lines' takeover of several Prudential Lines passenger/cargo ships and trade routes. The transfer included the Prudential's 'Santa M' Class ships *Santa Maria, Santa Magdalena, Santa Mercedes* and *Santa Mariana* on a bareboat charter basis, which meant that Delta was practically the owner of the vessel and was responsible for crewing, maintenance, provisioning and repairs. Painted in Delta funnel colours and given new voyage numbers, the 'Santas' continued on the San Francisco-round South America route.

In May 1982, Holiday Inn announced that it was seeking a buyer for Delta Line on the grounds that its passenger/cargo operation did not fit in with its hospitality-related interest. Within a year, Thomas

Designed by George Sharp, Del Mar *was the last of the trio for Delta Line* (Frank O. Braynard collection).

Crowley had purchased the company; Crowley Maritime was a giant towing and barge operation based in San Francisco.

In December, Crowley promptly withdrew *Santa Mariana* from service. Although the remaining three ships were carrying good passenger loads, fares in 1983 ranged from $9,615 to $18,510 (£6,009 to £11,569) per person for a 54-day cruise, and the 'Santas' were not running at a profit. Huge American union wages, increasing port charges, mounting maintenance and fuel costs and limited container-carrying space all spelled economic disaster. To stop these mounting losses, Crowley decided in 1984 to suspend all Delta's passenger services. The first vessel to be withdrawn was *Santa Mercedes* in May, followed by *Santa Maria* in October and finally *Santa Magdalena* that November. The next year, Crowley ceased all shipping operations under the name of Delta Line.

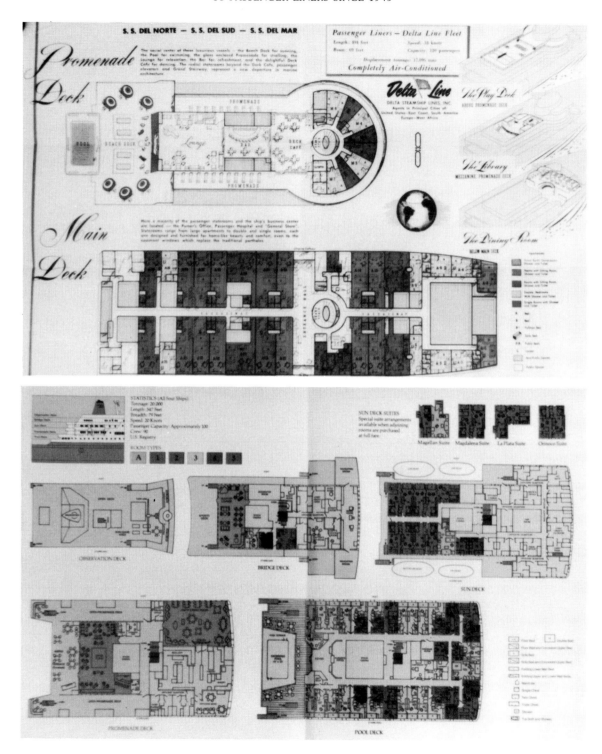

Left *Deck plan of the Delta trio* (Author's collection).
Below left *Deck plan of the Delta 'Santa M' Class quartet* (Author's collection).

1 *Del Norte* 1946-1967

Ingalls Shipbuilding Corporation, Pascagoula, Mississippi, 1946.

10,073 gross tons; 494 × 69 ft (151 × 21 m); geared turbines; single screw; 17 knots; 120 passengers. Launched 11/1/1946.

MV 29/11/1946 New Orleans-Buenos Aires. 1967 Ceased carrying passengers. 1969 8,638 tons. 1972 Scrapped at Kaohsiung.

2 *Del Sud* 1947-1967

Ingalls Shipbuilding Corporation, Pascagoula, Mississippi, 1947.

10,073 gross tons; 494 × 69 ft (151 × 21 m); geared turbines; single screw; 17 knots; 120 passengers. Launched 22/2/1946.

MV 28/3/1947 New Orleans-Buenos Aires. 1967 Ceased carrying passengers. 1969 8,638 tons. 1972 Scrapped at Kaohsiung.

3 *Del Mar* 1947-1967

Ingalls Shipbuilding Corporation, Pascagoula, Mississippi, 1947.

10,073 gross tons; 494 × 69 ft (151 × 21 m); geared turbines; single screw; 17 knots; 120 passengers. Launched 17/5/1946.

MV 13/6/1947 New Orleans-Buenos Aires. 1967 Ceased carrying passengers. 1969 8,638 tons. 1972 Scrapped at Kaohsiung.

4 *Santa Maria* 1978-1984 (c)

Bethlehem Shipbuilding Corporation, Sparrow's Point, Maryland, 1963.

11,188 gross tons; 547 × 79 ft (167 × 24 m); steam turbines; single screw; 20 knots; 121 first class passengers. Launched 9/10/1962 for Grace Line (see page 123). 1978 Chartered by Delta. FV 17/6/1978 San Francisco-Vancouver-San Francisco-round South America. 1984 Laid up at Alameda. 1985 Returned to Prudential and laid up (see page 167). 1988 Towed to Taiwan and scrapped.

5 *Santa Magdalena* 1978-1984 (c)

Bethlehem Shipbuilding Corporation, Sparrow's Point, Maryland, 1963.

11,219 gross tons; 547 × 79 ft (167 × 24 m); steam turbines; single screw; 20 knots; 121 first class passengers. Launched 13/2/1962 for Grace Line (see page 122).

1978 Chartered by Delta. FV 1/7/1978 San Francisco-Vancouver-San Francisco-round South America. 1984 Laid up at Alameda. 1986 *Santa Magdalena* (PSS Steamship Co). Continued in lay-up. 1988 Towed to Taiwan and scrapped.

6 *Santa Mercedes* 1978-1984 (c)

Bethlehem Shipbuilding Corporation, Sparrow's Point, Maryland, 1964.

11,188 gross tons; 547 × 79 ft (167 × 24 m); steam turbines; single screw; 20 knots; 121 first class passengers. Launched 30/7/1963 for Grace Line (see page 123).

1978 Chartered by Delta. FV 21/7/1978 San Francisco-Vancouver-San Francisco-round South America. 1984 Laid up. 1984 *Patriot State* (Massachusetts Bay training ship).

7 *Santa Mariana* 1978-1983 (c)

Bethlehem Shipbuilding Corporation, Sparrow's Point, Maryland, 1963.

11,188 gross tons; 547 × 79 ft (167 × 24 m); steam turbines; single screw; 20 knots; 125 first class passengers. Launched 5/11/1962 for Grace Line (see page 123).

1978 Chartered by Delta. FV 7/8/1978 San Francisco-Vancouver-San Francisco-round South America. 12/1982 Laid up at Alameda. 1985 Transferred to PSS Steamship Co. 1988 Towed to Taiwan and scrapped.

Moore-McCormack Lines

(1917-1969)

As young men, Albert V. Moore and Emmet McCormack were both interested in shipping. They became good friends, and Moore quit his job to join McCormack's infant trading firm. The partnership of Moore & McCormack Company Inc was organized on 9 July 1913 with a capital of $5,000 and a visionary faith in the future of trade with South America.

The company's first assignment was the hauling of dynamite from Wilmington, Delaware, to Rio de Janeiro. To carry out this explosive task, the gentlemen acquired the ageing *Montara*, built in 1881. Although only 2,562 gross tons with a length of 315 ft (97 m) and a beam of 22 ft (7 m), she was the company's first 'real' ship. When *Montara* arrived in Rio in 1913, she was the first American ship to enter that harbour for 26 years.

Moore & McCormack entered the passenger business with *Saga* in 1917, and during the First World War she was the only ship sailing between the United States and Rio. In 1938 the 'Good Neighbour Fleet' — *Uruguay, Brazil* and *Argentina* — set course for Rio and points south under the banner of a M & M subsidiary, American Republic Line.

Restyled Moore-McCormack Lines in 1938, the company embarked on an ambitious building programme of four 150-passenger ships. The war intervened, however, and the US Government requisitioned the newly-completed ships together with the 'Good Neighbour Fleet'. Upon the return of peace, Moore-McCormack's trio were handed back to them and converted again into liners. *Argentina* was the first to depart for South America in January 1948. All three carried the funnel markings of Moore-McCormack.

In the late 1940s, Moore-McCormack, together with the US Maritime Commission, conducted some studies on the eventual replacement of the 'Good Neighbour' trio. Several alternative proposals were put forward: a quintet of 22-knot cargo passenger ships sailing from New York weekly on a 35-day cycle with a 125-passenger capacity load; a quartet of 27-knot cargo passenger ships sailing on a 28-day cycle with accommodation for 250 passengers; or two faster ships sailing on alternate weeks with a capacity of 550 passengers. Incorporated in the design was cargo storage space and handling facilities and a shallow draught of no more than 28 ft (8m) to permit navigation of the River Plate and the approaches to Buenos Aires.

The passenger business reached its peak in 1952 when the trio carried a record-breaking 25,000 passengers. Thereafter the numbers declined, resulting in the retirement of *Uruguay* in 1954. It was not until 1956 that Moore-McCormack ordered replacements. Designed by Bethlehem Steel Company, they were not the original quintet or quartet, but a handsome pair of 15,000-ton liners, capable of carrying 553 passengers, all in outside cabins with private facilities, and 4,470 tons of cargo. Their names, according to an early waterfront rumour, were to be *North America* and *South America*.

Built and completed by Ingalls Shipbuilding Corporation of Pascagoula, and named *Brasil* and *Argentina*, the pair made their debut on the South America run in 1958. During *Brasil's* delivery voyage from Pascagoula to New York, a horrendous discovery was made — there was no toilet paper to be found

Above right Uruguay *sailing past the skyline of New York* (E.W. Johnson/SSHSA Collection).

Right Brazil *still in wartime colours* (Moore-McCormack Lines).

Above Argentina *anchored in a Caribbean port* (Frank O. Braynard collection).

on board! Walter Hamshar, shipping editor of the *New York Herald Tribune*, who was giving a group tour of the ship, came upon the strong box and insisted to see what was inside. *Voilà* — forty boxes of toilet paper!

A unique feature of each ship was its funnel. There was what appeared to be a traditional funnel amidships, but the base was used as a radio room and the open top was reserved for nude sun bathing (this was closed in the 1963 refit). The real funnels were placed aft in the form of twin up-take pipes. Passage fares for an eleven-day voyage to Rio in 1960 ranged from $575 to $1,920 (£205 to £686), and sixteen days to Buenos Aires ranged from $675 to $2,375 (£241 to £848).

The new ships enabled the old *Brazil* and *Argentina* to be withdrawn and laid up in 1957 and 1958 respectively. Both were sold to the breakers in 1964. In 1963, the new *Brasil* and *Argentina* were refitted by Bethlehem Steel in Baltimore. Each emerged with an additional lounge and cabins on a new top deck. Besides their regular South American run, the twins could be found cruising the Caribbean, African and the North Cape/Baltic regions. On one such cruise to the latter region during the summer of 1962, which included a call at Leningrad, passengers caught a preview of the Cuban missile crisis. They reported seeing guns, missiles and tanks out on the open pier, with

Above right Brasil's *maiden arrival in New York* (Courtesy Peter M. Warner).

Right Brasil *after her 1963 refit* (Moore-McCormack Lines).

Argentina passing the skyline of lower Manhattan (Moore-McCormack Lines).

a few Greek-flagged freighters taking on those supplies. For as little as $36 (£13) a day, passengers were able to sail in 1965 on a 63-day 'Round Africa' cruise, and in 1969 a 32-day South America voyage ranged from $1,310 to $3,075 (£546 to £1,281).

By the mid-1960s, the fashionable set jetted to Copacabana and Ipanema and foreign-flagged companies were courting and winning over the American cruise passenger. Revenue began to plummet while operating costs, coupled with union demands, were rocketing. Part of the labour cost problem stemmed from hiring such renaissance persons as 'bread boys'

whose sole duty was to take rolls out of the basket and place them on the passengers' side plates. The union strike during the summer of 1965, and subsequent labour problems over the next few years, crippled Moore-McCormack, as they did United States Lines and Grace Line ships. In order that Moore-McCormack could curtail its losses, it withdrew *Brasil* and *Argentina* from service in 1969 and laid them up at Baltimore. This brought an end to the company's passenger liner operations and the losses to which all its liners contributed. If there was a sunny side to the demise of Moore-McCormack's passenger business, it was the fact that the union members now had all the vacation time in the world. Meanwhile, Moore-Mac's profitable freighters continued to ply the South America and Southern Africa routes carrying cargo and twelve passengers.

In 1982 the shipping division of Moore-McCormack was purchased by United States Lines and its fleet incorporated into the new owner's schedule. Moore-McCormack Resources continued without its maritime interest and became an active corporation specializing in the mining and building materials fields, and controlled several small vessels on the Great Lakes for its own use.

1 *Uruguay* 1938-1954

Newport News Shipbuilding & Drydock Co. Newport News, Virginia, 1928.

20,237 gross tons; 601 × 80 ft (183 × 24 m); turbo-electric drive; twin screw; 17 knots; 500 first class passengers. Launched 1/10/1927 as *California* (American Line).

1934 17,833 tons. 1937 Sold to US Maritime Commission and rebuilt, 20,183 tons, with one funnel. 1938 *Uruguay* (American Republic), managed by Moore & McCormack. FV 22/10/1938 New York-La Plata. 1942 Troop-transport. 1943 Collided with US Navy tanker off Bermuda, 13 killed. 1946 Returned to Moore-McCormack. FV 12/2/1948 New York River Plate service. 1954 Laid up in James River. 1963 Sold for breaking up. 1964 Scrapped.

2 *Brazil* 1938-1957

Newport News Shipbuilding & Drydock Co, Newport News, Virginia, 1928.

20,614 gross tons; 613 × 80 ft (187 × 24 m); turbo electric; twin screw; 17 knots; 500 first class passengers. Launched 18/10/1927 as *Virginia* (American Line).

1933 18,298 tons. 1937 Sold to US Maritime Commission and rebuilt, 20,614 tons, with one funnel. 1938 *Brazil* (American Republic), managed by Moore & McCormack. FV 8/10/1938 New York-River Plate. 1942 Troop-transport. 1946 Returned to Moore-McCormack. FV 5/1948 New York-River Plate service. 12/1957 Laid up. 1964 Scrapped.

3 *Argentina* 1938-1958

Newport News Shipbuilding & Drydock Co, Newport News, Virginia, 1929.

20,707 gross tons; 613 × 80 ft (187 × 24 m); turbo electric; twin screw; 17 knots; 500 first class passengers. Launched 10/7/1929 as *Pennsylvania* (American Line).

1933 18,200 tons. 1937 Sold to US Maritime Commission and rebuilt, 20,164 tons, with one funnel. 1938 *Argentina* (American Republic), managed by Moore & McCormack. FV 5/11/1938 New York-River Plate. 1942 Troop-transport. 1946 Returned to Moore-McCormack. FV 15/1/1948 New York-River Plate service. LV 8/1958 New York-River Plate, then laid up. 1963 Sold for breaking up. 1964 Broken up in New Jersey.

4 *Brasil* 1958-1969

Ingalls Shipbuilding Corporation, Pascagoula, Mississippi, 1958.

14,984 gross tons; 617 × 86 ft (188 × 26 m); geared turbines; twin screw; 21 knots; 553 first class passengers. Launched 16/12/1957.

MV 12/9/1958 New York-Buenos Aires. 1963 Rebuilt, one deck added, 15,257 tons. 9/1969 Laid up at Baltimore after North Cape cruise. 1971 Sold to Holland-America. 1972 *Volendam* (Holland-America), rebuilt, 715 passengers, 23,395 tons. 1974 Laid up at Hampton Roads. 1975 *Monarch Sun* (Monarch Cruises). 1976 15,361 tons. 1979 *Volendam* (Holland-America). 1984 Sold to C.Y. Tung. 1984 *Island Sun* (C.Y. Tung). 1984 Laid up. 1985 *Liberté* (American Hawaii) (see page 55). 1987 Laid up. 1987 *Canada Star* (Bermuda Star Line). 1988 *Queen of Bermuda* (Bermuda Star Line).

5 *Argentina* 1958-1969

Ingalls Shipbuilding Corporation, Pascagoula, Mississippi, 1958.

14,984 gross tons; 617 × 86 ft (188 × 26 m); geared turbines; twin screw; 21 knots; 553 first class passengers. Launched 12/3/1958.

MV 12/12/1958 New York-Buenos Aires. 1963 Rebuilt, one deck added, 15,257 tons. 1969 Laid up at Baltimore. 1971 Sold to Holland-America. 1972 *Veendam* (Holland-America), rebuilt, 713 passengers, 23,372 tons. 1974 Laid up at Hampton Roads. 1976 *Monarch Star* (Monarch Cruises). 1976 15,631 tons. 1978 *Veendam* (Holland-America). 1984 Sold to C.Y. Tung. 1984 Chartered to Bahama Cruises, renamed *Bermuda Star*, 671 passengers.

New York & Porto Rico
Steamship Company
(1899-1949)

The New York & Porto Rico Steamship Company was established in 1885 to carry freight southbound to Puerto Rico and the Dominican Republic, and bring back sugar on the return leg. Passenger services commenced in 1899 with the steamers *Ponce* and *San Juan*. In 1908, the NY & PR became part of the holding company of Atlantic, Gulf and West Indies Steamship Company (AGWI).

In all, the NY & PR operated a fleet of ten liners before the war. The only survivor of the conflict was *Borinquen*, which was returned in 1946. While she was refitting, AGWI chartered *Marine Tiger* in 1946 to operate an austerity service between New York and San Juan. Once *Borinquen* was ready in June 1947, *Marine Tiger* was handed over to United States Lines management.

Increasing air competition (flights between New York and San Juan) and escalating operating costs forced the NY & PR to abandon the service, and in

Borinquen *of New York & Porto Rico Steamship during wartime* (US Signal Corps/SSHSA Collection).

1949 *Borinquen* was sold to Bull Lines. Four years later, AGWI went into liquidation and all its associated lines ceased to exist.

1 *Marine Tiger* 1946-1947 (c)

Kaiser Company Inc, Vancouver, Washington, 1945.

14,420 tons; 523 × 71 ft (159 × 21 m); steam turbines; single screw; 16 knots; 850 tourist class passengers. Launched 23/3/1945 as troop-ship for US Maritime Commission.

1946 Chartered to AGWI. FV 1946 New York-San Juan. 6/1947 Handed over to USL management. 1949 To Maritime Commission. 1966 *Oakland* (Litton Industries). 17,184 tons, 684 ft (210 m) 1975 Transferred to Reynolds leasing. 1987 Scrapped in Taiwan.

2 *Borinquen* 1931-1949

Bethlehem Shipbuilding Corporation, Quincy, Massachusetts, 1931.

7,114 gross tons; 466 × 60 ft (142 × 18 m); steam turbines; single screw; 16.5 knots; 271 first class, 90 second class passengers. Launched 24/9/1930.

MV 26/2/1931 New York-San Juan. 1942 Army transport. 1946 returned to owners. FV 20/6/1947 New York-San Juan. LV 8/1949. 1949 *Puerto Rico* (A.H. Bull) (see page 71). 1954 *Arosa Star* (Arosa Line). 1959 *Bahama Star* (Eastern Steamship) (see page 97). 1969 *La Jenelle* (Western Steamship Co). 13/4/1970 Destroyed in gale off California.

Northland Transportation Company

(1935-1947)

In 1923 the Sunny Point Packing Company began sailing the wooden steamer *Bellingham* to its packing plant in Hydra, Alaska. Additional ships were purchased and in 1927 the Northland Transportation Company was formed to provide regular passenger and freight sailings between Puget Sound and Hydra via Ketchikan, Alaska.

During the war its ships served to carry army personnel and supplies to Alaskan bases, and five years later, three of its ships were returned. Two were sold, leaving only *North Sea* to continue sailing in 1946. On 13 February 1947, *North Sea* became stranded near Bella Bella, and her 85 passengers were taken to Vancouver in the steamer *Prince Rupert*. An attempt was made to salvage her, but the ship broke

her back. This ended the company's passenger trade and the following year Northland merged with Alaska Steamship Company.

North Sea 1936-1947

Bethlehem Shipbuilding Corporation, Wilmington, Delaware, 1918.

3,133 gross tons; 312 × 45 ft (95 × 14 m); steam turbines; single screw; 12 knots; 145 first class, 202 second class passengers. Launched 16/4/1918 as *Plainfield* (US Shipping Board).

1922 *Mary Weems* (Baltimore & Carolina Steamship). 1927 *Admiral Peoples* (Admiral Line). 1934 *North Sea* (Northland Transportation) FV 14/4/1935 Seattle-Alaska. 14/5/1935 Ran aground on Marsh Point. 1941 Chartered by War Shipping Administration. 1946 Returned and resumed service. 13/2/1947 Wrecked on Porter Reef, Bella Bella, BC (Canada).

North Sea *sailed between Seattle and Alaskan ports to the north* (Symors/SSHSA Collection).

Pacific Cruise Lines

(1947-1949)

Under the guidance of the Skinner and Eddy Corporation, owners of the Alaska Steamship Corporation, Skinner and Eddy embarked upon the luxury cruise market by creating Pacific Cruise Lines in 1947. Within a short time, the company spotted its prize, *Corsair*.

Corsair was a $2 million yacht constructed in 1930 for J.P. Morgan, son of the international turn-of-the-century financier. She had only six large staterooms for no more than 10 guests, about as many people as Morgan could tolerate at one time. After an eventful career with him, *Corsair* was turned over to the British Admiralty in 1940. After the war, she was brought by undisclosed buyers and placed under Panamanian registry. Sighted by Pacific Cruise Lines,

she was purchased, taken to Todd Shipyards in New York for repair and overhaul, then sailed to the Victoria Machinery Depot in Victoria, Canada, for conversion to a luxury cruise vessel. In charge of her interior was the firm of William Schorn Associates of New York who were to fit accommodation for 85 passengers.

Transformed into a luxurious cruise 'liner', *Corsair* made her debut on 29 September 1947 offering two-week cruises from Long Beach, California, to Acapulco. During the summer of 1948, she was switched to Alaskan waters. A company brochure announced 'Thirteen glorious days ...the first de luxe cruise ever offered to Alaska! The first combination de luxe cruise to Mt McKinley Park ever offered! The first passenger ship ever to discharge passengers at Whittier! The first special train for cruise passengers from Whittier to McKinley National Park!' Emphasis was also placed on her former life

The former yacht of J.P. Morgan, Corsair *(Frank O. Braynard collection).*

and owner, and the sybaritic surroundings that awaited the 85 fortunate souls. *Corsair* left Vancouver on her first Alaskan cruise on 4 June, and ended the season with the 11 September departure. Fares ranged from $690 (£171) for a double to $860 (£213) for a suite. Those were indeed luxury fares for 1948! The autumn and winter saw her return to Long Beach for her Mexican cruises, then in the summer of 1949 she operated out of Vancouver again.

The end of *Corsair* came during one of her autumn Mexican Riviera cruises. On 12 November 1949 she struck a rock and was beached at Acapulco, where her 55 passengers were put ashore in lifeboats. She was examined by her owners then abandoned as a total constructive loss.

Corsair 1947-1949

Bath Iron Works, Bath, Maine, 1930.

2,700 gross tons; 344 × 43 ft (105 × 13 m); turbo-electric; twin screw; 18 knots; 85 first class passengers. Launched 10/4/1930 for J.P. Morgan.
1949 To British Admiralty in convoy patrol service. 1945 Sold. Panamanian registry. 1946 Purchased by Pacific Cruise. FV 29/9/1947 Long Beach-Acapulco. FV 4/6/1948 Vancouver-Whittier. 12/11/1949 Struck rock and beached at Acapulco, abandoned.

Pacific Far East Line

(1971-1976)

Pacific Far East was established in 1946 to carry cargo between California and the Far East. In October 1970, the company concluded negotiations with Matson for the purchase of *Mariposa* and *Monterey* for $5.5 million each. Four years later, John Alioto, son of San Francisco's mayor, purchased Pacific Far East Line.

The 'golden bear' logo was placed on the ships' funnels in January and February 1971 and they continued to ply the South Pacific trade. However as deficits rose on the South Seas run due to low passenger and freight bookings, *Mariposa* and *Monterey* spent more time cruising to Hawaii and other destinations. Among the more unusual cruises was a 56-day Mediterranean cruise that departed from Los Angeles on 16 April 1971 by *Monterey*, and

a 77-day North Cape cruise in *Mariposa* that left San Francisco on 2 May 1977.

The $17.6 million federal subsidy expired on the two liners in 1978. This subsidy was necessary in order to keep fares competitive with the growing foreign competition. Members of Congress from California and Hawaii tried to introduce legislation in Congress to grant the company an extension, but Pacific Far East officials did not show much enthusiasm; they were more interested in selling the ships to raise cash to shore up their balance sheet.

The first ship to be laid up was *Monterey* in January

Monterey of Pacific Far East Line at Portland, Oregon (James L. Shaw).

1978, followed in April by *Mariposa*. Later that year Pacific Far East declared bankruptcy and went out of business.

1 *Mariposa* 1971-1976

Bethlehem Shipbuilding Corporation, Quincy, Massachusetts, 1953.

14,812 gross tons; 563 × 76 ft (172 × 23 m); steam turbines; single screw; 20 knots; 365 first class passengers. Launched 7/11/1952 as *Pine Tree Mariner* for US Maritime Administration.

1956 *Mariposa* (Matson) (see page 135). 1970 Sold to Pacific Far East Line. FV 22/1/1971 San Francisco-Sydney. LV 20/3/1978 San Francisco-Honolulu-Los Angeles, arriving San Francisco 9/4/1978. 1978 Laid up. 1979 Sold to World Airways and laid up at Oakland. 1980 Sold to American World Line (C.Y. Tung), towed to Hong Kong and laid up. 1983 *Jin Jiang* (China Ocean Shipping, Beijing). 1984 Transferred to Shanghai Jin Jiang Shipping.

2 *Monterey* 1971-1976

Bethlehem Shipbuilding Corporation, Sparrow's Point, Maryland, 1952.

14,799 gross tons; 563 × 76 ft (172 ×23 m); steam turbines; single screw; 20 knots; 365 first class passengers. Launched 29/5/1952 as *Free State Mariner* for US Maritime Administration.

1956 *Monterey* (Matson) (see page 135). 1970 Sold to Pacific Far East Line. FV 16/2/1971 San Francisco-Sydney. LV 7/12/1977 San Francisco-Sydney-San Francisco, arriving 19/1/1978. 1978 Laid up. 1979 Sold to World Airways and laid up at Oakland. 1980 Sold to American Maritime Holdings and laid up at San Francisco. 1987 *Monterey* (SS Monterey Limited Partnership Forecast) (see page 174).

Panama Railroad Company
(Panama Canal Company)
(1896-1981)

The predecessor of the Panama Canal Company was the Panama Railroad Company, re-organized in 1896, and Columbian Line, founded in 1894. Columbian Line ran a fleet of steamers from New York to Colon where the ships would discharge their freight and passengers. Both were then hauled across Panama by railroad to the Pacific, and thence either up to West Coast ports or down the west coast of South America.

During its construction and upon its completion, the Panama Canal needed huge amounts of construction materials and, later, manpower to operate it. Panama Railroad and its ships were able to supply these, and it was only fitting that Panama Railroad's *Ancon* should officially open the Canal on 15 August 1914 when she became the first ocean-going steamer to transit through the waterway on a ceremonial passage from the Atlantic to the Pacific.

Two years before the American entry into the Second World War, Panama Railroad took delivery of three sister ships — *Panama, Ancon* and *Cristobal* — at a cost of $5 million each. They were the first ships to be built with perfectly level decks from bow to stern, an innovation introduced by their designer, George Sharp. On board the liners for their 202 passengers to enjoy were a mirrored dining salon, lounges, a swimming pool, cabins with private facilities and air-conditioning throughout.

Of the three, *Ancon* was in the forefront of wartime action. She witnessed the sinking of six ships and was the subject of aerial attacks in European waters and the Pacific. She also captured an Italian submarine, was an assault ship at Normandy,

Panama Canal's Panama (Courtesy Peter M. Warner).

Above left Ancon *as an army transport during the Second World War* (Frank O. Braynard collection).

Left *The main lounge of the* Cristobal *during the Second World War* (Frank O. Braynard collection).

Above Cristobal *saluting the tug as she sails for Panama* (Frank O. Braynard collection).

participated during the landing on Okinawa and, finally, was one of the first Allied ships to steam into Tokyo Bay in August 1945. Wedged between the US battleships *Missouri* and *South Dakota*, *Ancon* played host to over 150 war correspondents, photographers and newsreel technicians, and from her decks came the news of the Japanese surrender.

After the war, the trio returned to their previous schedules of shuttling passengers and freight between New York and Cristobal. Departures were from New York's Pier 64, West 24th Street, with sailing time usually scheduled for 4 pm; round trips usually lasted fourteen days. In 1951, one-way fares, to Cristobal, a five-day voyage, ranged from $160 to $300 (£57 to £107). The round trip was priced at $288 to $540 (£103 to £193).

In the re-organization of 1953, Panama Railraod divested itself of its ships and created the Panama Canal Company to operate the vessels which were being subsidized in part by the railroad profits. This subsidy was most clearly evident in passenger fares. In a four-year period, the fares were increased by less than nine per cent. The 1955-56 one-way rate to Cristobal, a seven-day voyage via Haiti, was $175 (£63), with a fifteen-day round trip voyage ranging from $315 to $550 (£113 to £196). The deficits of the ships began to mount, and in 1957 the Panama Canal Company sold *Panama* to American President Lines. Four years later, decreasing traffic and pressure from Panama's Panama Line led the Panama Canal Company to suspend all non-government passenger services. *Ancon* was laid up and then sold in 1962 to the Maine Maritime Academy. *Cristobal* was switched to operate out of New Orleans, carrying government personnel only, until she was sold for breaking up in 1981.

1 *Panama* 1939-1956

Bethlehem Steel Company, Quincy, Massachusetts, 1939. 10,021 gross tons; 493 × 64 ft (150 × 19 m); steam turbines; twin screw; 17 knots; 202 first class passengers. Launched 24/9/1938.

MV 27/4/1939 New York-Cristobal. 13/6/1941 *James Parker* (US Army transport). 15/5/1946 *Panama*. 1948 9,978 tons. 1953 Panama Railroad became Panama Canal Company. 1957 *President Hoover* (APL) (see page 66). 1965 *Regina* (Chandris Cruises). 1973

Regina Prima (Chandris Cruises). 1979 Laid up at Piraeus. 1986 Scrapped.

2 *Ancon* 1939-1961

Bethlehem Steel Company, Quincy, Massachusetts, 1939. 10,021 gross tons; 493 × 64 ft (150 × 19 m); steam turbines; twin screw; 17 knots; 202 first class passengers. Launched 10/12/1938.

MV 22/6/1939 New York-Cristobal. 1/1942 US Army transport. 1946 Re-entered New York-Cristobal service. 1948 9,978 tons. 1953 Panama Railroad became Panama Canal Company. 1961 Laid up. 1962 Sold for breaking up in Wilmington.

3 *Cristobal* 1939-1981

Bethlehem Steel Company, Quincy, Massachusetts, 1939. 10,021 gross tons; 493 × 64 ft (150 × 19 m); steam turbines; twin screw; 17 knots; 202 first class passengers. Launched 4/3/1939.

MV 17/8/1939 New York-Cristobal. 1/1942 US Army transport. 1946 Returned to service. 1948 9,978 tons. 1953 Panama Railroad became Panama Canal Company. 1961 Ceased carrying commercial passengers. 1962 FV New Orleans-Cristobal. 9/1981 Withdrawn from service and scrapped at Brownville, Texas, in December.

Peninsular & Occidental Steamship Company

(1901-1969)

Henry M. Flagler, owner of the Florida East Coast Steamship Company, was primarily a developer and railroad man interested in reaching Havana, via Key West, by railroad and thence by water. Together with the Plant Steamship Company, Florida East Coast formed the Peninsular & Occidental Steamship Company (P & O) in 1901, named in imitation of the famed British shipping concern Peninsular & Oriental. The American P & O was 50 per cent owned by Flagler and 50 per cent by Plant Steamship. In 1902 the Atlantic Coast Line (railroad), which evolved from the Plant estate, took over 50 per cent ownership. P & O was to be the pioneer in developing the tourist business to Havana, and indirectly develop Miami as a cruise port.

For the 1901-02 season, P & O operated nine ships on the Tampa-Key West-Havana route. As the ships grew old, replacements, both new or chartered, were brought into use. There was little deviation through the decades from the original itinerary set up in 1901, except for the addition of Miami and Nassau, which became a route in itself.

In 1945, P & O had only two ships — *Florida* and *Cuba*. The latter was built in 1921, sold in 1946 to 1. Messina & Company, renamed *Pace* and operated in the Mediterranean and down to East Africa. *Florida*, built in 1931, was sent to Newport News for re-conversion to a passenger ship; she emerged in 1947 and commenced sailings from Miami to Havana, and in 1954 to Nassau.

In the autumn of 1954, P & O announced that they wanted to return to the Tampa-Key West-Havana service. For this route they acquired *Denali* from Alaska Steamship Company in 1954 and placed her in service in January 1955 as *Cuba*. Fares for her inaugural season were $35 (£13) one way and $59.50

(£21) round trip, with a supplementary room charge of $10 (£4) without facilities and $15 (£5) with.

To lower costs and solve labour disputes, P & O announced in 1955 the formation of two Liberian corporations to take over the ships. The Blue Steamship Company took over *Florida* on 7 September and the White Steamship Company took over *Cuba* in October, fresh from drydock and with the name *Southern Cross* painted across both sides of her foresection and stern. *Southern Cross* undertook Caribbean cruises from Miami, with a twelve-day voyage starting at $220 (£79) without facilities to $385 (£138) with shower and toilet.

The political crisis in Cuba caused P & O to abandon Havana. *Southern Cross* was withdrawn from service in 1957, laid up, and eventually scrapped in 1960, while *Florida* was switched to Miami-Nassau sailings. In 1966, 'festive' three-day cruises ranged from $59 to $120 (£21 to £43), four-day cruises from $74 to$130 (£26 to £46) and overnight one-way trips $30 to $55 (£11 to £20).

During the early 1960s the Florida East Coast Railroad and the Atlantic Coast Line disposed of their interests in P & O. Labour problems, an ageing vessel and new safety regulations (as a result of the *Yarmouth Castle* and *Viking Princess* disasters) were issues P & O did not want to address. Therefore *Florida* was laid up in the autumn of 1966 and sold to a Canadian concern in 1967 for use as a hotel for Expo '67. P & O chartered the Zim liner *Jerusalem*, renamed her *Miami* and billed her as the 'largest ship in Miami-Nassau service'. After two years, the charter on *Miami* expired and she was returned to Zim who sold her to Eastern Steamship. Her departure ended 68 years of Peninsular and Occidental service, of which the last thirteen had been under foreign flags.

Above *P&O's* Florida at Nassau (Everett E. Viez/SSHSA Collection).

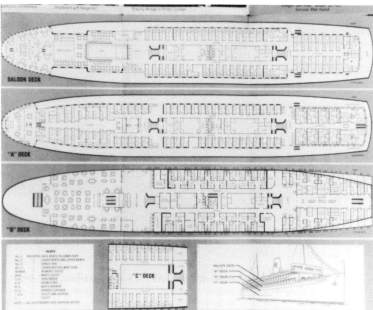

Left *Deck plan of* Florida (Author's collection).

Above right *P&O's chartered* Miami (A. Duncan).

1 *Florida* 1931-1966

Newport News Shipbuilding & Drydock Company, Newport News, Virginia, 1931.

4,945 gross tons; 387× 56 ft (118 × 17 m); steam turbines; twin screw; 19 knots; 612 first class, 130 second class passengers. Launched 7/3/1931.

MV 4/6/1931 Tampa-Key West-Havana. 24/1/1936 Collided with Swedish freighter *Trolleholm* in Havana harbour. 1942 US Army transport. 1946 Returned to P & O. FV 2/1947 Miami-Havana. 1966 Laid up. 1967 'Le Palais Flottant' (floating hotel at Montreal Expo '67). 1968 Scrapped in Spain.

2 *Cuba* 1954-1955
Southern Cross 1955-1959

Newport News Shipbuilding & Drydock Company, Newport News, Virginia, 1927.

4,302 gross tons; 336 × 51 ft (102 × 16 m); steam turbines; twin screw; 12 knots; 354 passengers.

Launched 30/6/1927 as *Caracas* (Atlantic & Caribbean Steam Navigation).

1938 *Denali* (Alaska Steamship) (see page 22). 1954 *Cuba* (P & O). FV 15/1/1955 Tampa-Key West-Havana. 1955 *Southern Cross* (P & O) FV 27/10/1955 Miami-Caribbean. 1960 Scrapped at Antwerp.

3 *Miami* 1966-1968 (c)

Deutsche Werft AG, Hamburg, 1958.

9,900 gross tons; 488 × 65 ft (149 × 20 m); steam turbines; twin screw; 19.5 knots; 566 first class passengers. Launched 9/5/1957 as *Jerusalem* (Zim Lines).

1966 Chartered to P & O. FV 11/1966 Miami-Nassau. 1968 Returned to Zim. 1969 *New Bahama Star* (Eastern Steamship) (see page 97). 1972 *Bahama Star* (Eastern Steamship) (see page 97). 1975 *Bonaire Star* (Venzolana de Cruceros del Caribe), laid up at Mobile, never sailed. 1979 Sold for scrap. 3/10/1979 Sank in Pacific while under tow.

Premier Cruise Lines

(1983 to date)

Greyhound Corporation had its eye on the Florida cruise market for a number of years. Finally, the management of its subsidiary, Florida Export, created another subsidiary, Premier Cruise Lines, with Bruce Nierenberg as its executive vice president. Premier purchased Costa Cruises' *Federico C*, built in 1958, and under the firm of A & M Katzourakis redecorated her to the tune of $14 million.

Unlike other new cruise companies, Premier decided not to enter the highly competitive port of Miami, but instead to concentrate its efforts on central Florida. Hence the company chose Port Canaveral as the home port for its ship. There they could tap the market potential of central and north Florida, make use of Port Canaveral's new $3.5 million cruise terminal facility, and, most importantly, tap the market of nearby Walt Disney World's visitors. Premier could offer three-day and four-day Bahamas cruises with the remainder of the week spent at Walt Disney World — a very clever marketing move. To entice newcomers to cruising, Premier was not offering hot dogs and hamburgers, but full course meals. Emphasis was placed on the cruise atmosphere, service, cuisine and the personal touches one found at the better hotels — for instance, a complimentary array of elegant, personal bath items.

Christened the 'Star Ship' *Royale*, the red-hulled liner departed from Port Canaveral on her first voyage to Nassau on 26 March 1984. Her passengers could lounge in the Club Universe, dine in the Galaxy dining room, catch a show in the Starlight Cabaret, get a drink at the Mars Bar or dance in the Outer Limits Disco. From the operational end, the accountants were also dancing with the stars. For her first eight months of operation, 'Star Ship' *Royale*

'Star Ship' Royale *of Premier Cruise Lines arriving at Nassau* (M/M Willie Tinnemeyer).

garnered 90 per cent of her passengers from the highly competitive Florida market.

Capitalizing on *Royale's* success, Premier acquired *Oceanic* from Home Lines in 1985 for $20 million. Another $10 million was invested in improving the rechristened 'Star Ship' *Oceanic* which included painting the hull red, refurbishing all public rooms and fitting a fifth berth in many cabins to accommodate families. On 25 April 1986 'Star Ship' *Oceanic* set out for the Bahamas from Port Canaveral.

Premier's tapping of the 'Magic Kingdom' market paid dividends in 1985 when Disney World designated Premier as 'The Official Cruise Line of Walt Disney World', a relationship that was mutually beneficial as each could use the other's name in its promotions.

To ensure profitable operations, Premier's 'Star Ships' are registered in Panama and staffed by an international crew, not subject to American labour laws.

Since early 1987, Greyhound had been in protracted negotiations with Home Lines over the acquisition of their *Atlantic* and *Homeric*. In April 1988, Holland-America purchased the two ships, and assigned its contract to purchase *Atlantic* to a new holding company put together by Citibank in New York. In June, Greyhound Corporation, Premier's parent, leased *Atlantic*, and after a 'major conversion' in November which increased her passenger capacity

from 1,306 to 1,600, *Atlantic* entered Premier's three-day and four-day Port Canaveral-Bahamas service on 19 December under a long-term lease.

1 *Royale* 1984

Ansaldo SpA, Sestri Ponente, 1958.

15,483 gross tons; 606 ×78 ft (185 × 24 m); steam turbines; twin screw; 20 knots; 1,255 first class passengers. Launched 31/3/1957 as *Federico C* (Costa Armatori).

South America-Italy and Miami-Italy service. 1984 *Royale* (Premier). FV 26/3/1984 Port Canaveral-Nassau.

2 *Oceanic* 1985

Cantieri Riuniti dell'Adriatico, Monfalcone, 1965.

27,644 gross tons; 782 × 96 ft (238 × 29 m); steam turbines; twin screw; 26 knots; 1,562 first class passengers. Launched 15/1/1963 as *Oceanic* (Home Lines).

1985 *Oceanic* (Premier). FV 25/4/86 Port Canaveral-Bahamas.

3 *Atlantic* 1988 (c)

Constructions Navales & Industrielles de la Méditerranée, La Seyne, 1981.

19,337 (30,000 in company literature) gross tons; 672 × 90 ft (204 × 27 m); FIAT diesels; twin screw; 23 knots. Launched 9/1/1981 for Home Lines.

1988 Sold to Holland-America, then leased to Premier. FV 19/12/1988 Port Canaveral-Bahamas.

'Star Ship' Oceanic *arriving at Port Canaveral* (M/M Willie Tinnemeyer).

Princess Cruises

(1965-1974)

After several failed attempts by other companies to start a regular cruise service from the West Coast to Mexico, Stanley B. McDonald, a Seattle industrialist, entered the field in 1965 and gave it a try. He formed a company and 'time-chartered', Canadian Pacific's *Princess Patricia* (the ship was leased for a period of time fully crewed and the charterer was responsible for general maintenance and marketing). The word 'Princess' was used on all Canadian Pacific coastal ships, and since its first vessel was a 'Princess' liner, the company was appropriately named Princess Cruises. *Princess Patricia* inaugurated the company's first series of fourteen-day Mexico cruises from Los Angeles on 3 December 1965 with rates from $430 (£154) for an outside upper and lower berth without private facilities to $1,095 (£391) for the Acapulco Suite on Upper Deck.

Princess Patricia's first season was a financial success, and she was again chartered for the 1966-67 winter season. This time the cruises ranged from three to fourteen days. In the meantime, Princess sought a larger and newer ship for its popular cruises. Just completed for a Sardinian firm was *Italia*, which was looking for an operator. McDonald time-chartered the brand-new ship, added the prefix 'Princess' to her name on the brochures (she was never actually registered under the new name) and set her course for the West Coast. *Italia's* arrival meant the return of *Princess Patricia* to Canadian Pacific in April 1967 after the winter season.

Italia made her maiden voyage from Genoa to Los Angeles, via the Panama Canal. After playing host to hundreds of travel agents who marvelled at her decor and the television set in every cabin, *Italia* headed south for Mexico on 16 December 1967. Her fourteen-day itinerary took in La Paz, Puerto Vallarta,

Acapulco and Mazatlan, with fares starting at $450 (£161) for an inside upper and lower berth to $1,350 (£482) for a one-room suite on Promenade Deck.

Princess Cruises' turnover mounted and in 1968 they time-chartered Costa's *Carla C*. She was dubbed *Princess Carla* in the brochures (though never registered as such), and she departed Nassau on 4 December 1968 on her positioning voyage to Los Angeles, whence she departed on 19 December for Mexico. Fares for an eleven-day cruise calling at Puerto Vallarta, Acapulco and Mazatlan ranged from $385 to $1,925 (£160 to £802). The arrival of *Carla C* relieved *Italia* for other duties, and during the summer of 1969 she inaugurated Princess's Alaska programme. Minimum fares for double occupancy ranged from $495 (£206) for an inside upper and lower berth to $1,395 (£581) for a one-room suite. That autumn, on 30 October, *Italia* embarked on a 42-day South Seas Cruise. *Carla C* was kept on the Mexican Riviera route for the entire summer and autumn.

For a brief two-year period, Princess Cruises was owned by Bose Cascade, but McDonald bought the company back in 1970.

Italia and *Carla C* maintained the same schedule pattern in 1970; however, *Carla C* was recalled by Costa during the autumn to replace one of its ships, *Fulvia*, destroyed by fire in July. This left *Italia* to carry on the Mexican programme in the winter, a Caribbean trip in the spring and autumn and Alaska during the summers of 1971 and 1972.

Above right Princess Patricia *started operations for Princess Cruises* (Canadian Pacific).

Right Italia *of Princess Cruises* (Author's collection).

162

Left Carla C. *Note the name-plate behind the funnel* (Author's collection).

Below left Island Princess *anchored at Acapulco* (Princess Cruises).

The unsuccessful *Island Venture* was time-chartered from Flagship Cruises and delivered to Princess in the autumn of 1972. She was renamed *Island Princess*, had the Princess mermaid affixed to her funnel, and was then dispatched on 28 November 1972 on her positioning voyage from Fort Lauderdale to Los Angeles. From there she made a seventeen-day cruise to Hawaii, and upon returning commenced her pattern of winter and early spring Mexican cruises. *Italia* was sent further south on 13 February 1973 when she departed Los Angeles on a 43-day 'Carnival in Rio Cruise', for which each passenger paid from $2,010 to $6,780 (£773 to £2,608).

Princess returned *Italia* to Sunsarda Navigation in 1973. It, in turn, chartered her to Costa Armatori who took delivery in the winter of 1974, so Princess was again left with only one ship, *Island Princess,* for the summer season. In mid-1974, Princess Cruises was purchased by the giant British shipping firm of Peninsular & Oriental (P & O) who were eager to acquire Princess' expertise and marketing techniques in the North American cruise market. P & O's *Spirit of London*, until then unsuccessful, was spruced up, renamed *Sun Princess* and placed on the Mexican Riviera run during the winter of 1975. Sensing financial success, P & O purchased *Sea Venture*, renamed her *Pacific Princess* and sailed her west in the spring of 1975 to join her sister ship, *Island Princess*. Now P & O, under the banner of Princess Cruises, had a modern fleet that was ready to star in the American television series 'The Love Boat'.

Though retained by P & O as president of the company, McDonald left Princess Cruises in 1983 to start another shipping company, Sundance Cruises (see page 175). Today Princess Cruises operates *Island Princess, Pacific Princess, Sun Pacific,* and *Royal Princess* in Alaskan, Caribbean, Mediterranean, Mexican and Pacific waters.

1 *Princess Patricia* 1965-1966, 1966-1967 (c)

Fairfield Shipbuilding & Engineering Company, Glasgow, 1949.

5,911 gross tons; 374 × 56 ft (114 × 17 m); steam turbines; twin screw; 23 knots; 346 first class passengers. Launched 5/10/1948 for Canadian Pacific.

1949 Canadian Pacific's coastal service from Vancouver. 1963 Overhauled and refitted as a cruise ship. 1965 Chartered to Princess. FV 3/12/1965 Los Angeles-Mexico. LV 17/4/1967 Los Angeles-Victoria, BC. 1967 Returned to Canadian Pacific.

2 *Italia (Princess Italia)* 1967-1973 (c)

Cantieri Navale Feszegi Shipyards, Trieste, 1967.

12,219 gross tons; 492 × 68 ft (150 × 21 m); Sulzer diesels; twin screw; 20 knots; 467 first class passengers. Launched 28/4/1965 as *Italia* (Sunsarda Navigation, Sardinia).

1967 Chartered by Princess Cruises as *Princess Italia.* MV 16/11/1967 Genoa-Los Angeles. FV 15/12/1967 Los Angeles-Mexico. FV 3/6/1969 San Francisco-Alaska. 1974 *Italia* (Costa Armatori). 1984 *Ocean Princess* (Ocean Cruise Lines).

3 *Carla C (Princess Carla)* 1968-1970 (c)

Ateliers et Chantiers de France, Dunkirk, 1952.

19,942 gross tons; 600 × 80 ft (183 × 24 m); steam turbines; twin screw; 22 knots; 754 first class passengers. Launched 31/10/1951 as *Flandre* (French Line).

1968 *Carla C* (Costa Armatori). 1968 Chartered by Princess Cruises as *Princess Carla*. FV 10/1/1969 Los Angeles-Mexico. 1970 *Carla C* (Costa Armatori). 1974 New diesel engines installed. 1986 *Carla Costa* (Costa Crociere SpA).

4 *Island Princess* 1972-1974 (c)

Nordseewerke, Emden, 1972.

19,907 gross tons; 554 × 80 ft (169 × 24 m); FIAT diesels; twin screw; 20 knots; 767 first class passengers. Launched 6/3/1971 as *Island Venture* (Flagship Cruises).

1972 *Island Princess* (P & O). Chartered to Princess. FV 28/11/1972 Fort Lauderdale-Los Angeles. FV 18/12/1972 San Francisco-Hawaii. FV 9/2/1973 Los Angeles-Mexico.

Prudential Lines

(1974-1978)

Founded in 1933 as the Prudential Steamship Company, Prudential gained its early experience in Mediterranean shipping, as well as in service to the Far East and other parts of the world. During the Second World War, Prudential broadened its experience by operating twenty ships for the US Government.

The postwar period was one of great growth for Prudential. In 1954, Spyros P. Skouras joined the company and initiated progressive policies that benefitted shippers and further stimulated Prudential's growth. When Spyros S. Skouras Jr was elected President in 1960, he began restructuring the line's operations and schedules, and nine years later he was ready to acquire a passenger fleet.

On 19 December 1969, Skouras announced the $44.5 million acquisition of Grace Line (see page 110). Included in the sale were the passenger ships *Santa Rosa, Santa Paula, Santa Magdalena, Santa Mariana, Santa Maria* and *Santa Mercedes*. Prudential-Grace was formed in 1970 and the ships continued their normal operations. By this time, the federal operating subsidy for *Santa Rosa* and *Santa Paula* had expired, and federal support for the 'Santa M' Class was also coming to an end. Prudential-Grace withdrew *Santa Rosa* and *Santa Paula* from service and closed the passenger accommodation on the 'Santa M' Class. *Santa Paula* was eventually sold in 1972 to Sun Line, and in August 1974 *Santa Rosa* was turned over to the US Maritime Administration.

Prudential-Grace resumed passenger operations in 1972 with *Santa Mariana*. The first trip left Vancouver on 27 June and after calls at Seattle/Tacoma, San Francisco and Los Angeles the liner sailed for the Panama Canal and proceeded to circumnavigate South America. *Santa Mariana* was joined in quick succession by *Santa Maria* and *Santa Mercedes*.

In September 1974, the name Grace was dropped from usage and the company reverted to Prudential Lines, the sole owner of the three remaining 'Santas'. *Santa Magdalena* was returned to passenger service under Prudential ownership in October 1974, enabling the company to provide a monthly passenger and container service to South America. The ships were marketed under the banner of Prudential Cruises, and 1974 rates for a 51-day Circle South America cruise started out at $3,380 (£1,414) for an inside upper and lower berth with bath to $6,280 (£2,628) for a twin-bedded cabin with a tub.

The executives at Prudential really never got into the swing of running a passenger operation. In addition, the ships were outmoded. Passenger capacity was limited to 125 and cargo capacity was also restricted, which in short meant that the ships were not paying dividends. Hence, at the first opportunity, in 1978, Prudential chartered out on a bareboat basis *Santa Maria, Santa Magdalena, Santa Mercedes,* and *Santa Mariana* to Delta Line. When Delta ceased passenger operations in 1984, the ships were laid up in California.

Prudential Lines remained active in the maritime world until the spring of 1986 when they entered into Chapter 11, filing for bankruptcy.

1 *Santa Magdalena* 1974-1978

Bethlehem Shipbuilding Corporation, Sparrow's Point, Maryland, 1963.

11,219 gross tons; 547 × 79 ft (167 × 24 m); steam turbines; single screw; 20 knots; 125 first class passengers. Launched 13/2/1962 for Grace Line (see page 122).

10/1974 Prudential Lines. FV 10/1974 San Francisco-round South America. 1978 Chartered to Delta (see page 139). 1984 Laid up. 1985 *Santa Magdalena* (PSS Steamship Co Inc), laid up. 1988 Towed to Taiwan and scrapped.

2 *Santa Mariana* 1974-1978

Bethlehem Shipbuilding Corporation, Sparrow's Point, Maryland, 1963.

11,188 gross tons; 547 × 79 ft (167 × 24 m); steam turbines; single screw; 20 knots; 125 first class passengers. Launched 5/11/1962 for Grace Line (see page 123).

1974 Prudential. FV 9/1974 San Francisco-round South America. 1978 Chartered to Delta (see page 139). 1983 Laid up. 1985 *Santa Mariana* (PSS Steamship Co Inc), laid up. 1988 Towed to Taiwan and scrapped.

3 *Santa Maria* 1975-1978

Bethlehem Shipbuilding Corporation, Sparrow's Point, Maryland, 1963.

11,188 gross tons; 547 × 79 ft (167 × 24 m); steam turbines; single screw; 20 knots; 125 first class passengers. Launched 9/10/1962 for Grace Line (see page 123).

1974 Prudential Lines. FV 9/1974 San Francisco-round South America. 1978 Chartered to Delta (see page 139). 1984 Laid up. Returned to Prudential, continued in lay-up. 1988 Towed to Taiwan and scrapped.

4 *Santa Mercedes* 1974-1978

Bethlehem Shipbuilding Corporation, Sparrow's Point, Maryland, 1964.

11,188 gross tons; 547 × 79 ft (167 × 24 m); steam turbines; single screw; 20 knots; 125 first class passengers. Launched 30/7/1963 for Grace Line (see page 123).

1974 Prudential Lines. FV 10/1974 San Francisco-round South America. 1978 Chartered to Delta (see page 139). 1984 Laid up. 1984 *Patriot State* (Massachusetts Bay training ship).

Santa Magdalena *of Prudential Lines (Author's collection).*

Royal Fiesta Cruises

(1985 to date)

According to Trevor White, executive vice president of Royal Fiesta, the company was created in 1985 and is owned by a large number of 'American' stockholders, including himself. At the time of writing, he said that the line had been scouring the world for at least two years looking for a suitable vessel, before settling on *Saint Colum I*, a passenger-car ferry that operated between Ireland and England. Eight million dollars is the projected cost for the purchase, conversion and refurbishing of the vessel into the cruise ship *Fiesta Princessa*.

During 1987, Royal Fiesta's chairman, Bill Folz, was negotiating with three shipyards in Europe, and once the conversion is completed Royal Fiesta plans to inaugurate a service in March 1988 from St Petersburg, Florida, to Mexico and the Caribbean. The reason why St Petersburg was selected was the void left by Commodore Cruise Lines' *Boheme*. Mr White stated '. . . *Boheme* had 87 per cent and better load factors every week, proving that this is a very good market and a strong niche'. The ship would fly the Pana-

manian flag and, added Mr White, 'we hope and are reasonably certain to become one of the first cruise lines with a US deck and engine crew'. It remains to be seen whether Royal Fiesta will succeed, considering that the competition is spending hundreds of millions on new 'super-liners' staffed by inexpensive crew, while Royal hopes to make do with spending $18 million on a third-hand 5,000-ton ship with an American union crew that will no doubt demand union wages.

Fiesta Princessa 1988 (proposed)

Schichau-Ges Uunterweser AG, Bremerhaven, 1973.

5,285 gross tons; 392 × 59 ft (119 × 18 m); Pielstick diesels; twin screw; 21 knots; over 700 first class passengers. Launched 1973 as *Saint Patrick* (Irish Continental Line).

1983 *Saint Colum I* (Allied Irish Banks & Allied Irish Investment Bank). 1987 *Fiesta Princessa* (Royal Fiesta). Proposed FV 3/1988 St Petersburg-Mexico.

Royal Hawaiian Cruise Lines

(1980)

Royal Hawaiian was formed in 1980 by Othmar Grueninger, a former Carras Lines official, who acquired the laid-up *Monterey* from World Airways Inc. The plan was for her removal to Bethlehem Steel in San Francisco for repairs, Coast Guard inspection and a $2 million refit which was to include the addition of forty new cabins.

In a 21-page brochure issued by Royal Hawaiian, the company stated that '*Monterey* is the first American all-passenger ship back in service. American flag, American crew, American service...' The brochure continued that, 'SS *Monterey* initiated the concept of unhurried elegance that has since become the great American tradition in the Pacific'. The

inaugural cruise was set for 2 March 1980 from San Francisco to Honolulu, whence *Monterey* would commence seven-day inter-island Hawaii cruises. Three trips from Honolulu to the West Coast were also scheduled for 1980.

Monterey never sailed, not even to Bethlehem Steel. Royal Hawaiian failed to come up with the $3 million purchase price. A $4.5 million loan from the Economic Development Administration did not materialize, and the company owed back rent for office space. *Monterey* remained in the possession of World Airways, and Royal Hawaiian faded into history.

Silver Star Line

(1952-1957)

Silver Star Line represented Arnold Bernstein's second attempt to enter the American maritime field. His first was in 1948 with Continental, although before the war he had founded Arnold Bernstein Line (see page 69) and acquired Red Star Line in 1935.

Anxious to resume his transatlantic service, Bernstein purchased *Nilla*. This vessel was completed in 1943 as HMS *Bruizer*, a Landing Ship Tank (LST). She was acquired by a Belgian firm in 1946 and subsequently laid up. During the winter of 1950, a Swiss financier, Vasile Winkler, purchased her and had her towed to Hamburg for planned reconstruction into the passenger ship *Nilla*. Bernstein spotted this bargain, and purchased her in 1950 for a

transatlantic service that was to begin in July of that year. However, Bernstein had to wait another 18 months for his ship. According to *Lloyds Registry of Shipping 1954-1955*, *Silver Star* was registered under Cia Naviera Estrella de Plata SA, marketed under the banner of Silver Star Line, with bookings handled by Arnold Bernstein Shipping.

Company literature on the vessel has been difficult to locate and the only reliable sources are the *Official Steamship Guide* and the *New York Times*. According to the latter, *Silver Star* arrived in New York on 22

Silver Star *docked at Nassau* (Everett E. Viez/SSHSA Collection.

January 1952 for inspection by travel agents before sailing on 24 January for Miami. A description by the paper stated that she carried 420 passengers in rooms holding one to four persons and that each room had running water and pressure ventilation. Among her passenger amenities were four bars, including one devoted exclusively to soft drinks, eight public rooms and three dance floors.

Silver Star departed from Miami on her first seven-day cruise on 29 January for Havana-Vera Cruz. She made a total of ten such cruises that first season, including a thirteen-day voyage to the Caribbean. On 9 May she made her first New York departure to Havana, Nassau and Miami, a ten-day voyage; in all, she completed ten such cruises. From 1 February to 4 April 1953, *Silver Star* was based out of Miami and alternated between four-day cruises to Havana and Nassau and seven-day cruises to Kingston and Nassau. She returned to New York on 29 May 1953 to undertake seven-day, nine-day and ten-day cruises. Following her summer schedule which ended in August, she was laid up until May 1954.

Silver Star returned to service on 28 May 1954 out of Washington, DC, becoming the first cruise ship to be based there. Her schedule called for four additional seven-day cruises that departed on 4 June, 21 August, 28 August and 4 September. That summer she also sailed from Charleston, North Carolina, on 12 and 16 June to Nassau, from New Orleans for five Havana trips in July, and from Savannah, Georgia, where she departed on 11 August for Havana.

On 19 September 1954 she left Washington for Bremerhaven with rates starting at $140 (£50) for an inside cabin and $160 (£57) for an outside. Upon her return to the States, a winter programme out of Miami commenced on 5 February 1955. *Silver Star* spent the summer of 1955 sailing from Washington, DC, New Orleans and Charleston on cruises to either Bermuda or Nassau/Havana. That winter she was based out of Miami, and returned north to undertake her summer programme from Washington and Charleston, during which she made six voyages to Bermuda. According to available literature, *Silver Star* made her last sailings on the Miami-Havana cruise route. At the conclusion of her 1957 winter season in April, the vessel was sold to Argentinian interests.

Silver Star 1952-1957

Harland & Wolff, Belfast, 1943.

5,101 gross tons; 404 × 49 ft (123 × 15 m); steam turbines; twin screw; 18 knots; 420 passengers. Launched 1943 as HMS *Bruizer*, Landing Ship Tank (LST).

1946 *Nilla* (Enterprises Chimiques et Electriques, Vilvorde, Belgium). 1950 *Nilla* (Vasile Winkler). 1950 *Silver Star* (Silver Star Line). FV 29/1/1952 Miami-Vera Cruz. FV 9/5/1952 New York-Havana-Nassau. FV 28/5/1954 Washington-Bermuda. FV 19/9/1954 Washington-Bremerhaven. 1957 *Ciudad de Santa Fe* (Cia de Nav Fluvial Argentina). 1968 Scrapped in Argentina.

Society Expeditions

(1974)

Founded as the Society for the Preservation of Archaeological Monuments in 1974 by T.C. Swartz, Society Expeditions was a natural spin-off established that year with the concept of providing educational wildlife and cultural tours to remote destinations such as the Galapagos Islands, the South Pacific, Greenland, Antarctica, the Amazon and New Guinea. The company began cruises in 1977 with *World Discoverer*, chartered from Discoverer Reederei. She underwent a brief refit and commenced sailing in July to the aforementioned areas.

World Discoverer sailed the distant oceans and seas until 1984 when Heritage Cruises took her over. Within a year she was returned to her German owners and chartered again by Society in May. Also in 1984, Society Expeditions and Heritage Hotels chartered *Lindblad Explorer* from Discoverer Reederei for an October delivery. Society invested $2 million to bring the newly-named Society Explorer up to date with a complete refurbishing. *Society Explorer* was ready to embark passengers at Singapore on 19 July 1985 for a thirteen-day cruise to Hong Kong. Following a positioning cruise to Nome, Alaska, she departed from that port on 23 August 1985 on an epic 32-day cruise to Halifax, Nova Scotia, via the North-west Passage. As *Lindblad Explorer* she had completed the first such journey in the reverse direction the previous September.

World Discoverer is registered in Liberia and *Society Explorer* is registered in the Bahamas. The captain and officers are German with the remainder of the crew being mostly Swiss and Filipino. Both vessels have special ice-strengthened hulls and superstructures for helicopter landings. In addition to the modern amenities for passengers to enjoy on board, there are special features such as zodiacs (large 'life rafts' with high-performance engines), super launches, a marine laboratory and a simulated bridge for passenger use. Guest lecturers are carried on every cruise to enhance passengers' knowledge.

Among the destinations offered by the ships in 1988 are twelve-day journeys in the Amazon between Manáus (Brazil) and Iquitos (Peru); fifteen-day cruises from Punta Arenas, Chile, to Antarctica; a 24-day voyage to Antarctica, South Georgia Islands and Falkland Islands; cruises to remote South Pacific islands; voyages along the coasts of China; and the grandest of them all, the North-west Passage from Dutch Harbor, Aleutian Islands (Alaska), to St Pierre Miquelon, Canada. All cabins are outside with private facilities, and average per diem rates ranged from $250 (£156) to $800 (£500), excluding air fare and port charges.

In August 1987, Society Expeditions was purchased by Heiko Klein, a West German shipping magnate, who also owns Discoverer Reederei, the company from whom Society leased its ships. Mr Swartz remained as an adviser with no financial stake in the company. It was also reported that with the infusion of Klein's wealth, Society was investigating the possibility of obtaining a third ship to be delivered in late 1989.

1 ***World Discoverer*** 1977-1984, 1985 (c)

Schichau-Unterweser AG, Bremerhaven, 1974.

3,153 gross tons; 287 × 50 ft (87 × 15 m); diesels; single screw; 12.5 knots; 140 first class passengers. Launched 1974 as *Bewa Discoverer* (Bewa Cruises), laid up.

1977 *World Discoverer* (Discoverer Reederei, West Germany). 1977 Chartered to Society Expeditions.

FV 4/7/1977. Returned to owners. 1985 Chartered again by Society.

2 *Society Explorer* 1985 (c)

Nystads Varv AB, Finland, 1969.

2,367 gross tons; 250 × 45 ft (76 × 14 m); diesels; single screw; 13 knots; 100 first class passengers.

Launched 18/6/1969 as *Lindblad Explorer* (Lindblad). 1984 Sold to Discoverer Reederei. 1984 *Society Explorer* (Society Expeditions). FV 19/7/1985 Singapore-Hong Kong.

Below World Discoverer (Society Expeditions).
Bottom Society Explorer (Society Expeditions).

SS Monterey Limited Partnership Forecast

(1984 to date)

After nine years laid up, *Monterey* (see Royal Hawaiian Cruise Lines) departed from San Francisco on July 17 1986 for Dillingham Marine in Portland, Oregon, to undergo hull inspection. This would be the first stop *en route* to returning to commercial service under the ownership of SS Monterey Limited Partnership Forecast, a firm established in 1984.

Shortly after its foundation, Monterey Limited entered into an exclusive sales and marketing agreement with Aloha Pacific Cruises Limited Partnership, a Virginian firm owned by James L. Kurtz. Monterey raised $16.8 million among 172 investors and in 1987 concluded the purchase of *Monterey* for $8.5 million from American Maritime Holdings Inc, a subsidiary of the International Organization for Masters, Mates and Pilots Union (IOMMP). In an effort to save American jobs on the liner, the union agreed to 'a fifteen-year no strike, no work stoppage, no slow-down contract in return for an exclusive jurisdiction over the supervisory workers on the ship and a ten per cent stake in the venture'. The other owners were Aloha Pacific with 20 per cent and investors representing 70 per cent of the ownership.

After extensive research, Aloha concluded that the demand for seven-day cruises in the Hawaiian Islands exceeded current capacity, and that its ship would present to the public a de luxe alternative to the present cruise-ships (*Independence* and *Constitution* — see page 55) operating in the Hawaiian market. Its market having been defined, *Monterey* underwent a $30 million refit, first at Tacoma Boatbuilding for superstructure work, then Wärtsilä Shipyard in Finland for interior redecoration that included a show lounge, casino, disco, swimming pool featuring two Jacuzzi whirpools and a theatre.

Monterey's first voyage was supposed to have been a 47-day cruise that departed from Copenhagen on 31 July 1988, sailing west and calling at ports all along the US eastern seaboard. Unfortunately, her 'state of the art' Sperry fin stabilizers were not ready on time and Aloha's president, John Broughan, believed that a transatlantic voyage without them would have been uncomfortable. Therefore *Monterey* sailed without passengers and arrived at Baltimore on 2 August. Following the installation of her stabilizers, and after a special two-day celebration for passengers in Washington DC, she sailed for Baltimore, whence she departed on 23 August for a 26-day cruise to Los Angeles and San Francisco, where she arrived on 15 September. After a night of festivities, *Monterey* sailed the next day on her 15-day 'Grand Homecoming Cruise' to Honolulu.

Monterey 1987

Bethlehem Shipbuilding Corporation, Sparrow's Point, Maryland, 1952.

14,799 gross tons; 563 × 76 ft (172 × 23 m); steam turbines; single screw; 20 knots; 639 first class passengers. Launched 29/5/1952 as *Free State Mariner* for US Maritime Administration.

1956 *Monterey* (Matson) (see page 135). 1970 *Monterey* (Pacific Far East Line) (see page 152). 1978 Laid up. 1979 Sold to World Airways, laid up at Oakland. 1980 American Maritime Holdings, laid up at San Francisco. 1987 *Monterey* (SS Monterey Limited Partnership Forecast).

Positioning voyage 21/7/1988 Turku-Baltimore. FV 23/8/1988 Baltimore-San Francisco. FV 16/9/1988 San Francisco-Honolulu-Hawaiian islands. FV 1/10/1988 Honolulu-Hawaiian islands.

Sundance Cruises
(1983-1986)

Having successfully launched and nurtured Princess Cruises into an international cruise line, seen by many on television, Stanley McDonald grew restless and sought new challenges northward. In 1983 he co-founded Sundance Cruises, Seattle, with the idea of a low-cost Alaska cruise vacation on which vacationers could take their cars or campers. The other partner was Silja Line, a Finnish ferry company.

Unlike Princess Cruises, which chartered its vessels, Sundance decided to purchase. The company's first ship was *Svea Corona*, a Silja Line ferry built for the Helsinki-Stockholm run. *Svea Corona* was renamed *Sundancer* and converted at Oskarshamn, Sweden, for $7 million into a cruise

ship/ferry. On board was a dining room with large picture windows, six bars, two swimming pools (one indoors), two spas, a sauna, a night club, disco, casino and sky bar. After a positioning voyage to Vancouver, *Sundancer* departed thence on 15 June 1984 on her first seven-day Alaskan cruise.

Misfortune struck the company on 29 June during *Sundancer's* third cruise. Due to an error of judgement on the pilot's part, *Sundancer* ran aground off Vancouver Island, sustained hull damage and had to return to the nearest dock, that of Crown Forest Pulp Mill in Ducan Bay. In August the company declared

Stardancer *in* Admiral Line *funnel colours* (Admiral Cruises).

the ship a total loss and put her up for sale.

Determined to try again, McDonald bought the unwanted DFDS liner/ferry *Scandinavia* in 1984. After finishing her Copenhagen-Oslo winter season in 1985, she was handed over to McDonald in May, and underwent a brief refit at Blohm and Voss. Renamed *Stardancer*, she provides comfortable accommodation for 968 passengers and garage space for 350 vehicles. All cabins have radios, closed-circuit televisions, and passenger amenities include a dining room, library, casino, night club, disco, pools, spa and health club.

Stardancer left Vancouver, BC, on 7 June on her first Alaskan Cruise. Because passengers could bring their vehicles, a unique feature of her schedule was that they could cruise one way. Vancouver to Skagway, three days, ranged from $334 to $828 (£261 to £647), or Skagway to Vancouver, four days, was $442 to $1,094 (£345 to £854). A seven-day cruise from $755 to $1,870 (£590 to £1,461). Vehicles were carried at $250 to $1,350 (£195 to £1,055), depending on their size and the duration of the trip.

Stardancer's Mexixan programmes commenced on 4 October, from Los Angeles to Puerto Vallarta. Like her Alaskan cruises, journeys could be taken in three-day or four-day segments, with vehicles accompanying their owners.

During the autumn of 1986, Sundance Cruises and the Norwegian concerns Eastern Cruise Lines and Western Cruise Lines amalgamated to form Admiral Cruises, thus bringing an end to the trade name Sundance Cruises.

1 *Sundancer* 1984-1984

Dubigeon-Normandie SA, Nantes, 1975.

12,576 gross tons; 502 × 73 ft (153 × 22 m); Pielstick diesels; twin screw; 22 knots; 700 first class passengers, 150 vehicles. Launched 19/7/1974 as *Svea Corona* (Silja Line).

1983 *Sundancer*. FV 15/6/1984 Vancouver BC-Skagway. 29/6/1984 Ran aground off Vancouver Island. 1984 *Pegasus* (Epirotiki Lines).

2 *Stardancer* 1985

Dubigeon-Normandie SA, Nantes, 1982.

26,747 gross tons; 607 × 88 ft (185 × 27 m); Burmeister & Wain diesels; twin screw; 21 knots; 968 first class passengers (1,606 berths), 350 vehicles. Launched 16/10/1981 as *Scandinavia* (DFDS).

1984 Purchased by Sundance Cruises. 1985. 1985 *Stardancer*. FV 7/6/1985 Vancouver-Skagway. FV 4/10/1985 Los Angeles-Puerto Vallarta. 1986 Transferred to Admiral Cruises.

United Fruit

(1899-1957)

Looking for cargo to carry during the off period in the New England fishing season, Captain Lorenzo Dow Baker decided to sail his 85-ton schooner, *Telegraph*, south in April 1870. He landed in Jamaica and chanced upon some half-ripe bananas; he had a few bunches loaded on to his ship and returned to Boston. The unfamiliar fruit was a sensation and he returned to Jamaica the next season. Business increased and he acquired more vessels. Captain Baker and an associate, Andrew Preston, subsequently founded the Boston Fruit Company in 1885 with working capital of $20,000. Five years later, on 3 October 1890, the company was incorporated in the State of Massachusetts with an authorized capital of $500,000.

Bananas were becoming a staple in the American diet, and Andrew Preston had grand designs. He wanted to merge the several banana importing firms along the US eastern seaboard and develop Central America for banana cultivation. Both designs were to become a reality, as in 1899 his dream came true with the merger of the major banana concerns into the United Fruit Company with Preston as President. The company thrived as ships were added to bring those profit-making bananas northward. By 1930, United Fruit was operating over thirty passenger-cargo ships which were popularly known among passengers as the 'Great White Fleet'.

When the United States entered the Second World War in 1941, United Fruit had fourteen passenger ships. All except *Antigua* were requisitioned, and all except *Sixaola* were returned to United Fruit ownership after the war. The older units were disposed of at the conclusion of their military commitments, and the six Mail Ships that survived were *Talamanca, Chirique, Antigua, Quirigua, Veragua*

and *Jamaica*, the first United Fruit ships to be built in America in the twentieth century.

Built in the early 1930s at a cost of $21 million, the Mail Ships were the result of the Jones-White Act that encouraged American companies to construct new tonnage and place them under the American flag. In return, the government would provide low-interest loans and probably a mail contract. Delivered between 1931 and 1933, the vessels were 6,900 tons each, were powered by turbo-electric engines and had refrigerated space for 50,000 bunches of bananas. They could also accommodate 100 passengers in first class cabins with hot and cold running water. For added comfort in the Tropics, a permanent swimming pool was built. Due to the prohibition law at that time, the ships were christened with a bottle of water gathered from the rivers in Central America. Each was returned to the New York-Havana-Cristobal-Port Limon service between 1946 and 1947.

As air travel became a more popular mode of transportation, an all-year-round passenger ship service between the United States and the Caribbean became impractical and unprofitable, especially with combination ships. Therefore, in 1952 United Fruit announced that it would withdraw from the profitless, passenger, sphere of action. *Quirigua, Veragua, Antigua* and *Talamanca* had their superstructures removed and were converted into freighters carrying only twelve passengers. They then continued to sail out of New York until the late 1950s.

Chiriqui and *Jamaica* were given a five-year reprieve by being switched to New Orleans whence they sailed to Havana (Cuba), Cristobal (Panama) and Puerto Barrios (Guatemala). In mid-1957 they were laid up and later that year sold to a German company.

In the late 1960s, United Fruit transferred its entire

Left Talamanca *was the first of six liners ordered by United Fruit in the 1930s* (A.B. Deitsch/SSHSA Collection).

Below left *Arriving in New York is* Chirique (Courtesy Peter M. Warner).

freighter fleet to British, Dutch and Honduran flags. During the last year of that decade, Eli M. Black's firm of AMK Corporation successfully acquired United Fruit by accumulating the stock. Under Black's chairmanship, profits declined, dividends were eliminated, the company's share of the banana market declined, and management was unable to deal with the turmoil in Latin America. In a series of buy-outs, sell-outs and trade-offs in the mid-1970s, United Brands subsequently took control of the AMK Corporation and its subsidiary, United Fruit. The company that was literally responsible for creating the economies of many Central American states had now disappeared into history.

1 *Talamanca* 1931-1952

Newport News Shipbuilding & Drydock Company, Newport News, Virginia, 1931.

6,963 gross tons; 447 × 60 ft (136 × 18 m); turbo electric; twin screw; 18 knots; 100 passengers. Launched 15/8/1931.

MV 23/12/1932 New York-San Francisco. FV 1/1932 San Francisco-Central America. 1937 New York-Cuba-Central America. 1942 *Talamanca AF-15* (US Navy). 1945 *Talamanca* (United Fruit). 1952 Reduced to twelve passengers. 1958 *Sulaco* (Elders & Fyffes). 1964 Scrapped in Belgium.

2 *Chirique* 1932-1957

Newport News Shipbuilding & Drydock Company, Newport News, Virginia, 1932.

6,963 gross tons; 447 × 60 ft (136 × 18 m); turbo electric; twin screw; 18 knots; 100 passengers. Launched 14/11/1932.

MV 24/3/1932 New York-San Francisco. FV 4/1932 San Francisco-Central America. 1937 New York-Cuba-Central America. 1941 *Tarazed AF-13* (US Navy). 1946 *Chirique* (United Fruit). FV 1952 New Orleans-Central America. 1957 *Blexen* (Union Handels, Germany). 1969 Scrapped at Kaohsiung.

Below *United Fruit's* Antigua (Frank O. Braynard collection).

Left Quirigua *in dry dock* (Frank O. Braynard collection).

Right Quirigua *after the removal of her passenger accommodation in 1952* (Moran Towing & Transportation Company).

Right *Last of the 'Great White Fleet' was* Jamaica, *commissioned in 1933 as* Peten (Frank O. Braynard collection).

3 *Antigua* 1932-1952

Bethlehem Steel Company, Quincy, Massachusetts, 1932.
6,982 gross tons; 447 × 60 ft (136 × 18m); turbo electric; twin screw; 18 knots; 100 passengers. Launched 28/11/1931.

MV 3/4/1932 New York-San Francisco. FV 4/1932 San Francisco-Central America. 1937 New York-Cuba-Central America. 1942 Store-ship for US Navy. 1944 Rammed by US Liberty ship *A.E. Christensen* near Pearl Harbor, badly holed and repaired. 1947 Back to United Fruit. 30/3/1949 Burned at New Orleans, beached in shallow water and repaired. 1952 Reduced to twelve passengers. 1958 *Tortuga* (Salenrederierna AB, Sweden). 1964 Scrapped at Bruges.

4 *Quirigua* 1932-1952

Bethlehem Steel Company, Quincy, Massachusetts, 1932.
6,982 gross tons; 447 × 60 ft (136 × 18 m); turbo electric; twin screw; 18 knots; 100 passengers. Launched 6/2/1932.

MV 8/6/1932 New York-Havana-Cristobal-Puerto Limon. 1941 *Mizar* (US Navy). 1946 *Quirigua* (United Fruit). 1952 Reduced to twelve passengers. 1958 *Samala* (Elders & Fyffes). 1964 Scrapped in Kaohsiung.

5 *Veragua* 1932-1952

Bethlehem Steel Company, Quincy, Massachusetts, 1932.
6,982 gross tons; 447 × 60 ft (136 × 18 m); turbo electric; twin screw; 18 knots; 100 passengers. Launched 23/4/1932.

MV 11/8/1932 New York-Havana-Cristobal-Puerto Limon. 1942 *Merak* (US Navy). 1946 *Veragua* (United Fruit). 1952 Reduced to twelve passengers. 1958 *Sinaloa* (Elders & Fyffes). 1964 Scrapped in Belgium.

6 *Jamaica* 1938-1957.

Newport News Shipbuilding & Drydock Company, Newport News, Virginia, 1933.
6,968 gross tons; 447 × 60 ft (136 × 18 m); turbo electric; twin screw; 18 knots; 100 passengers. Launched 15/8/1931 as *Segovia* (United Fruit). Burned and sank during fitting out. 1932 Raised and renamed *Peten* (United Fruit).

MV 2/3/1933 New York-Havana-Cristobal-Puerto Limon. 1937 *Jamaica* (chartered to Colombian Mail). 1938 Returned to United Fruit, and resumed service 16/4/1938. 1942 *Ariel* (US Navy). 1946 *Jamaica* (United Fruit). 1952 New Orleans-Central America. 1957 *Blumenthal* (Union Handels, Germany). 1969 Scrapped at Kaohsiung.

United States Department of Commerce

(1964-1965)

America's maritime technology reached its zenith with the commissioning of *Savannah*, the first ever nuclear-powered passenger ship, named in memory of her 1819 predecessor which pioneered transatlantic steamship voyages.

Designed by George Sharp, *Savannah* was authorized by an Act of Congress on 30 July 1956. Her keel was laid on 22 May 1958 by the New York Shipbuilding Corporation, Camden, NJ, and she was launched by Mrs Dwight D. Eisenhower on 21 July 1959. Completed in December 1961, *Savannah* embarked on trials lasting until April 1962.

Savannah's prime feature was her nuclear reactor representing the combined efforts of United States top marine nuclear scientists. It was 28 ft high, weighed 105 tons and was housed in a containment vessel of 2½ in heavy steel shielding weighing 2,500 tons; a secondary shielding consisted of layers of wood, concrete, polyethylene, steel sheets and 500 tons of lead plate. The fuel was 17,000 pounds of uranium oxide enriched in the fissionable uranium 235. A single core of fuel was sufficient energy to operate the ship for 300,000 miles during a period of three years.

Awaiting the fortunate 60 passengers were all outside cabins with private facilities located on A Deck, a dining room below on B Deck, and a main lounge, card room, writing room, veranda and swimming pool all located on Promenade Deck.

Savannah was owned by the United States Department of Commerce who appointed States Marine Lines to operate her. She departed from Yorktown, Virginia, on her maiden voyage on 20 August 1962 for Savannah, Georgia, then sailed on 'goodwill demonstration' voyages to northern Europe and the Mediterranean. After her 'goodwill' trips, she

Deck plan of Savannah (Author's collection).

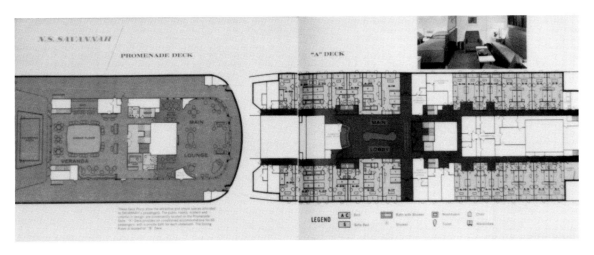

Above *The nuclear-powered* Savannah *about to dock in New York* (Moran Towing & Transportation Company).

Left *The main lounge, lobby and verandah of* Savannah (Author's collection).

settled down to ply the North Atlantic. Her first scheduled sailing with passengers left New York on 8 June 1964; on board were thirteen passengers bound for either Dublin, Bremerhaven, Hamburg or Southampton. Her next New York departure was on 30 July for Scandinavia, followed by Mediterranean sailings on 21 September, 8 November and during December. *Savannah's* capacity never exceeded 25 passengers on any of these trips. For that reason, coupled with the fact that it was expensive to maintain, the passenger accommodation was sealed up during the summer of 1965 and she sailed as a freighter. Simultaneously, that summer there were labour difficulties at States Marine Lines and the government decided to transfer management to the First Atomic Ship Transport (FAST) of American Export-Isbrandtsen Lines. She continued to make occasional transatlantic sailings until 1967. On 22 May of that year, she departed from New York for the Orient, and during the summer of 1968 she was refuelled for the first and last time. Her final outing was her 2 May 1970 sailing from Baltimore to the Far East.

At the conclusion of this Orient trip it was realized that she would never be economically viable. She had arrived during an age of change — to airfreight competition and containerization. She was also certainly not designed to compete with any existing passenger ship company. *Savannah* was more of a 'show boat' — America's ambassador of nuclear goodwill. For safety reasons she needed two to three times as many crew members on board, and finally some nations protested against her entry into their waters, notably, Japan.

Savannah was laid up at Galveston, Texas, following the completion of her Orient trip. During the latter part of 1971 her nuclear core was removed, and soon afterwards, in January 1972, she was towed to Savannah, Georgia, to become a museum.

Savannah 1964-1965

New York Shipbuilding Corporation, Camden, New Jersey, 1964

13,599 gross tons; 595 × 78 ft (181 × 24 m); nuclear reactor & steam turbines; single screw; 21 knots; 60 first class passengers. Launched 21/7/1959.

MV 20/8/1962 Yorktown-Savannah. 9/1962 'goodwill voyages'. 1964 15,585 tons. FV (commercial) 8/6/1964 New York-Europe. 22/5/1967 New York-Orient. 2/5/1970 Baltimore-Orient. 1970 Laid up at Galveston. 1971 Nuclear core remove. 1972 Towed to Savannah to become a museum.

United States Lines

(1921-1969)

At the end of the First World War, the United States Government found itself with a large fleet of ex-German liners which it placed under the control of the United States Shipping Board (USSB), a Department of Commerce agency. In 1920, many small German vessels, together with *Amerika* and *George Washington*, were handed over to a new concern, United States Mail Steamship Co, which operated the liners along with four American-built ships from America to France, Germany and England.

US Mail possessed very little capital and even less shipping experience; unable to fulfil its obligations, the USSB, through the District Court, ordered the return of its vessels on 21 August 1921. The USSB in turn appointed Albert Moore (Moore & McCormack), Kermit Roosevelt (Roosevelt Steamship Company) and W. Averill Harriman (United American Lines) as managing operators of US Mail, until the ships could be sold to private operators. The new operators managed the line under the title United States Lines (USL), with no interruption in service.

The first sailing under USL auspices was undertaken by *America*, the former *Amerika* of Hamburg-America; she sailed from New York on 27 August 1921 for Plymouth, Cherbourg and Bremen. She was eventually joined by other former German liners — *George Washington, Leviathan* and *Republic*, giving United States Lines a viable first class fleet, though slightly unbalanced since *Leviathan* had no consort. Six American-built '502' and '535' Class ships, so called for their overall length, were introduced between 1921 and 1922 to supplement the sailings of the luxury liners.

Financial losses by US Lines continued to increase thanks, no doubt, to the albatross of Prohibition. To arrest these losses, the USSB unanimously adopted the Teller resolution in July 1926 which called for the sale of US Lines to private American interests. (The USSB had been operating the ships alone since 1923 when United American Lines and Moore & McCormack withdrew as managing operators.) In 1929, Paul Wadsworth Chapman, a Chicago financier, paid $16,300,000 for the company and changed its name to United States Line Inc, of Delaware. Trading continued for two years under Chapman's direction, but when he failed to keep up his payments, the USSB announced a new organization, the United States Lines Company of Nevada, to take over operations.

In May 1943, the US Lines Company was merged with the International Mercantile Company of New Jersey and concurrently the company's name was amended to United States Lines Company of New Jersey.

After the war, *Mount Vernon* was chartered to US Lines by the US Maritime Commission and her name reverted to *Washington*, the name under which she had been owned by USL from 1933 to 1941. She undertook US Lines' first post-war sailing from New York on 2 April 1946 to Cobh and Southampton. *Washington* was followed on 6 April by the chartered liner *John Ericsson*, the former Swedish liner *Kungsholm, Brazil*, and *Argentina*. The latter proceeded to make six round voyages, commencing on 13 April 1946. *Washington* survived until October 1951, whereupon she was laid up. *John Ericsson* suffered a fire on 7 March 1947 and was sold to

Above right *A postwar shot of* Washington (Courtesy Peter M. Warner).

Right Marine Marlin *docked at a Manhattan pier* (National Archives, Washington DC).

Left *The first troop-transport to sail on austerity voyages for USL was* Marine Flasher *(National Archives, Washington DC).*

Below left Marine Flasher *was rebuilt in 1966 as the 17,814 tons, 684 ft (208 m)* Long Beach, *a container ship (Ingalls Shipbuilding).*

Right *An enthusiastic welcome is accorded* America *on her maiden arrival in New York on 29 July 1940 (Courtesy Peter M. Warner).*

Below America *at Newport News, with the building of* United States *in the background (Courtesy Peter M. Warner).*

Home Lines, and *Brazil* and *Argentina* were handed back to Moore-McCormack in August and September 1946.

These liners were followed by nine 'C4-S-A3' Class troop transports capable of carrying from 850 to 930 passengers, mainly in dormitories. They were all built by the Kaiser Company on the West Coast, and powered by double reduction geared turbines turning a single screw. The first of this class to sail under charter for US Lines was *Marine Flasher*, which left New York on 25 May 1946 for Southampton and Le Havre. Joining *Marine Flasher*, were *Marine Perch*, *Ernie Pyle*, *Marine Marlin*, *Marine Falcon*, *Marine Jumper*, *Marine Tiger*, *Marine Shark* and *Marine Swallow*. *Marine Falcon*, *Marine Jumper* and *Marine Tiger* were chartered in 1947 as a result of the disaster that befell *John Ericsson* and the reconditioning of *Washington*. *Marine Shark* and *Marine Swallow* joined USL in 1948, the latter being the last vessel to sail for USL, making her final voyage from New York on 25 August 1948.

Company literature pointed out that the above vessels were troop carriers with a limited number of staterooms, operated on an emergency basis to assist in transporting the large number of travellers who could not be accommodated otherwise. The rates in May 1948 from New York to Bremerhaven, Germany (eleven to twelve days), were as follows: $200 (£50) for A and B Deck staterooms and dormitories for between 6 and 38 per room, with meals served in A Deck dining room; $180 (£45) for dormitories accommodating 24 people with meals served in B Deck dining room; and $160 (£40) for men in open troop quarters ranging from 46 to 66 in a Section with meals in the B Deck dining room. To England and France $20 and $10 (£5 and £2) respectively were deducted.

America was discharged from military service in July 1946, given an overhaul, and then placed on US Lines' New York-Cobh-Southampton-Le Havre service on 14 November 1946. She was originally laid down for the United States Maritime Commission as a replacement for *Leviathan*, but during construction was transferred to US Lines. Upon completion, *America* became the largest, fastest and finest US passenger liner. Following her refit in 1946, she provided accommodation for 516 first class, 371 cabin class and 159 tourist class passengers. In 1951 her western terminus was extended to Bremerhaven.

United States: the building of a superliner

William Francis Gibbs had always been obsessed with building the ultimate American liner. Since the 1920s, he had been drawing up plans for an American superliner to compete successfully against the European liners, and which at the same time could be converted easily into a troop-ship for national defence. Finally, in the late 1940s, the US Government and the Maritime Administration, collaborating with United States Lines, accepted Gibbs' blueprints for a mammoth liner. A special enclosed drydock was prepared at Newport News, and the keel of the ship was laid on 8 February 1950. Secrecy surrounded her construction and many of the photographs reproduced here were considered top secret and only released in the 1960s. The Navy, which played a significant role in her design, particularly the machinery, wanted no information to leak out.

On 23 June 1951, the liner was christened *United States* by senator's wife Mrs Tom Connolly. An interesting anecdote reported in a maritime publication stated that the evening before, when water was being pumped into the drydock where the ship was being built, a group of Carolinians was employed in a rowing-boat clearing debris from the dock. By chance, one produced a bottle of corn liquor and, with one stroke, anticipated Mrs Connolly by several hours by naming the ship *United States*.

Completed a year later, *United States* was handed over to United States Lines ownership and became the pride of the American Merchant Marine. She was 53,329 tons, 990 ft (302 m) long and 101 ft (31 m) wide, enabling her to transit through the Panama Canal; she carried 913 first class, 558 cabin class and 537 tourist class passengers. A prime consideration in her construction was her ability to be transformed,

The steel frames of United States: *a photograph taken on 8 February 1950* (**left**), *construction of the aft end* (**above**) *and the forward part* (**right**) (Courtesy Peter M. Warner).

within a matter of hours, into a troop-ship carrying 14,000 men and their equipment. For that reason *United States'* interiors were rather plain. All first class and cabin class cabins had private facilities, but tourist class lacked that refinement.

Alcoa could not have been more pleased. Aluminium was everywhere — the decks, funnels, radar mast, lifeboats, furniture, decorations, interior partitioning and much of the plating of the superstructure — thereby making the 'Big U' virtually fireproof. Even the curtains were treated with fireproof chemicals. Steinway, however, refused to make an aluminium piano. That instrument, together with the butcher's chopping block, balsa wood in the bilge keel and lignum vitae in the propeller bossings, were the only places where wood could be found in the ship. Additional pieces of wood could be found on the person of Mr Gibbs whenever he boarded 'his' ship — he carried them for good luck. Although

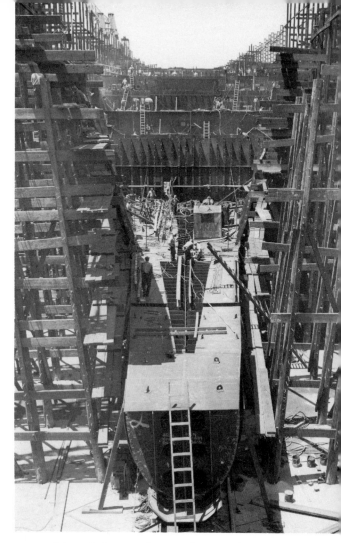

Above and opposite *The hull takes shape as the work proceeds on the building of* United States *(Courtesy Peter M. Warner).*

making her virtually fireproof, however, the aluminium gave her interiors an institutional look; luxurious interiors were not to be an important selling point to the public.

Under the command of Commodore Harry Manning, this $78 million technological wonder set from New York on her maiden voyage to Le Havre and Southampton on 3 July 1952 with 1,660 passengers on board. Powered by Westinghouse geared turbines, the quadruple screw liner steamed the 2,942 nautical miles from Ambrose Lightship to Bishop Rock in 3 days 10 hours 40 minutes at an average speed of 35.59 knots. Homewards, she

steamed from Bishop Rock to Ambrose Lightship in 3 days 12 hours 12 minutes at an average speed of 34.51 knots, so capturing the 'Blue Riband' and becoming the second ship actually to fly the large triangular 'Riband' from her mast up the Hudson River. This 'Riband' was contributed by the press on board who were overcome by enthusiasm and patriotism. (The only other ship to create and fly the 'Blue Riband' was *Normandie.*) *United States* brought home the Hales 'Blue Riband Trophy' in November 1952.

There was a rumour that on one westbound voyage in 1952 with Commodore Manning in command, *United States* caught up with *Queen Mary*, also heading west, and instead of simply overtaking her, Commodore Manning ordered his helmsman to circle the 'Queen' then sail on, thereby effectively

rubbing salt into the wound! *United States* never tried to top her own record, however, but in 1968 some of her engineering secrets were revealed. Her two engines could develop 240,000 horsepower, instead of 150,000 as was popularly believed, giving her a maximum speed of 42 knots. What good this speed would be against air attack in the 1950s was probably never given a thought. In addition, *United States* could transport a division of 14,000 troops for a distance of 10,000 miles without refuelling or reprovisioning (a guaranteed way to lose an entire division in the age of rockets and heat-seeking missiles!).

The 'All-American Team' of *United States* and *America* settled down in the 1950s to a quiet life of criss-crossing the Atlantic Ocean carrying the cream of seasoned travellers. Among them were the Duke and Duchess of Windsor who switched their allegiance from the Cunard 'Queens' to *United States*, not only to spite the British but also because of the good treatment they received on the latter. (How was Cunard treating them, one wonders?) In charge of

Left *The completed hull surrounded by scaffolding.* **Right** *Beginning the construction of the superstructure.* **Below** *The top of the sampan stack* (Courtesy Peter M. Warner).

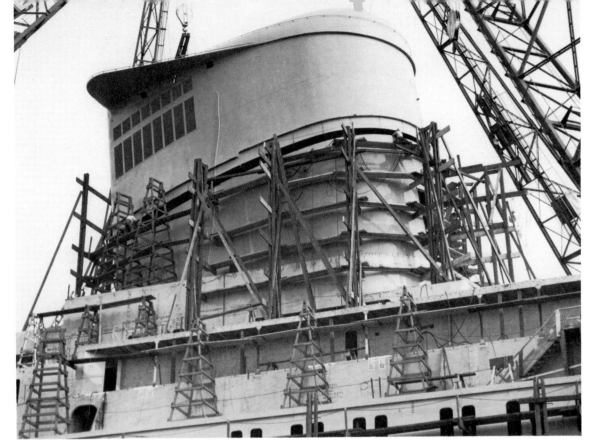

Above left and above *The fitting of the funnel, the scale of which is easily seen* **below left** *as it stands on the dockside waiting to be lifted into place* (Courtesy Peter M. Warner).

their comfort was Theodore Geautier who always made sure that they occupied the same suite — the Duck Suite. Both liners sailed from New York's Pier 86, West 46 Street. The 'fabulous' *United States* usually sailed at noon and five days later called at Le Havre

and Southampton, reaching Bremerhaven on the sixth day. *America*, described as 'a superb ship that offers all the refinements and luxuries of the most elegant living' departed usually at 4 pm and reached Cobh on the sixth day, Le Havre and Southampton on the seventh and Bremerhaven on the eighth. Passage fares over a seventeen-year period between New York and Southampton per person during the summer season were, in dollars (pounds), as follows:

	1952		1960		1969	
	Min	Max	Min	Max	Min	Max
First class						
United States	360 (129)	930 (332)	417 (149)	1,197 (428)	510 (213)	950 (396)
America	325 (116)	850 (304)	372 (133)	882 (315)	—	—
Cabin class						
United States	255 (91)	290 (103)	290 (104)	325 (116)	321 (134)	380 (158)
America	*220 (79)	275 (98)	*255 (*91)	310 (111)	—	—
Tourist class						
United States	*170 (*61)	*200 (*71)	*222 (*79)	252 (90)	*276 (*115)	*290 (*121)
America	*165 (*59)	210 (75)	*215 (*77)	250 (89)	—	—

*a four-berth cabin without private facilities.

Above *The unfinished upper decks of* United States (Courtesy Peter M. Warner).

Left *The almost completed* United States *minus the portholes in the superstructure* (Courtesy Peter M. Warner).

Right *The day of reckoning — the christening of the 'Big U'* (Courtesy Peter M. Warner).

In 1961, two events happened in *United States'* life. On 27 May, Congress passed PL 87-45 75S89 that allowed the liner to make cruises during the off season. The first of many left New York on 30 January 1962 and was a fourteen-day cruise to Nassau, St Thomas, Trinidad, Curacao and Cristobal, with a minimum rate of $520 (£186) for a cabin with private facilities. The second was that during her re-measurement it was discovered that her original registered tonnage of 53,329 was incorrect. She was now listed at 51,988 gross tons. This 1,342-ton difference brought with it lower tonnage dues. A further reduction to 44,893, then finally 38,216, was arrived at in 1967 without a single interior or exterior change. The reasons for these tonnage fluctuations

without alterations were due to an 1865 American law (see the explanatory notes on page 12). The goal of the tonnage reduction was to reduce the operating cost of this giant liner.

By the early 1960s, airlines were beginning to steal the best of the transatlantic traffic. As patronage switched to the air, steamship profits decreased, and in addition American steamship companies were facing increasingly vocal unions. The beginning of the end for United States Lines was a strike called by 680 unlicensed crew members of the National Maritime Union who were advocating the removal of senior engineer officer Louis B. Neurohr on charges that he 'locked a washroom to prevent its use by Negro and Puerto Rican crew members, of having refused to have them on his watch and of having insulted crew members'. When Mr Neurohr's union, the Marine Engineers' Beneficial Association, refused to remove him, the NMU members went on strike on 15 September 1963. Sharing the same front-page headline of 'America cancels sailing in dispute on racial charge' was 'Birmingham bomb kills 4 Negro girls in church; riots flare; 2 boys slain'.

The strike was finally settled in December with Neurohr pledging to refrain from actions that could be construed as biased in any way. *America* moved on 20 January 1964 from her lay-up berth at Todd Shipyards, Hoboken, first to Pier 86, then to Newport News. She resumed her transatlantic schedule on 7 February and completed thirteen round trips before being sold in November to Chandris Lines for $4.25 million on the proviso that the liner be made available to the United States in time of national emergency and that she could not be used in service to United States ports in competition with US ships. Chandris renamed its acquisition *Australis*, and placed her on its Australian emigrant service.

This left *United States* as the lone warrior for the next five years. There was always talk of building a

Above right *United States* is floated out of her building dock. *The purpose of this building technique was to hide her underwater works* (Courtesy Peter M. Warner).

Right *United States* is completely afloat for the first time on 23 June 1951 (Courtesy Peter M. Warner).

Above left United States *is towed to her fitting-out berth* (Courtesy Peter M. Warner).

Left *At fitting-out, her furnishings are installed and interiors completed* (Courtesy Peter M. Warner).

Above United States *heads for the Atlantic for her trials* (Courtesy Peter M. Warner).

sister ship in the 'fifties, but as time passed opposition to the scheme mounted in the Executive and Budget Departments at Washington.

In 1966, US Lines of New Jersey was organized into a holding company, with a wholly-owned subsidiary, United States Lines Inc, to operate the fleet. However, by now the writing was on the wall — *United States* was losing $8 million per year. Helping to contribute to this was a lay-up during the peak travel months of July and August 1965 because of striking union crew members asking for more money, shorter working hours, additional holidays and improved pension plans. In fact, from 1 January 1961 to 25 October 1969, labour unrest forced *United States* to cancel voyages on eleven different occasions. When she was sailing, revenue derived from passengers was

not sufficient to pay the crew and the sizeable fuel bills. Even on cruises she did not slow down — she dashed across to Africa and South America in 28 days, while a quick trip in 1969 to Cannes, Gibraltar and Bermuda occupied only 15½ days, and her ultimate voyage — a 'Great Adventure Cruise' that took her to Curacao, Rio de Janeiro, Cape Town, Port Elizabeth, Luanda, Tenerife, Dakar, Gibraltar, Lisbon and Funchal, departing on 23 January 1969 — was completed in 39 days with 750 passengers paying from $1,650 to $6,050 (£688 to £2,520) to sail in America's super-liner. Cabins without facilities cost $1,400 (£583). By 1969, *United States* had consumed $100 million in Government subsidies.

United States sailed unceremoniously on 25 October 1969 on her 726th crossing. In mid-ocean, Captain John S. Tucker received a wire advising him that the 9 November 21-day 'Autumn Adventure' cruise was cancelled and that once *United States* returned to New York on 7 November she would depart two days later for Newport News for an early annual overhaul. This rescheduling was to head off another threatened union strike. Once *United States* arrived at Newport News, she never sailed again. In

her seventeen-year career, she had logged 2,772,840 miles and carried 1,002,936 passengers across the Atlantic and 22,755 on cruises. In 1973 she was placed under the US Federal Maritime Administration, then five years later was sold to United States Cruises, a Seattle firm, which has plans to convert her into a cruise liner.

United States Lines ceased all passenger operations, including that of the freighters, in 1969 and during the autumn of that year was purchased for $71 million by Walter Kidde and Company Inc, who made the company a subsidiary in its building of a worldwide system of intermodal transportation. In 1978, Malcolm McLean, who founded McLean Trucking in 1934 and Sea-Land in 1956, obtained complete control of Walter Kidde & Co and thus of US Lines. By 1985, 'US Lines' competitors, American President, was offering a faster service to the Orient and Taiwan's Evergreen Marine had lower operational costs. After facing a nine-month loss of $237 million in December 1986, McLean put US Lines into bankruptcy, bringing to a close another great American shipping company.

1 Washington 1933-1941
Washington 1946-1951 (c)

New York Shipbuilding Corporation, Camden, New Jersey, 1933.

22,846 gross tons; 705 × 86 ft (215 × 26 m); steam turbines; twin screw; 20 knots; 1,150 single class passengers. Launched 20/8/1932.

MV 10/5/1933 New York-Cobh-Plymouth-Le Havre-Hamburg-Southampton-Cobh. FV 13/1/1940 New York-Naples-Genoa. 26/7/1940 New York-San Francisco. 1941 Sold to US Maritime Commission. 1941 *Mount Vernon* US troop-ship). 1946 Chartered to USL, renamed *Washington*. FV 2/4/1946 New York-Cobh-Southampton. 1947 Reconditioned. 2/4/1948 Resumed service. 1948 23,626 tons. 1949 29,627 tons. LV 10/10/1951 Hamburg-Le Havre-Southampton-Cobh-New York (arriving 19/10). 1951 Laid up. 1965 Scrapped at Kearny, New Jersey.

2 John Ericsson 1946-1947 (c)

Blohm & Voss, Hamburg, 1928.

16,522 (B 20,067) gross tons; 609 × 78 ft (185 × 24 m); B & W diesels; twin screw; 17 knots; 1,513 single class passengers. Launched 17/3/1928 as *Kungsholm* (Swedish-American).

1942 *John Ericsson* (US Government). FV 6/4/1946 New York-Southampton. LV 2/1947 Southampton-Le Havre-Cobh-New York. 7/3/1947 Damaged by fire in New York. 1948 *Italia* (Home Lines). 1965 Scrapped at Bilbao.

3 *Brazil* 1946 (c)

Newport News Shipbuilding & Drydock Company, Newport News, Virginia, 1928.

20,614 gross tons; 613 × 80 ft (187 × 24 m); turbo electric; twin screw; 17 knots; 385 first class, 365 tourist class passengers. Launched 18/10/1928 as *Virginia* (American Line), two funnels.

1938 *Brazil* (American Republic), one funnel. FV 6/4/1946 New York-Le Havre. LV 16/7/1946 New York-Southampton-Le Havre. 5 RV. 1946 Returned to Moore McCormack (see page 145). 1964 Scrapped in New York.

4 *Argentina* 1946 (c)

Newport News Shipbuilding & Drydock Company, Newport News, Virginia, 1928.

20,183 gross tons; 613 × 80 ft (187 × 24 m); turbo electric; twin screw; 17 knots; 500 single class passengers. Launched 10/7/1929 as *Pennsylvania* (American Line), two funnels.

1938 *Argentina* (American Republic), one funnel. FV 13/4/1946 New York-Southampton. LV 13/8/1946 New York-Southampton-New York. 6 RV. 1946 Returned to Moore McCormack (see page 145). 1964 Scrapped in New Jersey.

5 *Marine Flasher* 1946-1949 (c)

Kaiser Company Inc, Vancouver, Washington, 1945.

12,420 gross tons; 523 × 71 ft (159 × 21 m); steam

The maiden arrival of United States *in New York on 23 June 1952 (Courtesy Peter M. Warner).*

turbines; single screw; 16 knots; 914 tourist class passengers. Launched 16/5/1945 as troop-ship, US Maritime Commission.

FV 25/5/1946 New York-Southampton. 7/8/1946 One voyage for American Export (see page 46). LV 26/8/1949 New York-Southampton-Le Havre. 1949 Returned to US Maritime Commission, and laid up. 1966 *Long Beach* (Litton), 17,814 tons, 684 ft (208 m). 1975 *Long Beach* (Reynolds Leasing). 1987 Scrapped in Taiwan.

6 *Marine Perch* 1946 (c)

Kaiser Company Inc, Richmond, California, 1945.
12,420 gross tons; 523 × 71 ft (159 × 21 m); steam turbines; single screw; 16 knots; 901 tourist class passengers. Launched 28/6/1945 as troop-ship for US Maritime Commission.

The 'Big U' being manoeuvred into Pier 84 (Courtesy Peter M. Warner).

FV 30/5/1946 for USL and American Scantic jointly, New York-Bremen-Copenhagen-Oslo-Gothenburg (see page 67). 5/8/1946 LV ditto. 4 RV. 1946 American Export (see page 46). 1949 Laid up. 1965 *Yellowstone* (Rio Grande Transport, US). 14/6/1978 Sank after colliding with *Ibn Batouta*.

7 *Ernie Pyle* 1946-1949 (c)

Kaiser Company Inc, Vancouver, Washington, 1945.
12,420 gross tons; 523 × 71 ft (159 × 21 m); steam turbines; single screw; 16 knots; 869 tourist class passengers. Launched 25/6/1945 as troop-ship for US Maritime Commission.

FV 19/6/1946 New York-Le Havre. FV 26/9/1947 for USL and American Scantic jointly, New York-Le Havre-Copenhagen-Oslo-Gdynia (see page 68). LV 12/1947 ditto. LV 3/1949 Hamburg-New York. 1949 Returned to US Maritime Commission, and laid up. 1965 *Green Lake* (Central Gulf Steamship Company). 1978 Scrapped at Kaohsiung.

8 *Marine Marlin* 1946-1949 (c)

Kaiser Company Inc, Vancouver, Washington, 1945. 12,420 gross tons; 523 × 71 ft (159 × 21 m); steam turbines; single screw; 16 knots; 926 tourist class passengers. Launched 28/7/1945 as troop-ship for US Maritime Commission.

FV 16/9/1946 New York-Bremen. LV 7/1949 Bremen-New York. 1949 Returned to US Maritime Commission, and laid up. 1965 *Green Bay* (Central Gulf Steamship Company). 17/8/1971 Sunk in Qui Nhon harbor, South Vietnam.

9 *Marine Falcon* 1947-1949 (c)

Kaiser Company Inc, Vancouver, Washington, 1945. 12,420 gross tons; 523 × 71 ft (159 × 21 m); steam turbines; single screw; 16 knots; 900 tourist class passengers. Launched 27/4/1945 as troop-ship for US Maritime Commission.

FV 4/1947 New York-Southampton-Le Havre. LV 8/3/1949 New York-Hamburg-New York. 1948 Returned to US Maritime Commission. 1966 *Trenton* (Litton), 17,189 tons, 684 ft (208 m). 1975 *Borinquen* (Litton).

United States finally being docked at Pier 84 on a cold winter morning (Moran Towing & Transportation Company).

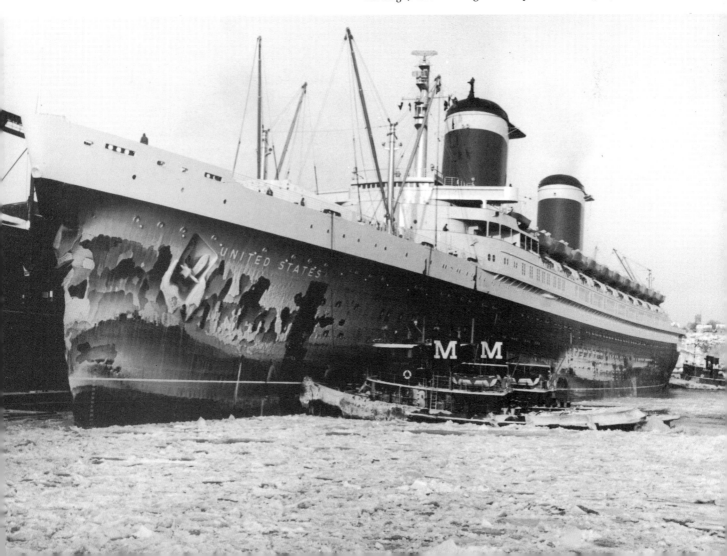

10 *Marine Jumper* 1947-1949 (c)

Kaiser Company Inc, Vancouver, Washington, 1945.
12,420 gross tons; 523 × 71 ft (159 × 21 m); steam turbines; single screw; 16 knots; 850 tourist class passengers. Launched 30/5/1945 as troop-ship for US Maritime Commission.

FV 6/6/1947 USL and American Scantic jointly, New York-Le Havre-Copenhagen-Oslo-Gdynia (see page 67). 27/9/1947 One voyage for American Export (see page 46). LV 11/8/1948 USL and American Scantic jointly. LV 7/1949 Bremen-New York. 1949 Returned to US Maritime Commission, and laid up. 1966 *Panama* (Litton), 17,184 tons, 684 ft (208 m). 1975 *Panama* (Reynolds). 1987 Scrapped in Taiwan.

11 *Marine Tiger* 1947-1949 (c)

Kaiser Company Inc, Vancouver, Washington, 1945.
12,420 gross tons; 523 × 71 ft (159 × 21 m); steam turbines; single screw; 16 knots; 850 tourist class passengers. Launched 23/3/1945 as troop-ship for

Left *Good Morning!* (Author's collection).
Below *Dinner aboard* United States *during one of her cruises* (Author's collection).

US Maritime Commission.

1946 Chartered to AGWI (see page 147). 1947 Chartered to USL. FV 24/6/1947 New York-Le Havre. LV 18/8/1949 New York-Southampton-Hamburg-New York. 1949 Returned to US Maritime Commission. 1966 *Oakland* (Litton), 17,184 tons, 684 ft (208 m). 1975 *Oakland* (Reynolds). 1987 Scrapped in Taiwan.

12 *Marine Shark* 1948-1949 (c)

Kaiser Company Inc, Vancouver, Washington, 1945.

12,420 gross tons; 523 × 71 ft (159 × 21 m); steam turbines; single screw; 16 knots; 930 tourist class passengers. Launched 4/4/1945 as troop-ship for US Maritime Commission

1946-1948 Sailed on charter to American Export (see page 44). 5/1948 One voyage for USL to Bremen, then back to American Export. 1949 USL. 11 RV. 1949 Returned to US Maritime Commission, and laid up. 1968 *Charleston* (Litton). 1984 Laid up. 1987 Scrapped in Taiwan.

13 *Marine Swallow* 1948 (c)

Kaiser Company Inc, Richmond, California, 1945.

12,420 gross tons; 523 × 71 ft (159 × 21 m); steam turbines; single screw; 16 knots; 850 tourist class passengers. Launched 21/6/1945 as troop transport. 1945 American President (see page 65). 1947 Laid up. 1948 USL. FV 26/7/1948 New York-Bremen. LV 25/8/1948 New York-Bremen. 2 RV. 1948 Laid up. 1965 *Missouri* (Meadowbrook Transport). 1974 *Ogden Missouri* (Ogden Missouri, Panama). *Linnet* (Linnet Shipping). 1978 Scrapped.

14 *America* 1946-1964

Newport News Shipbuilding & Drydock Company, Newport News, Virginia, 1940.

26,314 gross tons; 723 × 93 ft (220 × 28 m); steam turbines; twin screw; 22 knots; 516 first class, 371 cabin class, 159 tourist class passengers. Launched 31/8/1939.

MV 10/8/1940 New York-Caribbean cruise. 1941 *West Point* US troop-ship). 1946 *America*. FV 14/11/1946 New York-Cobh-Southampton-Le Havre. 1960 516 first class, 530 tourist class passengers, 33,961 tons. LV 9/10/1964 New York-Bremen. 1964 *Australis* (Chandris). 1978 *America* (Venture Cruises) (see page 213). 1978 *Italis* (Chandris), one funnel. 9/1979 Laid up in Piraeus. 1980 *Noga* (Intercommerce Corporation SA). 1984 *Alferdos* (Silver Moon Ferries).

15 *United States* 1952-1969

Newport News Shipbuilding & Drydock Company, Newport News, Virginia, 1952.

53,329 gross tons; 990 × 101 ft (302 × 31 m); Westinghouse geared turbines; quadruple screw; 31 knots; 913 first class, 558 cabin class, 537 tourist class passengers. 23/6/1951 Floated in building dock.

MV 3/7/1952 New York-Le Havre-Southampton (departing 10/7)-Le Havre-New York (arriving 15/7). Record passages in both directions. 1961 51,988 tons. 1962 44,893 tons. 1967 38,216 tons. LV 25/10/1969 New York-Le Havre-Southampton-Bremen (departing 1/11) Southampton-Le Havre-New York (arriving 7/11). Laid up at Newport News. 6/1970 Laid up at Norfolk. 1973 To US Federal Maritime Administration. 1978 Sold to US Cruises (Seattle).

Venture Cruise Lines

1978

Leonard Lansburgh, president of David Travels Inc, of Miami, had a simple idea. He wanted to offer a floating entertainment centre that would have three discos, two dance bands, four bars, a film theatre and a casino complete with 78 slot machines and assorted gambling paraphernalia, and charge an average of $77 (£42) per diem, in an effort to entice people, particularly the young, to sail. Together with Fred Kassner, owner of Liberty Travel and Gogo Tours, and GWV Travel of Newtown, Mass, they formed American Cruise Line and purchased the redundant Chandris liner *Australis* for $5 million.

America *departing on her first cruise* (Author's collection).

The company quickly ran into legal technicalities when American Cruise Lines of Haddam, Conn (see page 34), objected to the use of a name so similar to theirs. Therefore, the triumvirate renamed the company Venture Cruise Lines.

After being laid up for four months in Timaru, New Zealand, the *Australis'* engines were steamed and she proceeded to New York. There, the ship was delivered to Venture Cruises on 9 June 1978 and renamed *America*. A slight 'refit' was necessary before she was to embark on a summer programme of two-day to three-day cruises to nowhere, four-day to five-day cruises to Halifax and five-day cruises to Nassau.

The blue-hulled *America* departed on her first nowhere cruise on 30 June 1978 with 900 passengers aboard. The trip was chaos: many cabins were not ready, those that were occupied contained cockroaches, rats were scampering about, showers did not work, and normal necessities like toilet paper and bedsheets were unavailable. There was a 'mini-mutiny' aboard the liner and the captain was forced to return to New York and anchor in the lower bay. This action later resulted in a summons for disembarking passengers in New York bay by tender without a permit; around 200 passengers had chosen to disembark in this manner. The ship eventually docked and the problems were corrected.

Her next sailing was a five-day cruise to Nova Scotia which departed on 3 July. She returned to New York on 8 July with 641 grumbling passengers. The cockroaches, rubbish-filled swimming pools and other troubles had not been corrected. Publicity was bad.

By 13 July, the company had accumulated fines totalling $500,000, as well as the condemnation of the Public Health Service. There was no choice but to cease operation. Chandris repurchased its ship for $1,010,000, and on 6 September *America* quietly slipped away to Piraeus, Greece, where she was laid up.

America 1978

Newport News Shipbuilding & Drydock Company, Newport News, Virginia, 1940.

26,314 (B 34,449) gross tons; 723 × 93 ft (220 × 28 m); steam turbines; twin screw; 22 knots; 2,258 passengers. Launched 31/8/1939 as *America* (US Lines) (see page 211).
1941 *West Point* (US troop-ship). 1946 *America* (US Lines). 1964 *Australis* (Chandris). 1978 *America* (Venture Cruise). FV 30/6/1978 New York-nowhere. LV 3/7/1978 New York-Nova Scotia. 1978 *Italis* (Chandris), one funnel. 9/1979 Laid up in Piraeus. 1980 *Noga* (Intercommerce Corporation SA). 1984 *Alferdos* (Silver Moon Ferries).

Windstar Sail Cruises

(1984 to date)

Windstar Sail Cruises was organized in 1984 by Karl G. Andren, Jacob Stolt-Neilson Jr (co-owner) and Jean-Claude Potier. Mr Andren is a naturalized American citizen, the principal shareholder and chairman of the company, while Mr Potier serves as president. Mr Andren is also the owner of New York's Circle Line sightseeing boats as well as Dayline, a company which operates a Hudson River excursion boat during the summer months.

Windstar had a novel concept: to offer the luxury found on large cruise ships with the excitement of actually sailing in an intimate vessel capable of catering to no more than 148 passengers. The ships were designed by Wärtsilä Shipyard, Helsinki, and built in France. The first two vessels cost $65 million; the first, *Wind Star*, came down the slipways on 13 November 1985, followed in August by *Wind Song*. A second pair, *Wind Spirit* and *Wind Saga*, are to be delivered in 1988 and 1989 respectively. All four are registered in the Bahamas and employ Norwegian officers and an attentive European crew which helps keep costs down.

Wind Star was chartered by four different groups before commencing all-year round, seven-day Caribbean cruises on 13 December 1986 from Martinique to St Lucia, Bequia, Tobago Cays, Mayreau, Grenada, Palm Island, Mustique and St Lucia. Passage fare for the inaugural season was $2,250 (£1,406), plus airfare, while travel during the low season was $525 (£328) cheaper. *Wind Song* visited New York, Miami, Los Angelos, San Diego and San Francisco in May, June and July before heading for Tahiti, whence she commenced her first seven-day cruise on 24 July 1987 to Huahine, Tahaa, Bora Bora, Maupiti/Tupai, Raiatea and Moorea. Like *Wind Star*, all cabins are priced the same, but *Wind Song*

offers only one session — peak — and in 1987 a cabin for two was $2,635 (£1,647) per person, plus airfare. To ensure a smooth operation in Tahiti, *Wind Song* is captained by a Frenchman, and with Mr Potier as president, *Wind Star* will not experience the bureaucratic maze encountered by American Hawaii's *Liberté* (see page 55). Another interesting note is that *Wind Song* is the first passenger ship to have a woman chief engineer.

Wind Spirit will make her debut on 30 April 1988 from Venice, and after seven cruises will be switched to Monte Carlo on 25 June for a series of seven-day cruises to St Tropez, Sardinia, Corsica, Elba and Porto Fino. Following these she will make her debut in the Caribbean for her winter season of cruises.

On 30 May 1987, Holland-America Cruises' chairman, Nico van der Vorm, obtained 50 per cent ownership of Windstar Cruises. The partnership agreement would give Windstar necessary additional capital to finance the fourth ship, *Wind Saga*. Mr van der Vorm made it clear that 'this is strictly an investment on the part of Holland-America Line in what we consider to be a money-making venture, and both Windstar and Holland-America will be completely separate entities'. At the time of writing, Windstar is undecided as to the home base of *Wind Saga*.

A unique feature of the ships is their power plant, which utilizes a computer system to operate six sails on four masts that tower 204 ft (62 m) above the water-line. When the sails are not in use, the ships are propelled by diesel-electric engines. Another feature of the ships is their unstructured programmes

Windstar's first 'sailing' cruise liner, Wind Star *(Windstar Cruises).*

— passengers can relax, undisturbed by announcements, in the comfortable lounge, take in the sun on the spacious decks, or watch one of 350 videos, of which 80 are X-rated, in their cabins. When in port, passengers can enjoy the unspoiled beaches or partake in the many water sport activities using equipment carried on board the ship. To replenish expended energy, breakfast and lunch are served in the veranda which doubles at night as a discotheque. Dinner is served in the spacious dining room. In the evening, passengers retire to staterooms each of which includes a private bath, bar, refrigerator, colour television, multi-channel radio, video cassette player and safe.

1 **Wind Star** 1986

Société Nouvelle des Ateliers et Chantiers du Havre, Le Havre, France, 1986.

5,307 gross tons; 440 × 52 ft (134 × 16 m); diesel electric and sails; twin screw; 12 knots; 148 first class passengers. Launched 13/11/1985.

10/1986 Positioning voyage, Le Havre-Miami-St Lucia. FV 13/12/1986 St Lucia-Caribbean.

2 **Wind Song** 1987

Société Nouvelle des Ateliers et Chantiers du Havre, Le Havre, France, 1987.

5,307 gross tons; 440 × 52 ft (134 × 16 m); diesel electric and sails; twin screw; 12 knots; 148 first class passengers. Launched 20/8/1986.

5/1987 Positioning voyage, Le Havre-New York. 20/5/1987 Miami-San Diego-Los Angeles-San Francisco-Tahiti. MV 24/7/1987 Tahiti-South Pacific.

3 **Wind Spirit** 1988

Société Nouvelle des Ateliers et Chantiers du Havre, Le Havre, France, 1988.

5,307 gross tons; 440 × 52 ft (134 × 16 m); diesel electric and sails; twin screw; 12 knots; 148 first class passengers. Launched 6/1987.

MV (proposed) 30/4/1988 Venice-Yugoslavian fjords-Corfu-Malta. FV (proposed) 25/6/1988 Monte Carlo-Mediterranean. FV 1988 St Croix-Antigua.

4 **Wind Saga** 1989 (proposed)

Société Nouvelle des Ateliers et Chantiers du Havre, Le Havre, France.

5,307 gross tons; 440 × 52 ft (134 × 16m); diesel electric and sails; twin screw; 12 knots; 148 first class passengers. Proposed launch 1989.

Yarmouth Steamship Company

(1961-1966)

Webster and Roberts formed the Yarmouth Steamship Company in 1961 to operate ships on cruises. Their first purchase was *Yarmouth* from Eastern Steamship Lines. She was sent out west via the Panama Canal to San Francisco where she would make ten-day cruises to the Seattle World's Fair. Since *Yarmouth* flew the Panamanian flag, she had to disembark her passengers at Victoria, Canada, and they then took a ferry to Seattle. Like *Tradewind* in 1955 and 1956, *Yarmouth* circumvented the Jones Act by disembarking her passengers at a foreign port. When the Fair closed in the autumn, *Yarmouth* sailed back to Miami and commenced a series of twice-weekly cruises to Nassau, in direct competition with her once fleetmate *Bahama Star*.

The idle *Evangeline* was purchased by Yarmouth's subsidiary, Chedade Steamship Company, and promptly renamed *Yarmouth Castle*. She was then chartered to Caribbean Cruise Lines in 1964, for a series of summer cruises from New York. This charter arrangement collapsed in July, and *Yarmouth Castle* slipped quietly away to Miami. In December she set course for the Bahamas where she and *Yarmouth* were billed as the 'Fun Ships' offering 'four gala sailings' per week to Nassau and Freeport.

The end of Yarmouth Steamship can be traced to a fatal fire that befell *Yarmouth Castle*. She departed Miami for Nassau on 12 November 1965 with 371 passengers and a crew of 174. During the night of 13 November, a fire was discovered in cabin 610; it quickly spread and engulfed the liner. Forty minutes passed from the discovery of the fire to the sounding of the 'abandon ship' alarm. Passengers panicked as a few members of an inexperienced crew tried to help them find life jackets, life belts and their boat stations. The top officers, including Captain Voutsinas, were the first people off the ship, and when they tried to board *Finnpulp*, one of the rescue vessels, its captain was so incensed by their lack of seamanship that he refused to allow Captain Voutsinas and his party to board. *Bahama Star* arrived on the scene, and together with *Finnpulp* managed to rescue 458 people.

The publicity did much to upgrade safety standards aboard cruise ships, but destroyed Yarmouth Steamship. *Yarmouth* was withdrawn from service in December for a safety equipment check, and, proven satisfactory, was returned to service on 20 December. Passenger loading, however, was very low. Yarmouth then announced that it planned to 'order' two new ships in the 14,000 tons range, capable of carrying 650 passengers in 300 cabins, with a delivery date set for 1968. The announcement did little to allay the public fears about the company, and between January and March 1966, *Yarmouth* carried only 3,478 passengers on her twice-weekly trips to Nassau, a load factor of 28 per cent. With those numbers, the company announced it was withdrawing *Yarmouth* from service in April. She was laid up in Miami and given the name *San Andres*.

In 1967 she was purchased by Hellenic International Lines of Piraeus and renamed *Elizabeth A*. An ambitious series of Mediterranean 'Miracle Cruises' was planned for this forty-year-old lady, and it would have indeed been a miracle if she had made one of those cruises. Instead, she was taken to the backwaters of Piraeus and there laid up until 1979 when she was scrapped.

1 *Yarmouth* 1961-1966

William Cramp & Sons Shipbuilding Company, Philadelphia, Pennsylvania, 1927.

5,002 gross tons; 380 × 56 ft (116 × 17 m); steam turbines; twin screw; 18 knots; 450 first class passengers. Launched 6/11/1926 as *Yarmouth* (Eastern Steamship) (see page 93).

1954 *Yarmouth Castle* (Eastern — F.L. Fraser) (see page 96). 1955 *Queen of Nassau* (Eastern — F.L. Fraser) (see page 96). 1956 *Yarmouth Castle* (Eastern — F.L. Fraser) (see page 96). 1958 *Yarmouth* (Eastern — F.L. Fraser) (see page 96). 1961 *Yarmouth* (Yarmouth Steamship Company). FV 5/5/1962 San Francisco-Seattle. FV 10/1962 Miami-Nassau. 1966 *San Andres* (Yarmouth). 1967 *Elizabeth A* (Hellenic International Line). 1979 Scrapped.

2 *Yarmouth Castle* 1964-1966

William Cramp Shipbuilding Company, Philadelphia, Pennsylvania, 1927.

5,002 gross tons; 380 × 56 ft (116 × 17 m); steam turbines; twin screw; 18 knots; 350 first class passengers. Launched 12/2/1927 as *Evangeline* (Eastern Steamship) (see page 93).

1954 *Evangeline* (Eastern Steamship) (see page 97). 6/1964 Chartered to Caribbean Cruise Lines (see page 77). 7/1964 Back to Yarmouth. FV 12/1964 Miami-Nassau. 13/11/1965 Burned and sank in Caribbean, with the loss of 87 lives.

Appendix: New Companies

The companies listed below are firms that one day hope to have an American flagship in service.

Adventure Cruise Line (1984)

This Miami-based company is seeking Maritime Administration (MarAd) financing for a $24 million, 401 ft (123 m) passenger vessel to operate three-day and four-day cruises between Miami and Key West with calls at Fort Jefferson and Dry Tortugas. The 570-passenger vessel is to be built at Eastern Marine, Panama City, Florida, and delivered in 1987. At the time of writing, it is doubtful whether MarAd will back this venture.

American Flagships (1982)

Headquartered in New York, American Flagships propose to build two 800 ft (246 m) liners. Joseph Greenwell, president, has presented a fifty-page proposal to the Navy seeking its financial support, since the ships will incorporate some military features. The idea of building a dual-purpose ship — passenger liner and troop-carrier — is reminiscent of *United States*, but it is very unlikely that the US Navy will back the project, in view of the fact that one heat-seeking missile could destroy the ship and its men.

Contessa Cruises (1983)

Contessa Cruises, based in Houston, Texas, and a subsidiary of Bulkfleet Marine Corporation, contracted Giannotti & Associates of Annapolis to design two 18,000-ton ships to be delivered during 1986 by Marine Power & Equipment Co of Seattle. Each ship would be 543 ft (167 m) long and carry 800 passengers on eight decks in double and single cabins. Amenities are to include swimming pools, theatres, night clubs, racketball courts and jogging tracks. They are intended to operate out of Gulf Coast ports to the West Coast, Mexico and Alaska. However, during the summer of 1984 Merrill Lynch Capital Market Group, the organization in charge of raising funds for the project, withdrew its financial services.

Constitution Cruise Lines (1987)

Headed by Rick Williams, Constitution Cruise Lines was negotiating during 1987 for a vessel to commence operations in the summer of 1988. Her home port will be Philadelphia and cruises are planned for the summer to Bermuda and Canada.

Galveston Cruise Line (1983)

Galveston Cruise Line is owned by Gulf Pacific Cruise Lines Inc, a firm owned in turn by Giannotti & Associates, the naval architects. Giannotti himself is one of four partners, the others being the Tower Capital Corporation, Jamestown Metals Marine Sales and one other unnamed partner.

Raising money independently for their ship through loan guarantees and limited partnerships, it is hoped to construct the liner *Galveston* at the Tacoma Boatbuilding Company. The $110 million liner would be 11,353 tons, 550 ft (169 m) long and powered by diesel engines giving the vessel a speed of 18 knots. She would carry 800 passengers and operate along the Gulf Coast and West Coast. Giannotti at one time negotiated for the conversion of *Monterey* (see page 135), then owned by American Maritime Holdings, a subsidiary of the International Organization for Masters, Mates and Pilots.

Signet Cruise Lines (1984)

Signet, a Houston-based company, awarded a design contract to the Wärtsilä shipyard in Helsinki for two 25-27,000-ton cruise ships capable of accommodating 850 passengers. The ships are to be constructed in the United States and outfitted in Europe with delivery set for 1988. They would fly the American flag.

Sun Coast Cruises (1987)

The newest entrant into the cruising field is Sun Coast Cruises, established in 1987 by Adam Whitley, chairman of the line, and two local partners. Based in Pensacola, Florida, the company hopes to purchase a vessel and operate it on five-night cruises from Pensacola to Playa de Carmen and Cozumel, Mexico, and twelve-hour excursions along the Gulf Coast. It was anticipated that the service would commence in the summer of 1987.

United States Cruises (1978)

The idle *United States* (see pages 191-206) was purchased for $5 million from the US Federal Maritime Administration in 1978 by Richard Hadley

of the Pacific Building Corporation, a construction and real estate firm in Seattle. Mr Hadley gave a down payment of $1 million and formed United States Cruises (USC) Inc of Seattle which intends to spend $30 million refurbishing her into a 1,200-passenger cruise liner. Some of the features Mr Hadley will incorporate will be six gourmet restaurants, four swimming pools and the only full-sized tennis court afloat. In preparation for her eventual overhaul, *United States* was moved on 2 May 1980 from Pier 2 at Norfolk International Terminal to the Norfolk Shipbuilding and Drydock's Titan floating dry dock for a hull inspection, prior to her final purchase. She was given a clean bill of health, and Mr Hadley paid another $1 million to the Federal Administration. On 19 March 1981, USC made the final $3 million payment on *United States*.

USC then began a search to find a suitable yard to convert its prize. In 1984, the German shipyard, Howaldtswerke Deutsche Werft, won the contract to refurbish the speed queen at a cost of $130 million. An auction of her furnishings was held in Norfolk on 8-14 October 1984, with a planned visit to an American yard for the installation of one deck then on to the Dominican Republic to remove the asbestos before proceeding to Germany.

In a letter dated 27 May 1987, George A. Sotir, president of United States Cruises, stated '...we are still aggressively pursuing the selection of the shipyards and the arranging of the financing to secure the eventual return of the SS *United States* to passenger cruising service...on seven-day cruises alternating between San Francisco and Los Angeles to the Hawaiian islands.' He did point out, however, that service would not commence until 1989.

Bibliography

Albion, Robert Greenhalgh. *Seaports South of Sahara.* New York: Appleton-Century-Crofts Inc, 1959.

Bonsor, N.R.P. *North Atlantic Seaway,* Vol 1. New York: Arco Publishing Company, 1975.

Bonsor, N.R.P. *North Atlantic Seaway,* Vols 2-5. Jersey: Brookside Publications, 1978, 1979, 1980.

Braynard, Frank O. *Famous American Ships.* New York: Hastings House, 1978.

Braynard, Frank O. *Lives of the Liners.* New York. Cornell Maritime Press, 1947.

Braynard, Frank O. *The Big Ship.* Newport News: The Mariners' Museum, 1981.

Coleman, Terry. *The Liners.* New York: G.P. Putnam's Sons, 1977.

Cram, Bartlett W. *Picture History of New England Passenger Vessels.* Hampden Highlands: Burntcoat Corporation, 1980.

Dunn, Laurence. *Passenger Liners.* London: Adlard Coles Ltd, 1965.

Emmons, Frederick E. *American Passenger Ships.* Newark: University of Delaware Press, 1985.

Hales, Edward K. 'Ships, Shipowners & Seamen', (unpublished typewritten manuscript), 1984.

Hughes, Tom. *The Blue Riband of the Atlantic.* New York: Charles Scribner's Sons, 1973.

Kludas, Arnold. *Great Passenger Ships of the World,* Vol 5, 1951-1976. Cambridge: Patrick Stephens Ltd, 1977.

Kludas, Arnold. *Great Passenger Ships of the World,* Vol 6, 1977-1986. Wellingborough: Patrick Stephens Ltd, 1986.

Lee, Robert C. *Mr Moore Mr McCormack — and the Seven Seas.* Princeton: Princeton University Press, 1957.

Maxtone-Graham, John. *Liners to the Sun.* New York: Macmillan, 1985.

McCann, Thomas P. *An American Company.* New York: Crown Publishers Inc, 1976.

Melville, John H. *The Great White Fleet.* New York: Vantage Press, 1976.

Miller, William H. *Transatlantic Liners.* New York: Arco Publishing Inc, 1981.

Mississippi Shipping Company. *A Historical Sketch of the Mississippi Shipping Company Inc, 1919-1947.* New Orleans: Mississippi Shipping Company, 1947.

Moore-McCormack Lines. *A Profile of Maritime Progress 1913-1963.* New York: Moore-McCormack Lines Inc, 1963.

Morrison, John H. *History of American Steam Navigation.* New York: Stephen Daye Press, 1958.

Smith, Eugene W. *Passenger Ships of the World Past and Present.* Boston: George H. Dean Company, 1963.

Stindt, Fred A. *Matson's Century of Ships.* Modesto: Fred A. Stindt, 1982.

Waters, Harold. 'A Long Line of Ships: The American President Lines Story'. *The Compass,* Spring 1971, Vol XLI, No 2, pp 11-16.

Williams, David L., and De Kerbrech, Richard P. *Damned by Destiny.* Sussex: Teredo Books Ltd, 1982.

Periodicals

Lloyds Register of Shipping

New York Times

Official Steamship Guide. Various issues from 1937-1955. New York: Transportation Guides.

Steamboat Bill (Journal of the Steamship Historical Society of America).

Travel Weekly. News Group Publications Inc.

Index